National Football League Franchises

National Football League Franchises

Team Performances, Financial Consequences

Frank P. Jozsa Jr.

LEXINGTON BOOKS
Lanham • Boulder • New York • London

Published by Lexington Books
An imprint of The Rowman & Littlefield Publishing Group, Inc.
4501 Forbes Boulevard, Suite 200, Lanham, Maryland 20706
www.rowman.com

Unit A, Whitacre Mews, 26-34 Stannary Street, London SE11 4AB

British Library Cataloguing in Publication Information Available

Library of Congress Cataloging-in-Publication Data

ISBN 978-1-4985-3394-2 (cloth : alk. paper)
ISBN 978-1-4985-3395-9 (electronic)

∞™ The paper used in this publication meets the minimum requirements of American National Standard for Information Sciences Permanence of Paper for Printed Library Materials, ANSI/NISO Z39.48-1992.

Printed in the United States of America

To Indianapolis Colts and Carolina Panthers Fans

Contents

Abbreviations ix

Acknowledgments xi

Foreword xiii

Introduction xv

American Football Conference 1

1 East Division 3

2 North Division 29

3 South Division 55

4 West Division 81

National Football Conference 107

5 East Division 109

6 North Division 135

7 South Division 161

8 West Division 187

Conclusion 213

Appendix 217

Bibliography 227

Index 233

About the Author 237

Abbreviations

AAFC	All American Football Conference
AFC	American Football Conference
AFL	American Football League
AP	Associated Press
APFA	American Professional Football Association
CBS	Columbia Broadcasting System
CD	Central Division
CFL	Continental Football League
CMA	Country Music Award
D.C.	District of Columbia
EC	Eastern Conference
ED	East Division
ESPN	Entertainment Sports Programming Network
FCI	Fan Cost Index
F1	Formula 1
GCC	General Cinema Corporation
IPC	Indian Packing Company
LLC	Limited Liability Corporation
MLB	Major League Baseball
MLL	Major League Lacrosse

MLS	Major League Soccer
MSA	Metropolitan Statistical Area
MVP	Most Valuable Player
NBA	National Basketball Association
NCAA	National Collegiate Athletic Association
ND	North Division
NFC	National Football Conference
NFL	National Football League
NHL	National Hockey League
NLL	National Lacrosse League
PSL	Permanent Seat License
SD	South Division
SEC	Southeast Conference
SMU	Southern Methodist University
SNC	Snyder Communications
TMR	Team Marketing Report
WC	Western Conference
WD	West Division

Acknowledgments

While organizing, writing, and editing the manuscript for this book during 2015 and early 2016, a few individuals provided information for it and thus helped me in different ways. Most important to my project, Pfeiffer University's library director and assistant professor of library science Lara Little found numerous readings about National Football League franchises from such publications as *Business Week*, *Forbes*, *Fortune*, *SportsBusiness Journal*, and the *Wall Street Journal*, and then promptly forwarded them to me. I appreciate Lara's professionalism and her dedication to spend time and obtain articles, reports, and studies for me regarding the business, economics, finance, and operations of teams in the sport. Certainly Lara is a superstar librarian for the University's administration, faculty, and staff, and especially for the school's undergraduate and graduate students.

University of Michigan professor of sport management and codirector of the school's Center for Sport Management Rodney D. Fort explained how to analyze the historical performances and business success of franchises in the National Football League. He suggested I thoroughly research such important topics as these teams' attendances and ticket prices at home games and also their markets, owners, seasons, and postseasons. The coauthor of *Pay Dirt*, Professor Fort provides business and other historical data on professional sports teams at https://sites.google.com/site/rodswebpages/cod.

Others contributed to this book as follows: Rutgers University Librarian John Maxymuk told me about sources he used in authoring football books and wrote the Foreword; *Forbes* magazine sports editor Kurt Badenhausen alerted me to the publication of new financial information of pro football franchises in September 2015; Carolina Panthers/Cleveland Browns fan Bill Focht informed me about articles on NFL teams and their coaches and players; *Sporting News Yearbooks* editor Scott Ridge mailed and said for me to get permission to reuse a specific article from an editor at *Sporting News* magazine. I thank John, Kurt, Bill, and Scott for their assistance.

My fiancé and best friend Maureen Fogle allowed me to use her computer to organize and write a manuscript for this book. Despite spreading books and files on the carpet in our office and also needing time to rewrite, edit, and print copies of chapters, she understood how important this project was for me to complete and then submit a professional copy of it to Lexington Books on or before the due date. Once again, thanks to Maureen for her cooperation and patience particularly since my retirement as a business/economics professor from Pfeiffer University in 2007.

Frank P. Jozsa Jr.

Foreword

There are eleven NFL owners who are members of the Pro Football Hall of Fame in Canton, Ohio, as of 2015. Eight were founders of their franchise, and two others are sons who carried on their father's team. The eleventh owner, Charles Bidwill, bought the Chicago Cardinals in 1934 and died in 1947, although his family stills owns the franchise now located in Arizona. He appears to have been elected into the Hall of Fame primarily because he was a friend of George Halas and financially assisted the league's patriarch to hold onto his Chicago Bears during the Great Depression of the 1930s.

Former Cleveland Browns/Baltimore Ravens owner Art Modell has been a candidate for enshrinement in recent years, largely for his role in helping the league expand its television revenue, but also has run into popular opposition for having screwed the rabid Cleveland fan base by moving the team to Baltimore twenty years ago. Although no hero to Cleveland fans, Modell was revered by his ownership brethren for his profit-maximization skills.

In the NFL there is clearly a whole different level of competition that fans often do not perceive or care about, but that has an impact on the teams' performances on the field, and that is examined in *National Football League Franchises*. Even in the social democracy of the NFL with its soft safety net of guaranteed television revenue equally split among thirty-two league franchises and its hard salary cap to govern player expenses, the teams are run by competitive businessmen striving to get ahead in the league's money race.

The stability of NFL ownership is remarkable. It is an extremely expensive club to join, but once initiated, members rarely drop out. As of this writing, seven of the current thirty-two NFL franchises have known only one controlling family or ownership group: Chicago Bears since 1920; Pittsburgh Steelers since 1933; Kansas City Chiefs since 1960; Tennessee Titans since 1960; Cincinnati Bengals since 1968; Carolina Panthers since 1995; and Houston Texans since

2002. In addition, nine clubs have known just two controlling families or ownership groups: New York Giants since 1925; San Francisco 49ers since 1946; Indianapolis Colts since 1953; Buffalo Bills since 1960; Atlanta Falcons since 1966; New Orleans Saints since 1967; Tampa Bay Bucs since 1976; Jacksonville Jaguars since 1995; and Baltimore Ravens since 1996. Together, these represent one-half of franchises in the league.

Add in the community-owned Green Bay Packers and six teams with just three controlling families or ownership groups—Arizona Cardinals since 1920; Dallas Cowboys since 1960; San Diego Chargers since 1960; Oakland Raiders since 1960; Miami Dolphins since 1966; and Seattle Seahawks since 1976—and that is nearly three-quarters of the league. Moreover, of the remaining nine franchises, the New York Jets and Washington Redskins have the same owner for fifteen years; Philadelphia Eagles and New England Patriots each for twenty-one; Denver Broncos for thirty-one; and Detroit Lions for fifty-four. By this measure, that leaves the Cleveland Browns, St. Louis Rams, and Minnesota Vikings as the most volatile front offices. Is there a link between that and their on-the-field performances?

Author Frank Jozsa Jr. looks at factors like market value, gate receipts, operating income, ticket prices, market demographics, stadium deals, and marketing and social media strategies to provide an answer. While the landscape today is vastly different than ninety-five years ago when the NFL was founded as the American Professional Football Association, the principles that enabled the league to survive, grow, and eventually thrive remain the same. Although George Halas did not have a degree in marketing when he and co-owner Dutch Sternaman teamed with college phenomenon Red Grange and his agent C. C. Pyle in 1925, they demonstrated a firm grasp of business promotion that helped the struggling league find an audience.

When beloved Art Rooney mingled amiably with the kids in his economically challenged Pittsburgh neighborhood in the 1960s and 1970s, he demonstrated a mastery of the best kind of social media. And then there is the Green Bay Packers. The fact that the Packers have been one of the league's top teams for the past twenty-five years, able to drastically upgrade their stadium and attract top talent despite not having a wealthy ownership group, demonstrates there is no replacement for savvy, flexible leadership, and that the NFL is a fruitful source of study of basic and successfully applied business concepts, laws, and principles. For Jozsa's research, knowledge, and interpretation of the subject, read *National Football League Franchises*.

John Maxymuk
Head of Public Services
Paul Robeson Library
Rutgers University
Camden, New Jersey

Introduction

The most popular, prominent, and successful organization in American professional team sports emerged, developed, and matured from the early twentieth to twenty-first century. After struggling for two years as the American Professional Football Association, the organization changed its name to National Football League (NFL) in 1922.[1]

Despite internal problems such as franchise owner and player scandals and disputes, and also external issues as economic recessions and government legislation, teams within the league perform before audiences in regular-season games and then, if qualified, they compete against each other in playoffs to win titles and championships including a Super Bowl. Consequently the NFL and its teams have become increasingly important, newsworthy, and unique in American culture and sports history.

To organize and schedule games in each of its regular seasons and postseasons, the NFL encourages and promotes teams to exist for years and even decades within small, mid-sized, and large metropolitan areas and appeal to fans in local, regional, national, and even international sports markets. Essentially teams provide entertainment by competing in home and away games at various stadiums and on television networks, and by operating as commercial enterprises in order to generate maximum cash flows, revenues, and profits. For various reasons, however, some NFL clubs experienced financial problems because of inferior owners, coaches and/or players, an apathetic fan base, and/or they simply underachieved for periods while playing rivals in their division and/or conference.

PURPOSE AND SCOPE

As a result of researching such sport-specific sources as books, journals, magazines, media guides, newspapers, and websites, and studying demographic, economic, and financial data and other information, *National Football League Franchises* highlights and analyzes thirty-two teams' historical regular-season and postseason performances and provides a financial profile of them while being competitive, popular, and profitable or unprofitable enterprises. Certainly this is an appropriate, interesting, and special subject for various readers because it includes existing franchises and reveals how effectively each of them competes and also operates, prospers, and survives from a business perspective.

LITERATURE REVIEW

Several books focus on the history and commercialization of professional football and specifically the league's growth, maturity, and prosperity. This section reviews the contents of three titles because they include or refer to one or more concepts, themes, and topics discussed in *National Football League Franchises*. For other references on franchises and/or the NFL and its regular seasons and postseasons, the bibliography contains authors' names and their publications, and also specific dates and pages of articles, books, dissertations, Internet sources, and a media guide.

Published in 2010 by McFarland & Company, *Football Fortunes* analyzes NFL expansions and mergers, teams' territories and their relocations, role of stadiums and markets, and the short- and long-run effects of domestic and foreign affairs on the league's commercial strategies, competitiveness, and operations. Besides the history of the Super Bowl, international expansion, and prior but defunct professional football leagues in North America and Europe, the book also includes sections about such entities as NFL Films, the NFL Network, and NFL Properties. Because of its tables of data and other contents, *Football Fortunes* was used as a reference to research previous and current growth, problems, and trends of the sport.[2]

Scholarly and well-researched, *Pay Dirt* reveals and evaluates in part the market for and value of professional sports franchises, emergence and success of leagues in different sports, and the financial returns and economic risks of investing in professional teams. It has a 150-page technical and data supplement, an extensive bibliography of publications, and a detailed index of names, places, and terms. In short, *Pay Dirt* exposes the complex and entrepreneurial aspects of team sports and also merges factual and entertaining anecdotes with economic laws, models, and principals.[3]

For historical statistics about the league's seasons and postseasons by divisions and conferences and also teams' coaches and players, the *2015 Official NFL Record and Fact Book* contains such items as all-time individual and franchise records, a recent draft summary, veteran and first-year rosters, pro football Hall of Fame members, and a revised and updated chronological history of professional football since 1869. Compiled for use by the news media to aid in the reporting of games played by clubs in the NFL, it was extremely valuable as a reference book.[4]

In addition to these and other sports books, various websites were helpful and contributed to researching the league and performances and business aspects of its teams and their respective owners, coaches, and players. Some of these sites were, for example, http://www.pro-football-reference.com and http://www.sportsecyclopedia.com; http://www.forbes.com and http://www.sportsbusiness.com; http://www.sportingnews.com and http://www.charlotteobserver.com; and http://www.bizjournals.com and http://www.wsj.com. Collectively the literature included several types of readings from different but current and reputable sources.

BOOK OVERVIEW

After the front matter, which consists of the list of abbreviations, foreword, acknowledgments, and the introduction, this book includes eight chapters followed by the conclusion and then an appendix, bibliography, and index. While the front and back matter are self-explanatory, the chapters focus on teams in four divisions of the American Football Conference (AFC) and then those in the National Football Conference (NFC). Within each division of the conferences, there are two major sections—"Team Performances" and "Franchise Business." The former includes "Historical Results" and "Performance Highlights" as subsections while the latter consists primarily of "Team Financials" and "Business Highlights." The following are examples of topics in each chapter.

Chapter 1 examines the performances and business data of franchises in the AFC's East Division. Besides such things as number of titles and other performance characteristics of the Buffalo Bills, Miami Dolphins, New England Patriots, and New York Jets, the chapter also ranks their market value and total revenue in the league each from first to thirty-second.

Chapter 2 explores the performances and financial results of the Baltimore Ravens, Cincinnati Bengals, Cleveland Browns, and Pittsburgh Steelers of the AFC's North Division. It includes and ranks, for example, each of these teams' total wins and also their gate receipts and operating income.

Chapter 3 reveals and ranks performances and commercial statistics of the Houston Texans, Indianapolis Colts, Jacksonville Jaguars, and Tennessee

Titans of the AFC's South Division. There is information about their all-time winning percentages and number of playoff appearances, and estimated market values and earnings.

Chapter 4 highlights and ranks the performances and financial amounts of the Denver Broncos, Kansas City Chiefs, Oakland Raiders, and San Diego Chargers of the AFC's West Division. Their success in postseasons and amounts of player expenses, for example, are contained in the chapter.

Chapter 5 examines the performances and business success of the NFC's East Division teams. It examines and ranks, for example, the division and conference titles and the market values and income of the Dallas Cowboys, New York Giants, Philadelphia Eagles, and Washington Redskins.

Chapter 6 compares the performances and business results of the Chicago Bears, Detroit Lions, Green Bay Packers, and Minnesota Vikings—who jointly compete as rivals in the NFC's North Division. There is information about their results while performing in regular seasons and postseasons of the league in addition to each team's financial status as of early to mid-2015.

Chapter 7 describes and ranks the performances and financial data of the Atlanta Falcons, Carolina Panthers, New Orleans Saints, and Tampa Bay Buccaneers—who each play in the NFC's South Division. When and how they won division and conference titles and any championships including Super Bowls, while increasing their gate receipts and revenue at home games, are topics in the chapter.

Chapter 8 describes and ranks the performances and business success of the NFC's Arizona Cardinals, San Francisco 49ers, Seattle Seahawks, and St. Louis Rams in the West Division. Readers learn, for example, whether these teams had the most or least number of wins within their division and how they ranked financially among each other based on their debt-to-value ratios.

By linking and comparing the historical performances of NFL teams to financial information about them as business organizations, this book is unique and a worthwhile contribution to the literature on the sports industry. Although there are plenty of books on various aspects of the league, and specific clubs and their results in regular seasons and postseasons, none of them connects their popularity and all-time records with their recent but estimated economic value, net worth, and other financial data.

National Football League Franchises was written and published for current and prospective owners and executives of pro football franchises and potential investors in these organizations; the league's commissioner and his staff; practitioners and scholars who research the sports industry; college and university professors who teach undergraduate and graduate students with majors and/or minors in sports administration, business, economics, management, and/or history; and especially for fans of one or more NFL teams.

NOTES

1. After operating for two years as the American Professional Football Association and then renamed National Football League (NFL) in 1922, the league consisted of an Eastern Division and Western Division from 1933 to 1949. For the next three years the NFL had an American and National Conference and then during 1953–1966, an Eastern and Western Conference. From 1967 to 1969 these conferences included, respectively, a Capitol and Century Division, and Coastal and Central Division. When the professional American Football League folded after its 1969 season, several of its clubs joined the NFL. As a result the latter league's thirteen-team American Football Conference (AFC) and National Football Conference (NFC) each had three divisions—Eastern, Central, and Western. Because of expansion from 1971 to 2001 and other factors, the NFL restructured again in 2002 and placed four teams each in the East Division, North Division, South Division, and West Division of both the AFC and NFC.

2. Frank P. Jozsa Jr., *Football Fortunes: The Business, Organization and Strategy of the NFL* (Jefferson, NC: McFarland, 2010).

3. James Quirk and Rodney D. Fort, *Pay Dirt: The Business of Professional Team Sports* (Princeton, NJ: Princeton University Press, 1992).

4. *NFL Record & Fact Book 2014* (New York: NFL, 2014).

American Football Conference

Chapter One

East Division

Before the 2016 National Football League (NFL) season, which team or teams in the East Division (ED) of the American Football Conference (AFC) had the fewest number of all-time wins, lowest winning percentage, most titles and championships, largest number of playoff appearances? Did the Miami Dolphins, for example, have a higher estimated market value than the Buffalo Bills? How much was the total revenue of the New York Jets, gate receipts of the New England Patriots, and what amounts were their player expenses as a franchise and group?

To answer these and other questions, next are some interesting but important, newsworthy, and relevant facts that highlight the historical performances of four teams in the AFC's ED as of the league's 2015–2016, or simply 2015, season. Besides their winning percentage and number of wins, division and conference titles, NFL and Super Bowl championships, and postseasons, this information includes special coaches, players, and events regarding each of them while competing in the NFL's regular season and any playoffs. In the chapter's final section—labeled Franchise Business—are these franchises' success or failure as business enterprises both individually and in comparison to each other from a financial perspective.[1]

TEAM PERFORMANCES

Buffalo Bills

Founded by Ohio entrepreneur Ralph Wilson in 1959, the Bills were in the American Football League (AFL) from 1960 to 1969. The team tied for the ED crown in 1963 but lost the division title to the Boston Patriots in a playoff game. In 1964 and 1965, the Bills defeated the San Diego Chargers each year and won AFL championships. After winning the ED again in 1966 but losing to the Kansas City Chiefs in the league's championship game, the club was ineligible to play in the first Super Bowl. During the next three seasons Buffalo finished third, fifth, and fourth in its division. After the AFL's 1969 season and its merger with the NFL, the Bills became a member of the latter league.[2]

Historical Results

While existing in the AFC's Eastern Division from 1970 to 2001 and then the ED during 2002–2015, the Bills played 712 games and won approximately 46 percent of them. More specifically, they won eleven division plus conference titles but zero NFL or Super Bowl championships in thirteen playoff appearances. In comparison to other AFC teams as of the NFL's 2015 season, Buffalo ranked eighth in number of victories, twelfth in winning percentage, ninth in division titles, fifth in conference titles, tied for eighth with eight other AFC teams in number of total championships, and tied for eighth with the Chargers in qualifying for the playoffs (Table A.1).

Within their division the Bills had a higher winning percentage and more wins than the Jets, but fewer total titles and also championships than both the Dolphins and Patriots. For various reasons, these performances including four appearances in but zero Super Bowl wins indicate that the Bills had below-average teams for most of their forty-six seasons and as a competitor against others in their conference and league since 1970.

Compared to the performances of thirty-one other NFL teams as of their 2015 season, the Bills were nineteenth in total wins and ranked twenty-second in winning percentage, nineteenth in division titles, tied for tenth with the Bears, Lions, and Vikings in conference titles, tied for twentieth with several other teams each with zero championships, and tied for eighteenth in playoff appearances. These and other results prove that Buffalo's teams have been, on average, mediocre performers among the group while playing more than four decades in the league (Table A.2).

During NFL seasons there were several coaches and players with exceptional careers for Bills teams. In the former group was Marv Levy with 123 victories, Chuck Knox with 38, and Lou Saban with 32. Levy's teams played in eight postseasons including four Super Bowls, and he was AFC coach of the year in 1988 and 1993. With less than 10 wins each, Buffalo teams' least successful coaches have been John Rauch, Harvey Johnson, Jim Ringo, Hank Bullough, and Perry Fewell.[3]

Based on their performances in the AFC between 1970 and 2014, Buffalo players established records for the franchise. During their careers, for example, running back Thurman Thomas had the most rushing yards, quarterback Jim Kelley the largest number of touchdowns and most yards, receiver Andre

Reed the highest number of catches, and punter Brian Moorman the longest average distance on punts. For a single season, quarterback Drew Bledsoe led in passing yards, receiver Eric Moulds in catches, and specialist Terrence McGee in average yards per kickoff returns. In a single game, running back O. J. Simpson gained 273 yards, kicker Steve Christie made 6 field goals, and cornerback Nate Clements and several other players each intercepted 3 passes. For sure, these athletes set significant records for the Bills.

Since 1970 some Buffalo players were outstanding among all those on NFL teams. These included Most Valuable Player (MVP) and Associated Press (AP) offensive players of the year Simpson in 1973 and Thomas in 1991; defensive players of the year Bruce Smith in 1990 and 1996 and also Bryce Paup in 1995; defensive rookies of the year Jim Haslett in 1979 and Shane Conlan in 1987; and comeback player of the year Doug Flutie in 1998. However, through the 2014 season, Bills players had never won an AP offensive rookie of the year award.

For their great success in the sport, eight Buffalo players are in the pro football Hall of Fame. Chronologically these include Simpson in 1985, guard Billy Shaw in 1999, Kelly in 2002, and guard Joe DeLamielleure and receiver James Lofton in 2003, Thomas in 2007, Smith in 2009, and Reed in 2014. Besides them, coach Levy was inducted in 2001 and deceased owner/founder Wilson in 2009.

To honor their contribution to various Bills' teams in NFL seasons, at least twenty-nine players are in the franchise's Wall of Fame. Such athletes include, for example, quarterback Joe Ferguson, defensive tackle Fred Smerlas, center Kent Hull, linebacker Darryl Talley, center Jim Richter, cornerback Robert James, and safety Steve Tasker. Besides athletes among the group, there is former trainer Eddie Abramoski, general manager Bill Polian, vice president Patrick McGroder and of course, deceased founder/owner Wilson.

Performance Highlights

Based on such websites as www.nfl.com and www.pro-football-reference.com, Buffalo's most productive years in the NFL were 1980–1981, 1988–1993, 1995–1996, and 1998–1999. Between 1940 and 1999, the club qualified for twelve playoffs, won four AFC titles, and appeared in but lost four consecutive Super Bowls. Meanwhile the Bills failed to make playoffs in such years as 1970–1973, 1975–1979, 1982–1987, and 2000–2015. In sum, these periods denote when the club had its greatest and least success since 1970.

Home to the only NFL franchise to appear in four consecutive Super Bowls and renowned as the site of a 1993 wild-card playoff game during which the Bills overcame a 32-point deficit to defeat the Houston Oilers

41–38 in overtime, the 73,000-seat Ralph Wilson Stadium opened in August 1973 when originally named Rich Stadium. Twenty-six years later, luxury boxes were added and in 2007 a new, thirty-three by eighty-two feet Mitsubishi scoreboard. The field, which is fifty feet below ground level, received a new A-Turf Titan fifty surface in 2011.

Among thirty-one NFL venues, Ralph Wilson Stadium ranked twenty-first in a 2015 study. According to an article in an edition of *Sporting News*, the author wrote:

> The 42-year-old facility completed $130 million in renovations last year [2014] as the Bills set their sights on developing a new stadium in the future. Bigger concession stands, a sports bar, wider concourses and easier access to the stadium were among the improvements to their existing building, which was in desperate need of a facelift. Some pollsters rank Ralph Wilson Stadium among the NFL's best tailgate spots. Wings anyone?[4]

In 2007 the Bills stadium officially had 73,967 seats. Based on the club's market penetration that year, it was nearly twice as hard to achieve a sellout of home games in Buffalo then forty years ago given the city's population/stadium density percentage. However, this did not take into account how much easier it was for the Bills' NFL competitors to sellout their stadiums.[5]

Based on such things as their winning percentage in the ED and ticket prices at home games, and also Buffalo's weather conditions, population, population growth, and household per capita income, the Bills struggle to consistently attract enough fans to fill Ralph Wilson Stadium each year. Historically, for example, total attendances in regular seasons ranged from 274,441 to 547,126 in the 1970s; 302,360 to 622,793 in the 1980s; 523,763 to 635,881 in the 1990s; and 499,835 in 2000 to 571,240 in 2009 and then to 540,176 in 2014 and 559,047 in 2015. Thus, there have been large differences in the number of fans attending Bills' home games across forty-six NFL seasons.[6]

Mary Owen, the former Bills' executive vice president of strategic planning and one of the highest-ranking female team executives in the league, resigned from her position in October 2014 to operate the foundation of the club's late owner, her uncle Ralph Wilson. Owen is the first high-profile departure from the team since Wilson's death in March and left only a handful of senior female NFL team executives including Cincinnati Bengals' executive vice president Katie Blackburn, Miami Dolphins' vice president of football operations Dawn Aponte, and San Diego Chargers' executive vice president and chief financial officer Jeanne Black.

For the franchise to become more competitive in 2016 and thereafter requires several changes. First, the Bills need to hire experienced and successful coaches to be leaders and each season to challenge the Dolphins, Patriots, and Jets, and thus win more games in the ED. Second, the franchise must recruit more talented players including rookies and veterans at key positions on the field. Third, new owners Terry and Kim Pegula need to establish trust and professional relationships with their coaches and players and frequently encourage them to mature and succeed, and also to respect the franchise and its history. If these things occur, the Bills will improve and win more titles in future NFL seasons.

Miami Dolphins

In 1962 the AFL awarded an expansion franchise to lawyer Joe Robbie and actor Danny Thomas for a fee of $7.5 million. While playing in the league's ED from 1966 to 1969, the Miami Dolphins won only fifteen games and finished third and fourth each once and fifth twice. During most seasons the club scored fewest points among eight or nine other AFL teams. When the AFL and NFL merged in 1970, Miami joined the Baltimore Colts, Boston Patriots, Buffalo Bills, and New York Jets in the AFC's Eastern Division (renamed East Division in 2002).[7]

Historical Results

Since entering the NFL in 1970, the Dolphins have won 408 games or approximately 58 percent with thirteen division and five conference titles and also two Super Bowls in twenty-two playoffs. Among fifteen other AFC clubs before their 2015 season, the Dolphins ranked third in total wins, second in winning percentage, fourth in number of division and conference titles, tied for fourth with the Ravens and Broncos in championships, and second in total playoff appearances (Table A.1).

Within the league's ED, Miami has the most all-time wins and highest winning percentage with less total titles than the Patriots but more than the Bills and Jets combined, and also the highest number of playoff appearances. Given these results, the Dolphins were competitive and among the best performing teams in their division and conference during many NFL seasons from 1970 to 2015.

In comparison to the all-time records of thirty-one other NFL clubs as of the league's 2014–2015 season, Miami ranked twelfth in number of wins, second in winning percentage, tied for tenth with the Eagles in division titles, tied for eighth with the Redskins in winning their conference, and tied for eleventh with the Ravens and Raiders in number of championships. In addition the Dolphins had more total titles than ten AFC teams and historically, less playoff appearances than only the Steelers. Thus, Miami's NFL team has been outstanding percent-wise at winning games in regular seasons and being competitive during the majority of forty-six years against clubs in their conference and also the NFC (Table A.2).

There have been a number of outstanding coaches and talented players for the franchise. For the former group, Coach Don Shula won 274 games during his twenty-six years with the club which included several division and conference titles plus Super Bowl championships in 1972 and 1973. Shula was also AFC coach of the year in 1970. Besides him, Dave Wannstedt and Jimmy Johnson each coached for four seasons and their teams had, respectively, 43 and 38 victories in addition to appearances in two and three playoffs. Alternatively, less effective coaches for Miami were Jim Bates, Nick Saban, Cam Cameron, Todd Bowles, Tony Sparano, and since 2012, Joe Philbin.

Some Dolphins players established records during their years with the club. Regarding career achievements, for example, fullback Larry Csonka had the most rushing yards and quarterback Dan Marino most passing yards and touchdowns while free safety Jake Scott led in interceptions, running back Mercury Morris in average yards on kickoff returns, wide receiver Mark Duper in receiving yards, and placekicker Olindo Mare in total points.

For a single season, leaders included such athletes as Ricky Williams in rushing yards, Mark Clayton in total receiving yards, Brandon Fields in average distance per punt, Jeff Ogden in average punt returns, Dick Westmoreland in interceptions, and O. J. McDuffie in number of catches. Meanwhile single-game records were set by such players as Bob Griese in passing touchdowns, Chris Chambers in number of receptions, Brian Hartline in yards as a receiver, Paul Warfield along with Mark Ingram and Ronnie Brown in total touchdowns and points, and Dick Anderson in interceptions. Because of these men's skills and determination to excel and win games, Miami was a successful AFC team in some years.

Several Dolphins players earned and received awards for their abilities. To illustrate, quarterback Marino was NLF MVP and AP offensive player of the year in 1984 for setting league records of 5,084 yards and 48 touchdown passes while leading his club to division and conference titles. In addition, running back Troy Stradford was AP offensive rookie of the year in 1987; Dick Anderson defensive player of the year in 1973, Doug Betters in 1983, and Jason Taylor in 2006; A. J. Duhe defensive rookie of the year in 1977, John Overdahl in 1986, and Tim Bowens in 1994; and Chad Pennington comeback player of the year in 2008.

Among all-time coaches and players for the franchise as of 2015, ten Dolphins are in the pro football Hall of Fame. Warfield, Csonka, and center Jim Langer were inducted in the 1980s; Griese, guard/tackle Larry Little, coach Shula, and center/tackle Dwight Stephenson in the 1990s; and Marino, Thomas, and linebacker Nick Buoniconti in the 2000s. In short, these individuals had great careers with Miami while playing against opponents in the AFC.

Performance Highlights

Since joining the NFL in 1970, the Dolphins' most productive periods were the 1970–1974, 1981–1985, and 1997–2001 seasons. Most importantly the team won its division and conference and then Super Bowl VII to complete an unblemished 17–0–0 record in 1972 and Super Bowl VIII in 1973, and it appeared in five consecutive playoffs in the early 1970s and 1980s, and late 1990s to 2001. In contrast to these NFL seasons, Miami teams' worst performances included such years as 1975–1977, 1986–1989, 2002–2007, and 2009–2015. Because of wrong owner decisions, inferior coaches, underachieving and injured players and their lack of morale, the franchise had more losses than wins during most of these years and failed to qualify for playoffs in the AFC.

While playing in the 70,000 to 80,000-seat Orange Bowl until 1987, the Dolphins usually had support from local fans. The team, for example, established an NFL single-game record with 74,961 ticket sales in 1973. After deciding to own a privately funded stadium, the franchise unveiled a new 73,000-seat venue named Joe Robbie Stadium in 1987. Following 1995, it was renamed Pro Player Stadium and then Dolphin Stadium, Land Shark Stadium, and since 2010, Sun Life Stadium. Since its construction, the facility has hosted five Super Bowls, two Major League Baseball (MLB) World Series, four BCS National Championship Games in college football, the second round of the 2009 World Baseball Classic, and WrestleMania XXVIII. The stadium is also one of four potential sites for the 2019 and 2020 Super Bowls.

In a recent study of thirty-one NFL stadiums, Sun Life Stadium ranked twenty-eighth. The study's author revealed this about the venue:

> The Miami Dolphins' Sun Life Stadium has played host to some huge games, including five Super Bowls, but changes are needed in an arena criticized for its atmosphere. And the Dolphins chiefs know that, as they've already started work on $350 million plans to transform the stadium. Every single seat has been ripped out, and huge corner chunks have been removed, ready for massive changes. After this season, a roof will be put in place, and the whole thing will be transformed into a European football-style area akin to the San Siro. Expect to see this stadium shoot up the list in 2016.[8]

Because of its performances against rival AFC teams and other factors such as market size and density, population growth and per capita income, Miami successfully attracts fans to its home games at Sun Life Stadium and earlier at the Orange Bowl. In fact the club's attendances ranged from 339,698 to 557,881 in the 1970s; 238,951 to 542,951 in the 1980s; 476,858 to 593,851 in the 1990s; and from 496,659 to 560,280 in the 2000s. Similar to other

NFL teams playing in their division, more people demanded to see Dolphins games during winning than losing seasons.

Based on decreases in population/stadium size ratios of AFC teams since 1970, it has become much easier for the Dolphins to sell out their home games than for the ED's Bills, Patriots, and Jets. For various demographic, economic, and social reasons, Miami's ratio ranked second highest while New England's placed ninth, New York's seventeenth, and Buffalo's twenty-fifth. Simply put, the Dolphins penetrated their market to a greater extent and more effectively compared to competitors.

In 2015 Emory University researcher Michael Lewis developed a Social Media Equity index to determine which NFL teams over- or underperform with respect to their Twitter following. His model controlled for such factors as market size and short-term winning percentages but removed stadiums' capacity restraints and teams' ticket-pricing policies. For the best fan base among the AFC's ED clubs, the Dolphins ranked twenty-third but followed the Patriots at third, Jets at ninth, and Bills at sixteenth. Regarding other teams in the index, the Pittsburgh Steelers were first and Arizona Cardinals thirty-second. In other words, the Dolphins underperformed according to their fans' expectations on social media.[9]

From 2002 to 2015 Miami played in one wild-card game and lost it despite an 11–5–0 record that season in the ED. During this period seven different coaches failed to lead, motivate, and teach Dolphins players enough to win a title. Except in 2008 the club's quarterbacks, running backs, and defensive and offensive linemen, as a group, have been mediocre or worse at their positions.

Based on these results, the franchise's owners and administrators need to be involved and smart to get more production from their coaching staff and roster of players. Specifically such things as improvements in scouting and drafting college athletes and increasing the team's payroll, teamwork, and work ethic are ways for them to accomplish better results. Otherwise, the Patriots will continue to dominate the AFC's ED and frequently defeat the Dolphins in crucial games.

New England Patriots

Businessman Billy Sullivan Jr., who had a strong sports promotional background, was the founder and owner of the Boston Patriots. One of eight teams in the inaugural season of the renegade AFL, this was the fourth attempt at permanently locating a professional football team in Boston, Massachusetts, following the former Boston Bulldogs, Redskins, and Yanks. During their history in the AFL, the Patriots played two years at Boston University's Nickerson Field and one at Harvard's stadium, six at the Boston Red Sox's Fenway Park, and finally one at Alumni Stadium.[10]

From 1960 to 1969, the Patriots had five winning seasons including 1963 when they lost the AFL championship game to the San Diego Chargers. Coached by Mike Holovak the club's most prominent players were wide receiver/placekicker Gino Cappelletti, who became the league's all-time highest scorer, and running back Jim Nance, who established AFL rushing titles in 1966 and 1967. One year after a disappointing 1969 season and then merger of the leagues, the Patriots joined the NFL and became a member of the league's AFC. In 1971, the team changed its name from Boston to New England Patriots.

Historical Results

While competing in the conference's ED from 1970 to the 2015 season, New England had 399 all-time victories, 56 percent of their total games. More specifically its teams won seventeen division and eight conference titles, and also four Super Bowls in twenty-two playoff appearances. Among AFC teams as of the league's 2015 season, the Patriots ranked fourth in number of wins, third in winning percentage, second in division titles, tied for first with the Steelers and Broncos in conference titles, second in NFL and Super Bowl championships, and tied for third with the Broncos in playoff appearances (Table A.1).

Compared to others in the ED, New England had the most titles and championships but less wins and a lower winning percentage than the Dolphins. Consequently, the Patriots have been very competitive and also successful for many seasons in their division and conference during their forty-six-year-old history.

When compared to the all-time records of thirty-one NFL clubs as of their 2015 season, New England ranked thirteenth in number of wins, fourth in winning percentage, eighth in division titles, tied for third with the Broncos, Steelers, and Cowboys in winning their conference, and tied for eighth with the Lions in number of championships. In addition they have more total titles than fourteen AFC teams and historically, less playoff appearances than only the conference's Dolphins and Steelers. Since 1996 the Patriots have appeared in sixteen playoffs, were superior percentage-wise at winning their games in regular seasons and titles in postseasons, and extremely competitive during these years while playing teams in the AFC and across the league (Table A.2).

Since 1970, there have been some well-known, popular coaches and many talented players employed by the Patriots franchise. The former group includes Bill Belichick with 181 wins and then Raymond Berry with 51, Chuck Fairbanks 46, and Bill Parcells 34. In fifteen seasons to 2014–2015, Belichick's teams appeared in twelve playoffs and won four Super Bowls. While he was NFL coach of the year in 2003, 2007, and 2010, Parcells won the award in the AFC in 1994, Berry in 1985, and Fairbanks in 1976. In contrast to them, such coaches as John Muzar, Phil Bengtson, Ron Erhardt, Ron Meyer, Rod Rust, and Dick MacPherson each had fewer than 25 victories.

Some New England players set records and had outstanding careers, single seasons, and a single game for the club. Among the career leaders is Tom Brady in passing touchdowns and yards, Sam Cunningham in rushing yards, Wes Welker in receptions, Tom Tupa in punting average, and Adam Vinatieri in number of field goals and total points. Single season record holders include, for example, running back Corey Dillon, punt returner Julian Edelman, field goal kicker Stephen Gostkowski, and kickoff return specialist Raymond Clayborn. For three single game records, Tony Collins had 212 yards in 1983; Andre Carter 4 sacks in 2011; and Randy Moss 4 touchdowns in 2007. Certainly these players established memorable records for the franchise.

The following Patriots players received special awards for their achievements. Brady was NFL MVP and AP offensive player of the year in 2007 and 2010 for his passing and leadership abilities. The AP also honored offensive rookies of the year John Stevens in 1988, Leonard Russell in 1991, and Curtis Martin in 1995; defensive rookie of the year Mike Haynes in 1976 and Jerod Mayo in 2008; and co-comeback player of the year Tedy Bruschi in 2005, Brady in 2009, and Rob Gronkowsi in 2014. Interestingly New England players have not won an award for AP defensive player of the year. In short, quarterback Brady and these other players received recognition for their great performances in different ways.

Among coaches and players of the franchise while in the NFL since 1970, six of them are in the pro football Hall of Fame. Besides Coach Bill Parcells, the players are guard John Hannah, cornerback Mike Haynes, running back Curtis Martin, and linebackers Junior Seau and Andre Tippett. They and others such as founder/owner Billy Sullivan, radio broadcaster Gil Santos, linebacker Steve Nelson, quarterback Steve Grogan, and wide receiver Stanley Morgan are also in the Patriots Hall of Fame. In the future, current owner Robert Kraft and quarterback Brady will be inducted into both Halls.

Performance Highlights

Since entering the NFL in 1970, the Patriots most productive periods were 1985–1986, 1995–1998, 2003–2007, and 2009–2015. During these seasons they dominated the ED and won eight conference titles and participated in seven Super Bowls. Despite Brady's injury and failure to play in 2008, New England still finished 11–5 and second in the ED. In contrast to these years, the club's worst performances occurred in 1970–1975, 1979–1981, and 1988–1993. Except for 1980, the team was inconsistent and not competitive, had coaching and ownership problems, and its players were mediocre and did not perform to their potential.

After playing its home games at 30,323-seat Harvard Stadium in the Allston neighborhood of Boston for one season, the team moved in 1971 to 60,764-seat Foxboro Stadium—located about twenty-five miles south of Boston—and then in 2002, to 68,756-seat Gillette Stadium in Foxborough, Massachusetts. During most of these years the club's attendances were variable but then really improved especially in the early 2000s. For example its home-game attendances ranged from 245,537 to 475,081 in the 1970s; 149,051 to 482,572 in the 1980s; 308,442 to 477,423 in the 1990s; and from 463,722 in 2000 to 550,048 in 2014. Rather than simply view games on television, Patriots fans increasingly became spectators at Gillette Stadium because of the team's competitiveness and winning division and conference titles and also Super Bowls especially led by coach Belichick and quarterback Brady.

In a recent article about thirty-one NFL venues, Gillette Stadium ranked nineteenth. According to an article in an edition of *Sporting News*, the author wrote:

> The Kraft family, owner of the Patriots, privately built the 13-year-old facility and has kept it up to speed over the years. The newest addition is the Cross Insurance Pavilion and Business Center, a 20,000-square-foot space for special events in the stadium's west side. Last year, the team filled an open space in the south end with a new club, an improvement that upset some fans who could not afford to pay for the premium upgrade. Patriot Place, a mall-like collection of bars, restaurants, and retail stores next to the stadium, provides plenty of eating and drinking options on game day.[11]

Based on a 2015 study designed to determine which NFL teams over- or underperform with respect to their Twitter following, the Patriots had the third-best fan base while the Jets ranked ninth, Bills thirteenth, and Dolphins twenty-third. According to the study's Social Media Equity index, New England finished behind the Steelers and Cowboys but ahead of twenty-nine other franchises in the league because of its passionate fans and their enthusiasm and support particularly at home games in Foxborough.

When Brady retires and/or becomes seriously injured in a game, and then replaced by a different quarterback, the Patriots will likely not continue their record of championship seasons. Although Belichick is a smart, shrewd, and successful coach, he may need to change his team's strategy and rely more on defense than offense to win games. If the Bills, Dolphins, and Jets improve their performances, they will become more confident and likely challenge New England in the ED. Consequently the organization, including franchise owner Robert Kraft and his staff, must ultimately prepare for one or more seasons without most of their current but outstanding players.

New York Jets

When the AFL formed in 1959, it granted sports broadcaster Harry Wismer a charter to own and operate a new franchise in the league. Named New York Titans as of the 1960 season, the organization was plagued with controversy for three years. Although the club had minor success by winning nineteen games, it was a disaster financially and not popular among football fans. Meanwhile, Wismer feuded about his franchise's debts with AFL Commissioner Joe Foss.[12]

In February 1963, Wismer sold his club for $1 million to a five-man group headed by prominent entertainment industry executive David "Sonny" Werblin. Shortly thereafter, Werblin changed the team's nickname from Titans to Jets and hired Web Ewbank as head coach. After moving from the antiquated Polo Grounds to newly constructed Shea Stadium in 1964, the Jets set an AFL attendance record at 45,665. Led by quarterback Joe Namath, they improved enough to win Super Bowl III in 1968 and another division title in 1969. One year later, the AFL and NFL merged with the Jets joining the Colts, Dolphins, Bills, and Patriots in the AFC's ED.

Historical Results

From the NFL's 1970 to 2015 season, the Jets had 318 victories while establishing a winning percentage of just 44 percent. In fact they won two division titles but zero conferences and championships in twelve playoff appearances. Among sixteen AFC teams as of 2015, New York ranked ninth in number of wins and only fourteenth percentage-wise and also fourteenth with the and Jaguars in division titles, tied for twelfth with the Browns, Texans, Jaguars, and Chiefs in conference titles, and tied for eighth with eight other clubs in Super Bowl championships since 1970 (Table A.1).

Within the ED, the Jets had worse performance results than the Bills, Dolphins, and Patriots. Because of problems with its managers and players, this New York NFL team has been below average competitively while playing games against division and AFC rivals during many of its regular seasons.

Compared to the all-time performances of thirty-two NFL clubs before their 2016 season, the Jets ranked twentieth in number of wins, twenty-fourth in winning percentage, thirtieth in division titles, tied for twenty-eighth with the Browns, Texans, Jaguars, and Chiefs in winning their conference, and tied for twentieth with twelve other teams each with zero NFL plus Super Bowl championships. In addition the Jets have fewer total titles than the majority of AFC teams and historically, ranked tenth in the conference and tied for twentieth among the league in playoff appearances. As such, Jets teams have been inferior while playing other clubs during most seasons since 1970 (Table A.2).

Despite these dismal results, the Jets had a few impressive coaches and several talented players since 1970. In the former group were Joe Walton with 54 wins, Rex Ryan 46, Walt Michaels and Herman Edwards each 41, and Bill Parcells 30. Although Walton, Ryan, Michaels—AFC coach of the year in 1978—and Edwards had their teams in consecutive playoffs, they failed to win a conference title. Alternatively, the club's least successful coaches were Charley Winner, Pete Carroll, Ken Shipp, Lou Holtz, Rich Kotite, and Al Groh.

Some players established individual records for the franchise. During their careers, for example, running back Curtis Martin led in most rushing yards, quarterback Namath in passing yards and touchdowns, receiver Don Maynard in number of receptions and total touchdowns, and Pat Leahy in field goals and points. For a single season, record-holders include such athletes as quarterback Vinny Testaverde in passing touchdowns, receiver Al Toon in number of receptions, and specialist Bobby Humphrey in kickoff returns. Single game records were set by Clark Gaines in number of receptions, Ty Law and many others in interceptions, Wesley Walker in total touchdowns and points, and Mark Gastineau and John Abraham in sacks. As a group, these Jets players had truly unforgettable seasons.

Besides athletes who set Jets franchise records, a few of the club's players received AP awards during 1970–2014. Erik McMillan was defensive rookie of the year in 1988, Hugh Douglas in 1995, Jonathan Vilma in 2004, and Sheldon Richardson in 2013, while Chad Pennington won comeback player of the year in 2006. No team members, however, earned such awards as NFL offensive and defensive player of the year or offensive rookie of the year.

For their outstanding years in the sport, eight former Jets are in the pro football Hall of Fame. By year of induction, these were coaches Weeb Ewbank in 1978 and Bill Parcells in 2013, and players Joe Namath in 1985, Don Maynard in 1987, John Riggins in 1992, Ronnie Lott in 2000, Art Monk in 2008, and Curtis Martin in 2012.

Performance Results

While in the NFL, the Jets' most productive periods were 1981–1982, 1985–1986, 2001–2002, and 2009–2010. Although the club failed to win a conference title or Super Bowl, these seasons featured Jets teams with winning records who qualified for the playoffs. Alternatively, some of their least impressive regular seasons consecutively included 1970–1981, 1987–1990, 1992–1997, and 2011–2014. During the latter periods, ED titles were won primarily by the Dolphins and Patriots. Thus Jets teams frequently struggled to compete due to coaching problems, inferior players, and such factors as ineffective offensive and defensive lineups, poor leadership, and lack of teamwork.

Because the New York-New Jersey metropolitan area is a very large and lucrative sports market, the franchise has maintained an excellent attendance record at its home games. For example, these numbers ranged from 309,473 to 441,099 in the 1970s; 182,349 to 541,832 in the 1980s; 385,154 to 548,012 in the 1990s; and in the 600,000s each season from 2000 to 2015. While playing at 80,242-seat Giants Stadium in East Rutherford, New Jersey, and later at 83,000-seat MetLife Stadium, the Jets have sold out their games for more than two decades. Despite teams in other professional sports, the NFL has become extremely popular in the region among fans and the media.[13]

In a recent study of thirty-one NFL venues, MetLife Stadium ranked seventeenth. According to an article about it in an edition of *Sporting News*, the author wrote:

> Some say the squabbles between the Jets and Giants during stadium development resulted in a drab facility. But technology brings flexibility for branding the building green or blue depending on which team is playing a home game. The team can flip merchandise displays in minutes. As for special events, the stadium still does big business with concerts and truck shows, just like its predecessor, old Giants Stadium. The light rail provides convenience for fans in New York traveling to New Jersey Meadowlands, and stadium officials over the years have created a "railgating" experience for those coming by train. Everyone else is tailgating in the lots surrounding the stadium.[14]

Researchers at Emory University in Atlanta created a study in 2015 to determine which NFL teams tend to over- or underperform with respect to their followers on Twitter. Among ED clubs the Patriots had the best and most fervent fan base with the Jets finishing ninth, Bills thirteenth, and Dolphins twenty-third. According to the study's Social Media Equity index, the Jets ranked ahead of twelve other AFC franchises in part because of enthusiasm and support from their fans regardless of the team's expensive nonpremium and premium ticket prices at home games, and recent losing seasons. In other words, the club has a relatively large number of followers according to responses from them on Twitter.

For most of their forty-five years in the league, Jets teams have been subpar at winning games in regular seasons and failed to be competitive during many of them. Nevertheless, they are popular enough on weekends to attract thousands of fans to their stadium and entertain them especially when playing the ED's Bills, Dolphins, and Patriots, and also the NFC's Eagles, Giants, and Redskins.

To win another division title and its conference, the franchise needs commitments from its owners and executives to prepare and implement plans, become more informed about professional football, and make smarter decisions with respect to recruiting and hiring administrators, coaches, and players. Eventually an opportunity to improve in the ED will occur for the Jets when the Patriots' Tom Brady retires. The Bills and Dolphins, meanwhile, are vulnerable rivals but nevertheless eager to defeat other clubs and win their divisional games. If Ryan Fitzpatrick continues to develop his skills and becomes a much better quarterback in 2016 and thereafter, the Jets will challenge opponents for a conference title like they did in 2009 and 2010.

FRANCHISE BUSINESS

Besides performing as teams in NFL regular season and postseason games, professional football franchises are commercial enterprises. To that end, their economic objective is to earn maximum revenue and obtain the greatest amount of profit on a fiscal basis from their operations. Although they share revenues with each other from such sources as national television contracts and some other deals, it is important for them to efficiently allocate resources, determine and distribute payrolls, set nonpremium and premium ticket prices for home games, and schedule investments in short- and long-term assets. To reveal and manage these activities, this section focuses on different parts of four franchises' business and how these organizations rank and succeed or not succeed from a financial perspective.

Buffalo Bills

Three years after hip surgery and also failing in health, the Bills' ninety-five-year-old founder/owner Ralph Wilson died in his home during March 2014 and left controlling ownership of the Bills franchise to his wife, Mary. Shortly thereafter, Wilson's estate offered the franchise for sale to any individual or group who promised to keep the team in Buffalo. With assistance from investment bank Morgan Stanley, the estate sold the team in late 2014 for an estimated $1.4 billion to entrepreneur Terry Pegula and his wife Kim.[15]

Born in 1951 and raised in Carbondale, Pennsylvania, Terry attended Scranton Preparatory School. After graduating from there, he enrolled in Penn State University as a math major and to continue in school, entered the Petroleum and Natural Gas Engineering program with a scholarship. Upon receiving his Bachelor of Science degree in 1973, Pegula landed his first job with Getty Oil Company in Victoria, Texas.

For an opportunity to learn while acquiring more responsibility, Pegula left Getty Oil and joined Felmont Oil Company, a decision that brought him to Olean, New York, in 1975. Eight years later, Terry borrowed $7,500 from family and friends and founded East Resources Incorporated, an independent oil and gas exploration and development company. Over the next twenty-seven years, he built it into one of the largest privately held companies in America.

A billionaire fracker, Terry made a fortune in oil and natural gas before purchasing two professional sports teams. His East Resources company sold the bulk of its assets to Royal Dutch Shell for $4.7 billion in 2010 and then unloaded an additional seventy-six thousand acres of land and assets to American Energy Partners for $1.75 billion in June 2014. Even so, he still retained oil and gas assets in states like Pennsylvania, West Virginia, and Colorado, though he traded some of his oil investments to organize a sports empire beginning in 2011.

Nearly a year after selling assets to Shell Oil, Terry purchased the National Hockey League (NHL) Buffalo Sabres, his hometown team, for $189 million. He joined the NFL in 2014 when his $1.4 billion bid for the Bills eliminated groups led by singer Jon Bon Jovi and real estate tycoon Donald Trump. Eventually Pegula wants to build a new stadium for his football team and also supports a $172 million development complex in downtown Buffalo that features two ice rinks, a hotel, and restaurant.

A native of Rochester, New York, Kim Pegula is a graduate of nearby Houghton College with a degree in Communications and has been involved with East Resources since 1991. Together she and Terry also founded Black River Music Group, a country music label based in Nashville, Tennessee, and the Ayrault Sports Agency located in Charlotte, North Carolina.

Team Financials

According to recent financial information published in *Forbes* for sixteen teams in the AFC, the Bills ranked sixteenth in market value at $1.4 billion, tied for fourteenth in both total revenue at $296 million and gate receipts at $49 million, thirteenth in operating income at $44 million, and seventh in player expenses at $163 million. In addition the club's debt-to-value ratio was 14 percent and tied for eighth place with the Ravens and Raiders in the AFC (Table A.3).

Among four ED clubs as of 2015, Buffalo had the lowest amounts of the group except for the Dolphins' operating income of $41 million, Patriots' and Jets' player expenses, and the Patriots' debt-to-value ratio of 7 percent. In part, these results denote the Bills' status as a small-market franchise that struggles to be competitive with others in their division and conference especially from a financial perspective.

Compared to thirty-one other NFL clubs in their 2014 season, Buffalo was thirty-second in estimated market value, tied for twenty-eighth with the Bengals in revenue, tied for twenty-seventh with the Bengals in gate receipts, twenty-fourth in operating income, tied for sixteenth with the Buccaneers in player expenses, and tied for eighth with the Ravens and Raiders in percent of their debt-to-value ratio. Other than their debt and players expenses, the Bills are a low-ranked professional sports business enterprise that needs additional revenue from their operations at home games and Ralph Wilson Stadium to be a more productive, successful, and valuable franchise (Table A.4).

For several years a Chicago-based company named Team Marketing Report (TMR) has prepared and published a Fan Cost Index (FCI) for the home games of teams in professional sports leagues. To attend a game for a typical family with two kids, an FCI includes the costs of four average-priced tickets, two cheapest-priced draft beers, four each cheapest-priced soft drinks and hot dogs, parking for one car, and two each game programs and least-expensive, adult-size adjustable caps. Costs are determined by telephone calls with team representatives, venues, and concessionaires, and from questions asked during interviews.[16]

For the 2015 NFL season, the Bills' FCI was approximately $391 or thirtieth highest in the league. Listed from most to least amounts by item for one person, the club's nonpremium ticket prices averaged $64, parking and caps each $25, beer $9, hot dogs about $6, and soft drinks $5. Among three other ED teams, the Patriots had the highest FCI at $624 followed by the Jets at $553 and Dolphins at $398. While the San Francisco 49ers' index of $640 was first in the league, the Jacksonville Jaguars placed thirty-second at $347. Thus, Bills' games are relatively cheap to attend for fans at Ralph Wilson Stadium. This, in turn, boosts attendances and increases the franchise's revenue, gate receipts, and operating income from home games compared to a higher FCI especially for ticket prices.

Business Highlights

Using fifteen years of data of such things as NFL team performances, home-game ticket prices, market populations and household median incomes, Emory University researchers created an equity index to determine which clubs had the most avid, engaged, passionate, and/or supportive fans as of 2015. Among the AFC's ED teams, the Bills ranked twenty-eighth and above the Dolphins in thirty-second but below the Patriots who finished second and Jets fifth. For various reasons, Buffalo's fans are not very engaged or passionate about their football team but more avid than those of the conference's Jaguars, Raiders, Browns, and Dolphins.

In another index at Emory University titled NFL Social Media Equity, the Bills ranked sixteenth and ahead of the Dolphins in twenty-third but behind the Patriots in sixth and Jets in ninth. While this index measured which teams over- or underperform with respect to their Twitter following, the Jets had a more dedicated fan base than sixteen other NFL clubs including eight in the AFC.

Western New York's two major sports franchises, the Bills and NHL Sabres, are using a high-tech approach that focuses more on customer-purchasing behaviors and less on mass marketing. The teams used to compete with each other to sell their tickets until the Pegulas became owners of both of them and centralized some functions under the umbrella of Pegula Sports and Entertainment (PS&E). Formed after they bought the Sabres in 2011, the Pegulas believed that many different disciplines can cross over both entities and maximize business efficiencies. These include such functions as marketing, finance, creative services, business development, and media content. Essentially, PS&E ties together the Bills, Sabres, and region into one Buffalo brand.

Regarding their NFL franchise, co-owners Terry and Kim Pegula will keep the Bills in Buffalo. The terms of the club's ten-year lease with Erie County requires anyone moving them from the city to pay the county $400 million if that occurs before the end of the 2019 NFL season. It also allows public entities to get a court injunction preventing the Bills from relocating elsewhere. The lease, however, contains a significant provision that could let them flee to another place. Indeed a clause allows the team to terminate its lease—and escape all provisions tying the team to Buffalo—after its seventh year (2020) for only a $28.4 million penalty.[17]

Miami Dolphins

Four years after becoming owner of the Miami Dolphins, businessman Wayne Huizenga decided to sell his team. During February 2008, New York real estate billionaire Stephen Ross purchased 50 percent of the franchise and Dolphin Stadium and its surrounding land from Huizenga for $550 million with an agreement to later become managing general partner of the NFL franchise. Ross closed on the purchase for an additional 45 percent share in early 2009 with Huizenga retaining a 5 percent interest.[18]

Dolphins' owner Ross attended Miami Beach High School and the University of Florida, and then earned a Bachelor of Arts in Science from the University of Michigan, a Doctor of Jurisprudence from Wayne State law school, and a Master of Laws from New York University. He began his career in Detroit as a tax attorney, and Michigan University's business school bears his name. Once a minority partner of the NHL's New York Islanders, Stephen was part of a group attempting to bring baseball to Miami in the early 1990s, and before Huizenga, became founding owner of MLB's Florida Marlins. He also made an unsuccessful bid for the NFL's New York Jets in 1999.

As chairman of Related Companies, Ross was the developer behind America's largest private real estate project. His $15 billion mega development, Hudson Yards—a twenty-eight-acre neighborhood on Manhattan's West Side—broke ground in 2012. Meanwhile his company developed Hunter's Point South in Queens, the largest affordable housing complex built in New York City since the 1970s. One part of his fortune—the Time Warner

Center—was the subject of a *New York Times* investigation in 2015. The newspaper found that the skyscraper had become home for some shady, if undeniably wealthy, characters. Ross's Related Companies also owns the Equinox fitness centers.

According to *Financial Times*, Ross is participating with some Qatar investors to purchase the Formula 1 (F1) racing circuit from Bernie Ecclestone for an estimated $7–$8 billion. Ross's RSE Ventures business wants to buy at least 35 percent of the company, which controls the racing circuit, to bring fans of F1 events to Miami and promote high-end sponsorships and corporate hospitality at Sun Life Stadium. If Ross is successful with Qatar investors and F1, he might use the additional cash to improve his football team.[19]

Team Financials

Based on financial data published in Forbes for sixteen AFC franchises as of 2015, the Dolphins ranked eighth in both market value at $1.85 billion and gate receipts at $57 million, and also seventh in total revenue at $322 million, fourteenth in operating income at $41 million, and fourth in player expenses at $169 million. In addition the club's debt-to-value ratio was 19 percent, or second highest in the AFC (Table A.3).

Among four ED clubs as of 2015, Miami had the third-highest market value, revenue and gate receipts, smallest operating income among the group, most player expenses, and a lower debt-to-value percent than the Jets. These results, in part, reveal why financially this is an average professional football enterprise in the AFC and a mediocre business that operates in a midsized sports market but has problems earning profits while competing with others in its division and across the conference.

Compared to thirty-one other NFL clubs in 2015, Miami was fifteenth in market value, tied for sixteenth with the Saints in revenue, tied for eighteenth with the Falcons in gate receipts, twenty-sixth in operating income, seventh in player expenses, and tied for seventh with the Lions in their debt-to-value. Other than their debt ratio, the Dolphins are a mid to low-ranked business that needs to get more production and better results from coaches and players based on amounts in their contracts and also has to improve gate receipts and operations while playing home games at Sun Life Stadium. In short, this franchise should focus on becoming efficient and more profitable during its regular seasons from a financial perspective (Table A.4).

For several years a Chicago-based company named Team Marketing Report (TMR) has prepared and published a Fan Cost Index (FCI) for the home games of teams in professional sports leagues. To attend a game for a typical family with two kids, an FCI includes the costs of four average-priced tickets, two cheapest-priced draft beers, four each cheapest-priced soft drinks and hot dogs, parking for one car, and two each game programs and least-expensive, adult-size adjustable caps. Costs are determined by telephone calls with team representatives, venues, and concessionaires, and from questions asked during interviews.[20]

For the 2015 NFL season, the Dolphins' FCI was approximately $398 or twenty-eighth highest in the league. Listed from most to least amounts by item for one person, the club's nonpremium ticket prices averaged $65, a cap $26, parking $20, beer $8, hot dog $6, a program $5, and a soft drink $4. Among three other ED teams, the Patriots had the highest FCI at $624 and then the Jets at $553 and last the Bills at $391. While the 49ers' index of $640 was first in the league, the Jaguars placed thirty-second at $347. Similar to the Bills' FCI, Dolphins' games are relatively cheap to attend for fans at Sun Life Stadium. This, in turn, affects attendances and the franchise's revenue, gate receipts, and operating income from home games compared to a higher FCI especially for nonpremium and premium ticket prices.

Business Highlights

Using fifteen years of data on such things as NFL team performances, home-game ticket prices, and market populations and their median incomes, Emory University researchers created an equity index to determine which clubs had the most avid, engaged, passionate, and supportive fans as of 2015. Among the AFC's ED teams, the Dolphins ranked thirty-second and below the Patriots who finished second, Jets fifth, and Bills twenty-eighth. Consequently, Miami's fans are not very engaged or passionate about their football team and less avid and enthusiastic than those of the conference's other fifteen teams.

National brands tend to stick to the tried-and-true social media services: Twitter, Facebook, maybe a foray into Instagram. Determined to stay on the cutting edge, the Dolphins became the first professional sports team to use Meerkat, the video live-streaming app that has seen explosive growth since its launch in early 2015. Veering toward trends in social media strategy, the team was the first in the NFL to join Yo, an app that sends followers the word 'Yo' to signify a new video, audio clip, or other update. Furthermore, the club used Snapchat to tease images of Dolphins players reimagined as Marvel characters before released. Meerkat, meanwhile, is the new service that allows iPhone users to show their Twitter followers a live video of their surroundings. Viewers can respond with tweets, which show up in the app in real time. Videos disappear once the livestream is over.

To highlight this part of the chapter, Sun Life Stadium's modernization is moving ahead. The Miami-Dade County Commission approved Mayor Carlos Gimenez's plan for bonus payments to the Dolphins for hosting marquee events in exchange for owner Ross's payment of $350 million to renovate the team's stadium. The agreement, which is designed to help bring future events such as Super Bowls, college football championships, World Cup soccer matches, and other international soccer events, exists for twenty years. The renovations are expected to make the stadium a state-of-the-art facility and extend its ability to attract marquee events for the next quarter century.[21]

New England Patriots

Born in Brookline, Massachusetts, Robert Kraft graduated from Brookline High School in 1959 and four years later from Columbia University where he played on the school's lightweight football team. In 1965 Kraft received a Master of Business Administration degree from Harvard Business School.[22]

Kraft began his career with the Rand-Whitney Group, a packaging company he later acquired. In 1972 he founded International Forest Products and traded physical paper commodities on exchanges. Combined, these are the largest privately held paper and packing companies in the United States. In 1986 Kraft helped a group purchase WNEV-TV, a CBS affiliate in Boston and then continued investing in the entertainment industry by buying several Boston radio stations.

A Patriots fan since their ten years in the AFL, Kraft became a season ticket holder in 1972. Thirteen years later, he bought an option on a parcel of land which contained Sullivan Stadium, the Patriots' home site. Then in 1988 Kraft outbid competitors to acquire the stadium, which was in bankruptcy, for $25 million and renamed it Foxboro Stadium in 1990.

In 1992 Kraft rejected a $75 million offer to buy out the lease which would have allowed the Patriots team to move to another city. Instead, he paid a then-NFL record $175 million to St. Louis businessman James Orthwein and bought the team in 1995 with profits from his paper manufacturing conglomerate and pledged to keep it located in the Boston area. Upon purchasing the club, Kraft committed to bring a Super Bowl and state-of-the-art facility to New England. However, his follow-through on those promises exceeded expectations.

Team Financials

According to financial information published in *Forbes* for sixteen teams in the AFC as of 2015, the Patriots ranked first in market value at $3.2 billion and also in total revenue at $494 million, gate receipts at $100 million, and operating income at $195 million, and eighth in player expenses at $160 million. In addition the club's debt-to-value ratio was 7 percent and tied for ninth with the Bengals, Texans, Jaguars, and Chargers (Table A.3).

Among four ED clubs as of 2015, New England had the largest amounts except for player expenses of the Dolphins but the smallest debt ratio of the group. Essentially these results reflect the Patriots' status as a profitable, rich, and large-market franchise that succeeds in being superior in regular season and also competitive with others in its division and conference especially from a financial perspective.

Compared to thirty-one other NFL clubs as of their 2014 season, New England was second in market value, revenue and operating income, first in gate receipts, nineteenth in player expenses, and tied for nineteenth with several other clubs in its percent of debt-to-value ratio. Thus, the Patriots are a high-ranked and wealthy professional sports enterprise that generates enough revenue from operations and their home games at Gillette Stadium to be a productive, successful, and valuable franchise. Consequently, this club is a prosperous business from a financial perspective (Table A.4)

For several years a Chicago-based company named Team Marketing Report (TMR) has prepared and published a Fan Cost Index (FCI) for the home games of teams in professional sports leagues. To attend a game for a typical family with two kids, an FCI includes the costs of four average-priced tickets, two cheapest-priced draft beers, four each cheapest-priced soft drinks and hot dogs, parking for one car, and two each game programs and least-expensive, adult-size adjustable caps. Costs are determined by telephone calls with team representatives, venues, and concessionaires, and from questions asked during interviews.

For the 2015 NFL season, the Patriots' FCI was approximately $624 or fourth highest in the league. Listed from most to least amounts by item for one person, the club's nonpremium ticket prices averaged $122, parking about $40 and a cap $20, a beer almost $8, program $5, and a hot dog and soft drink each $4. Among other ED teams, the Jets' FCI was ranked seventh at $553, Dolphins twenty-eighth at $398, and Bills thirtieth at $391. While the San Francisco 49ers' index of $640 was first in the league, the Jacksonville Jaguars placed thirty-second at $347. Thus, Patriots games are very expensive to attend for fans at Gillette Stadium. However, because of its spectacular success in games and seasons since the early 2000s, New England makes plenty of revenue from gate receipts to be profitable despite relatively high nonpremium and premium ($566 each) ticket prices and other costs.[23]

Business Highlights

Using fifteen years of data on such things as NFL team performances, home-game ticket prices, and market populations and their median incomes, Emory University researchers created an equity index to determine which clubs had the most avid, engaged, passionate, and supportive fans as of 2015. Among the AFC's ED teams, the Patriots ranked second and ahead of the Jets at fifth, Bills at twenty-eighth, and Dolphins at thirty-second. For various reasons,

Patriots fans are very engaged and passionate about their football team, but less avid than those of only the Dallas Cowboys.

For other business news, the Patriots use their winning brand to generate revenue beyond the NFL. Adjacent to Gillette Stadium, for example, the Kraft family owns Patriot Place, which includes more than 1.3 million square feet of shopping, dining, and entertainment. It features such retailers as Old Navy and Victoria's Secret, and the region's only Bass Pro Shops and restaurants like CBS Scene, Davio's, Toby Keith's I Love This Bar & Grill, and Olive Garden. There is also interactive entertainment with 5 Wits' 20,000 Leagues and Espionage as well as Tour the Hall presented by Raytheon, which honors the greatest moments in Patriots' history.[24]

New York Jets

Born in 1947, Robert Wood Johnson IV was the great-grandson of one of the Johnson & Johnson founders. Nicknamed Woody, he was a teenager in 1965 when his father, then president of Johnson & Johnson, lost his position with the company after a feud within the family. During Woody's early twenties, both men died and his entry into the family business closed.[25]

For a time he drifted, moved to Florida, and worked in real estate. Despite a hippy appearance, Woody did well in business and augmented his considerable fortune with a successful cable company. In the early 1980s he thought about investing in an NFL franchise in Tampa, Florida, but decided it was a bad fit. Instead, he poured his energy into charitable and political fund-raising.

While attending the funeral of longtime Jets owner Leon Hess in 1999, Robert IV was impressed to see the entire Jets team in attendance. When the Hess family put the franchise for sale on the market, he moved quickly. Although experts placed the Jets' value then at roughly $250 million, the bidding war for it soared much, much higher. Ultimately the bidding came down to him and Charles Dolan, the owner of Madison Square Garden, NHL Rangers, and National Basketball Association (NBA) Knicks. When Woody bid $625 million and then increased it by $10 million at the deadline, Dolan dropped out of the process. This price tag was the highest ever for a New York sports franchise, and the third highest for an NFL team.

When he acquired the Jets, it had three advantages. First, it was the legend of Super Bowl III in 1969 when quarterback Joe Namath guaranteed and then delivered an upset win. Second, the franchise had the marketing cachet of being a New York–based team even though it played home games in a New Jersey stadium shared with, and named for, the rival NFL Giants. Third was Coach Bill Parcells, who led the Jets to the brink of the Super Bowl in 1999. But in January 2000 Parcells quit as did his potential replacement, Bill Belichick.

Team Financials

According to data and other financial information published in *Forbes* for sixteen teams in the AFC as of 2015, the Jets ranked second in market value at $2.6 billion, gate receipts at $77 million, and operating income at $118 million, tied for second with the Texans in total revenue at $383 million, and sixteenth in player expenses at $138 million. In addition the club's debt-to-value ratio was 23 percent, or the highest in the conference (Table A.3).

Among only ED clubs, New York Jets had the second largest market value, revenue, gate receipts and operating income, lowest payroll, and highest percent in debt-to-value. These results denote the team's profile as a large-market and wealthy franchise with significant debt but also one that struggles to win games and championships in its division and conference yet primarily succeeds from a financial perspective.

Compared to thirty-one other NFL clubs in 2015, New York was sixth in market value, tied for sixth in revenue, tied for fifth in gate receipts, fifth in operating income, thirty-first in players expenses, and third in debt to value. Despite the team's relatively small player expenses and large debts, the Jets are a rich and profitable sports enterprise from their operations and home games at MetLife Stadium. Nevertheless, the club needs to hire smart and productive coaches and recruit better players to be competitive across NFL seasons and become a more competitive, popular, and successful franchise (Table A.4).

For several years a Chicago-based company named Team Marketing Report (TMR) has prepared and published a Fan Cost Index (FCI) for the home games of teams in professional sports leagues. To attend a game for a typical family with two kids, an FCI includes the costs of four average-priced tickets, two cheapest-priced draft beers, four each cheapest-priced soft drinks and hot dogs, parking for one car, and two each game programs and least-expensive, adult-size adjustable caps. Costs are determined by telephone calls with team representatives, venues, and concessionaires, and from questions asked during interviews.[26]

For the 2015 NFL season, the Jets' FCI was approximately $553 or seventh highest in the league. Listed from most to least amounts by item for one person, the club's nonpremium ticket prices averaged approximately $106, parking $25, a cap $20, and program $10, hot dog $6, beer $5, and a soft drink $3. Among three other ED teams in the AFC, the Patriots had the highest FCI at $624 and then the Dolphins at $398 and Bills' $391. While the San Francisco 49ers' index of $638 was first in the league, the Jacksonville Jaguars placed thirty-second at $345. Thus, Jets games are relatively expensive to attend for fans at MetLife Stadium. Because of sellouts, however, this means more revenue, gate receipts, and operating income for the franchise from home games in part because of nonpremium and premium ($344 each) ticket prices.

Business Highlights

Using fifteen years of data on such things as NFL team performances, home-game ticket prices, and market populations and their median incomes, Emory University researchers created an equity index to determine which clubs had the most avid, engaged, passionate, and supportive fans as of 2015 but before the regular season. Among the conference's ED teams, the Jets ranked fifth and above the Bills at twenty-eighth and Dolphins at thirty-second but below the Patriots who finished second among all teams. For various reasons, the Jets have an avid and passionate fan base that is very engaged and passionate about their football team and similar to those of the Ravens and Bears.[27]

In April 2014, Moody's Investors Service assigned Baa3—three notches above junk ratings—to Jets Stadium LLC's $255 million of project revenue bonds and $297 million of parity debt, which combined are being used to finance the team's portion of MetLife Stadium. According to the financial report, the ratings reflect the high level of medium to long-term contracted revenues that support cash flow certainty due to the high level of support for the Jets and the team's large regional market (biggest in the nation) having one of the highest median incomes and concentrations of Fortune 500 companies. The ratings also incorporate the low level of capital expenditures required at the new stadium and recent debt reduction in which the team originally sold $650 million of bonds for its construction.[28]

NOTES

1. For the history of the NFL, see Frank P. Jozsa Jr., *Football Fortunes: The Business, Organization and Strategy of the NFL* (Jefferson, NC: McFarland, 2010), and James Quirk and Rodney D. Fort, *Pay Dirt: The Business of Professional Team Sports* (Princeton, NJ: Princeton University Press, 1992).
2. Two important references for the AFL and its teams' seasons and postseasons from 1960 to 1969 are "Teams," http://wwww.profootballhof.com, cited September 1, 2015, and "Teams," http://www.pro-football-reference.com, cited August 25, 2015.
3. Besides www.nfl.com, coaches and players performances, records, and awards are in the *NFL Record & Fact Book 2014* (New York: NFL, 2014) and "NFL Links," http://www.sportsecyclopdia.com, cited August 25, 2015.
4. Results appear in "Ranking All 31 NFL Stadiums," http://www.sportingnews.com, cited August 31, 2015. For another study, see Michael Potts, "Ranking All NFL Stadiums for 2015—From Worst to Best," http://www.whatculture.com, cited September 2, 2015.
5. "If the flight of people from the Buffalo area continues, it isn't going to matter how much marketing [former owner] Ralph Wilson or his successor does. This team will have no choice but to significantly reduce the size of the stadium to be more in line with the MSA [Metropolitan Statistical Area] totals, or to move to an area with a larger MSA." See K. C. Joyner, "N.F.L. Sellouts Have Become Easier, But Not for Bills," http://www.nytimes.com, cited September 2, 2015.

6. The historical attendances of NFL teams are in the data supplement on pages 488–94 of *Pay Dirt* and also in "Rod Fort's Sports Business Data," http://www.sites.google.com cited September 1, 2015.

7. Similar books, readings, and websites were used as sources for the performances of Miami Dolphins teams as for those of the Buffalo Bills, New England Patriots, and New York Jets.

8. This quote was from Michael Potts, "Ranking All NFL Stadiums for 2015—From Worst to Best."

9. See rankings of the Dolphins and other NFL teams in Manish Tripathi, "2015 NFL Fan Equity Rankings," https://scholarblogs.emory.edu, cited September 4, 2015 and Michael Lewis, "2015 NFL Social Media Equity Rankings," https://scholarblogs.emory.edu cited September 4, 2015.

10. Literature sources for the Patriots' performances were similar to those of the Bills, Dolphins, and Jets.

11. To evaluate the venue of all teams in the league, read "Ranking All 31 NFL Stadiums."

12. Jets performances are from the same books, readings, and websites as the Bills, Dolphins, and Patriots.

13. See "Rod Fort's Sports Business Data" and NFL attendances at http://www.espn.go.com.

14. The Jets' stadium and its amenities are evaluated in "Ranking All 31 NFL Stadiums."

15. "NFL Team Owners," http://www.biography.yourdictionary.com, cited December 24, 2015.

16. For each ED team in the AFC and NFC, see "2015 NFL Fan Cost Index," http://www.teammarketing.com, cited November 20, 2015.

17. Other information about the Bills business is contained in Daniel Kaplan, "Among Wilson's Legacies: A Small-Market Team, A Prescient Vote," *SportsBusiness Journal* (March 31, 2014): 29; and Bill King, "New Bills Owners' Passionate Vision of One Buffalo," *SportsBusiness Journal* (December 8, 2014): 1.

18. "NFL Team Owners."

19. Mike Ozanian, "Stephen Ross Wants F1 Because Fast Cars Will Make Dolphins Swim Faster," http://www.forbes.com, cited September 9, 2015.

20. "2015 NFL Fan Cost Index."

21. Miami seeks more income as discussed in Daniel Kaplan, "Dolphins See Potential for Tailgating Revenue," *SportsBusiness Journal* (August 17, 2015): 19; Don Muret, "Dolphins Boxes to Offer Comforts of Home," *SportsBusiness Journal* (February 2, 2015): 3; Sharon Terlep, "Why Ticket Brokers Hate the Dolphins," *Wall Street Journal* (October 2, 2015): D8.

22. For highlights of Robert Kraft's personal and business careers, "NFL Team Owners" has information about his success.

23. To compare the annual increase in FCIs among teams, see the "2015 NFL Fan Cost Index" and "2014 NFL Fan Cost Index," https://www.teammarketing.com, cited August 26, 2015.

24. Read about the Patriots franchise as a business in Abraham Madkour, "Patriots Build on Stadium's Year-Round Appeal," *SportsBusiness Journal* (September 7, 2015): 1 and "Patriots: Suite New Digs," *SportsBusiness Journal* (September 7, 2015): 40.

25. "NFL Team Owners."

26. "2015 NFL Fan Cost Index."

27. See the readings in Note 9 for the how the Jets ranked in these indexes.

28. For this franchise's financial goals, see such readings as Terry Lefton, "Jets Stroll Down 'Silicon Valley' with an Eye on Engagement," *SportsBusiness Journal* (June 15, 2015): 13; and Stu Woo, "New Jets Leaders Will Need Patient Flight Plan," *Wall Street Journal* (December 31, 2014): 1.

Chapter Two

North Division

Prior to the 2015 National Football League (NFL) regular season, which team or teams in the North Division (ND) of the American Football Conference (AFC) had the most titles and championships, least total losses in games, best winning percentage, and appeared in the largest number of playoffs? Were the Baltimore Ravens, for example, a more valuable franchise than the Pittsburgh Steelers, and did the Cincinnati Bengals or Cleveland Browns earn more total revenue, gate receipts, and operating income during a recent season?

To answer these and other questions about the operations of this sport, next are some interesting but important, realistic, and relevant facts that highlight the historical performances of four teams in the AFC's ND as of the league's 2015–2016, or simply 2015 season. Besides their winning percentage and number of wins, titles, championships, and playoff appearances, this information includes special coaches, players, and events regarding each of them while competing in the NFL's regular seasons and any playoffs. In the chapter's final section—labeled Franchise Business—are these franchises' success or failure as business enterprises both individually and in comparison to each other from a financial perspective.[1]

TEAM PERFORMANCES

Baltimore Ravens

Following the Colts' sudden, but necessary, relocation from Baltimore, Maryland, to Indianapolis, Indiana, in March 1984, the former city began efforts to attract another NFL team. When the league decided to expand and later add two clubs in the 1995 season, Baltimore was considered a prime site.

However, based on several factors including bids from various individuals and/or syndicates, NFL team owners awarded new franchises to Charlotte, North Carolina, and Jacksonville, Florida.[2]

After being rejected for expansion, Baltimore became home to a Canadian Football League (CFL) team nicknamed the Colts. Forced to change its name to Stallions when NFL Colts' owner Robert Irsay filed a lawsuit, the team won the league's Grey Cup in 1995. Despite the success of the Stallions in the CFL, Baltimore really sought an existing NFL franchise. In October 1995 the city's officials made a deal with Cleveland Browns owner Art Modell to move his team to Baltimore.

To prevent them from relocating, Cleveland filed an injunction in court to keep the Browns there until 1998 while several other lawsuits were filed by some fans and season ticket holders. After extensive talks between the league, Browns, and two cities, this led to a settlement between the city of Cleveland and NFL permitting Modell to immediately move his club to Baltimore. However, the Browns were required to leave behind their heritage and records including name, logo, colors, history, playing records, trophies, and memorabilia to be used, if approved, by an expansion team in Cleveland to begin play in 1999. This meant that the Baltimore team had an established roster with a new heritage, history, records, and name. Eventually "Ravens" was chosen as a nickname in honor of poet Edgar Allen Poe's famous book written while he lived in the city.

After relocation, Modell hired Ted Marchibroda to be head coach for his new team. Marchibroda was already well-known because of his reputation and accomplishments as head coach of the league's Baltimore Colts during the 1970s and Indianapolis Colts during the early 1990s. Cleveland Browns' former all-pro tight end Ozzie Newsome joined Modell's organization as director of football operations. He was later promoted to vice-president/general manager. In retrospect, these were the new club's decision makers and key personnel to open the 1996 NFL season.

Historical Results

While playing in the AFC's Central Division from 1996 to 2001 and then as a member of the ND during 2002–2015, the Ravens had 173 victories and won 54 percent of their games. As of the league's 2015 season, they won four division and two conference titles and also two Super Bowls in ten playoff appearances. Compared to other teams in their conference, Baltimore ranked twelfth in number of wins and fourth in winning percentage. In addition the club was eleventh in division titles, tied for seventh with the Bengals and Colts in conference titles, tied for third with the Dolphins and Raiders in number of NFL plus Super Bowl championships, and placed twelfth in postseason playoffs (Table A.1).

Regarding only ND teams in the AFC, the Ravens had the second fewest number of wins and highest percentage of them, but ranked only third with six titles. In short, this twenty-year-old club was above average in performances during several seasons and postseasons of the conference because of its dedicated coaches, talented players, and the vision and commitment of its owners to become involved each year in decision-making and therefore appreciate and invest resources and money in their franchise.

When compared to the performances of thirty-one other NFL teams as of their 2015 season, the Ravens ranked twenty-sixth in number of wins, seventh in winning percentage, twenty-fifth in division titles, tied for seventeenth in winning their conference, and tied for ninth with two Super Bowl championships. These and other results prove that Baltimore's NFL team has been, on average, competitive but not superior among the group while playing two decades in the league (Table A.2).

To achieve these results, Baltimore's teams had two excellent coaches and several competitive players. In the former group was Brian Billick with 85 wins and John Harbaugh with 81, while Coach Ted Marchibroda's three Ravens teams finished with a 16–31 record. Although the club had no coaches of the year in the league, Harbaugh has appeared in six playoffs in seven years and Billick appeared in four in nine years while each coach won one Super Bowl. If his teams continue to excel and win more championships, Harbaugh will be a future candidate for the pro football Hall of Fame.

As of 2015, some players had been outstanding performers and established records for the franchise at various positions on the field. During their careers as Ravens, for example, running back Jamal Lewis led in rushing yards; quarterback Joe Flacco in passing yards and touchdowns; safety Ed Reed in interceptions; and specialist Matt Stover in field goals and points. For a single season, Vinny Testaverde set records in passing yards and touchdowns; Derrick Mason and Michael Jackson in receiving passes; Sam Koch in punting average; Jacoby Jones in kickoff returns; and Ray Rice in number of touchdowns. In a single game, record holders include quarterback Tony Banks, receivers Priest Holmes and Qadry Ismail, and running back Marcus Robinson. Thus, these were great athletes in one or more NFL seasons for the Ravens.

Because of its relatively brief time as a member of the AFC, Baltimore had only a few winners of Associated Press (AP) awards before the league's 2015 season. Jamal Lewis was offensive player of the year in 2003; Ray Lewis won defensive player of the year in 2000 and 2003, Ed Reed in 2004, and Terrell Suggs in 2011; and Peter Boulware became defensive rookie of the year in 1997 and Suggs in 2003. Besides them, no other team players received AP awards for being offensive rookie of the year or comeback player of the year. Eventually more Ravens players will be honored for their accomplishments in games of NFL seasons.

Thus far, Baltimore has four players in the pro football Hall of Fame. Those inducted include cornerback/safety Rod Woodson in 2009; cornerback/kick returner/punt returner Deion Sanders and tight end Shannon Sharpe in 2011; and offensive tackle Jonathan Ogden in 2013. When eligible, former player Ray Lewis will enter the Hall of Fame because of his ability to play outstanding defense as a middle linebacker and being selected on several annual AFC and NFL all-pro teams.[3]

Performance Highlights

Among their years in the league, the Ravens most successful periods were 2000–2001 and 2008–2012, and 2014. Besides appearing in at least two playoffs during each period, they won a Super Bowl in 2000 and again in 2012. Such athletes as quarterbacks Tony Banks and Joe Flacco, running backs Ray Rice and Jamal Lewis, receivers Anquan Boldin and Shannon Sharpe, and defensive players Ray Lewis and Terrell Suggs were stars. Alternatively, the team's worst seasons were 1996–1999, 2002, 2004–2005, 2007, and 2013.

From 1996 to 1997, the Ravens played their home games at Baltimore's Memorial Stadium. Then in 1998 the team shifted from there to the newly constructed, multipurpose, 71,000-seat M&T Bank Stadium. As a result, the club's home attendances substantially increased because of the new stadium's amenities including its five levels, three hundred suites, ease of access, number and availability of concessions, and also padded club seats, luxury boxes, and an upper bowl.

Among NFL venues, M&T Stadium ranked sixteenth in a recent study. According to a publication about it in an edition of the *Sporting News*:

> In the last two years, the stadium has undergone $35 million in renovations touching most aspects of the 17-year-old facility. The upgrades include improved wireless infrastructure, a refresh of concession stands, new LED screens, and bars branded for Barcardi, Yuengling, Dogfish, and Captain Morgan. Also, outside the stadium, the Ravens Walk offers food and drink concessions at reduced prices compared with inside the facility. Last year, a new statute of Ravens legend Ray Lewis joined an existing monument to existing Hall of Famer Johnny Unitas, the original Johnny Football.[4]

Based on such things as their winning percentage in the ND, popularity and ticket prices, and also Baltimore's weather conditions, market size, population growth, and household per capita income, the Ravens consistently attract fans to their home games. Historically, for example, total attendances in regular seasons ranged from 471,665 in 1996 to 574,188 in 1999; 554,991 in 2001 to 568,660 in 2009; and from 569,817 in 2010 to 568,353 in 2014. If the club continues to successfully compete in its division and qualifies for the playoffs, M&T Stadium will be filled to capacity at all Ravens' home games and likely increase the franchise's gate receipts, revenues, and market value.[5]

Regarding the team's future, general manager Ozzie Newsome has been able to retool year-by-year and move forward with establishing a strong but balanced roster of players. Baltimore has missed the playoffs just three times since 2006, but in their 2016 and 2017 seasons they could have enough athletes to win the AFC and compete again in a Super Bowl. The reasons, in part, are because (a) Joe Flacco is an elite quarterback, (b) the offensive line is one of the best in their conference, and (c) besides Newsome and coach Harbaugh, the team has excellent offensive and defensive coordinators who teach and motivate their players to succeed.

To continue winning in postseasons, Baltimore must earn home-field advantage in the playoffs. Every team wants to be at home in the playoffs, but for the Ravens, this has been huge during the coach Harbaugh era. Since he replaced Billick and took over in 2008, Baltimore has a 45–11 record at home and 27–29 on the road in regular seasons through 2014. Except in 2013 and 2015, the Ravens made the playoffs every year but never won home-field advantage in the AFC since hiring Harbaugh. If they win their division, that is one home playoff game. If they win twelve games, that should be enough for two. What they really need, though, is for the rest of the conference to get as competitive as the ND has been in recent years, so the path to the Super Bowl will not be played on the road.

In sum, the Ravens have been a formidable team especially when they play mid-tier and marginal opponents in the AFC. Most seasons, the division's Steelers are Baltimore's strongest rival followed by the Bengals and then Browns. If quarterback Flacco stays healthy and Newsome continues his job as general manager, the franchise will likely win and thrive at least for the next few or more years.

Cincinnati Bengals

Plans to establish this franchise occurred three years before the team began playing in the AFL's 1968 season. Paul Brown, who enjoyed great success as the head coach of the NFL Cleveland Browns for seventeen seasons before departing in 1962, was eager to return to a job in professional football. After he met with Ohio Governor Jim Rhodes in 1965, they jointly agreed the state could accommodate and support another professional football team.[6]

Scheduled for completion by 1970, Cincinnati's city council approved the construction of 60,389-seat Riverfront Stadium in 1966. The next year, a group of investors headed by Brown was awarded an AFL franchise to begin playing in the league's 1968 season. Brown nicknamed his team Bengals to honor previous Cincinnati professional football franchises with the same name and performed in the 1930s and 1940s. Subsequently, he coached the Bengals for the club's first eight years.

Although the 1968 Bengals won their first two home games in 28,000-seat Nippert Stadium on the campus of University of Cincinnati, they finished the season 3–11–0 but with the most victories of any expansion team of the 1960s. After Cincinnati improved its performance to 4–9–1 in 1969 and finished fifth in the Western Division, Brown continued as head coach of the team.

Because of a merger between the AFL and NFL before their 1970 season, the Bengals, like other former AFL teams, joined the AFC and was assigned to its Central Division (CD) along with clubs based in Cleveland, Houston, and Pittsburgh. Cincinnati was a prime location, and, like Major League Baseball's (MLB) Reds, could attract sports fans from several medium-sized to large neighboring cities including Louisville and Lexington in Kentucky; Columbus, Dayton, and Springfield in Ohio; and Indianapolis, Indiana. Each of these cities is less than 125 miles from downtown Cincinnati.

Historical Results

While playing in the league's CD from 1970 to 2001 and then the ND during 2002–2015 the Bengals had 332 victories and won approximately 46 percent of their games. In addition they played well enough to earn nine division and two conference titles, but zero Super Bowls in fourteen playoff appearances. Compared to other AFC teams as of the league's 2015 season, Cincinnati was seventh in number of wins and ranked eleventh in winning percentage, and also tied for seventh with the Raiders in division titles, tied for seventh with the Ravens and Colts in conference titles, tied for eighth with eight other clubs in winning zero NFL plus Super Bowl championships, and tied for sixth with the Chiefs in number of playoffs. These results, in part, denote the franchise's historical competitiveness and results while performing in its conference during forty-six seasons in the league (Table A.1).

Among only ND teams as of 2015, the Bengals had the second most wins following the Steelers and third highest winning percentage after the Ravens and Steelers but more total titles than the Ravens and Browns combined. To be truly successful, however, the club needs to improve its performances in regular seasons and win another conference title and its first Super Bowl. Because of the Steelers, who dominate the conference's ND and the powerful Ravens, Cincinnati must become more consistent playing against its division rivals and win at least ten or eleven games each season to qualify for the playoffs.

Compared to the all-time performances of thirty-one other NFL teams as of their 2015 season, the forty-six-year-old Bengals tied for sixteenth in number of wins and also ranked twenty-first in winning percentage, tied for fifteenth in division titles and seventeenth in conference titles, and tied for eighteenth with zero Super Bowls. These and other results prove that, except for a few seasons including 2011–2015, Cincinnati's NFL team has performed below average competitively while playing more than four decades in the league (Table A.2).

Since 1970, Bengals teams had a number of successful coaches and also talented players who performed at different positions on the field. In the former group was Marvin Lewis with 100 victories, Sam Wyche 64, Paul Brown 48, and Forest Gregg 34. For winning eight games and the CD title but losing to the Ravens in the divisional playoffs, Brown was the AFC coach of the year in 1970. Thirty-nine years later, Coach Lewis also won the award when his team won the ND but then was defeated in the wild card playoff by the New York Jets. Alternatively, the club's least successful coaches include Homer Rice, Dick LeBeau, Bill Johnson, Dave Shula, and Bruce Coslet, who individually, had more losses than victories.

Some Bengals players performed well enough to establish career, single season, and single game records for the franchise. Career leaders, for example, include running back Corey Dillion in rushing yards; quarterback Ken Anderson in passing yards and touchdowns; receiver Chad Johnson in number of catches and yards; and cornerback Ken Riley in interceptions. For a single season, some record holders are punter Kevin Huber, punt returner Lemar Parrish, and kickoff return specialist Tremain Mack.

In a single game of a season Boomer Esiason remarkably passed for 490 yards; Shane Graham kicked 7 field goals; Larry Kinnebrew and two other players each had 4 touchdowns; Antwan Odom recorded 5 sacks; and Dillon, Kinnebrew, and Marvin Jones each scored 24 points. Indeed these and several other athletes were extraordinary performers for Bengals teams by setting career, single season, and/or single game records.

Including coaches Brown and Lewis, some Bengals players won NFL Associated Press (AP) awards. More specifically, Ken Anderson was offensive player of the year in 1981; Eddie Brown offensive rookie of the year in 1985 and Carl Pickens in 1992; and John Kitna comeback player of the year in 2003. For different reasons, Cincinnati had no players winning defensive player of the year or defensive rookie of the year awards from 1970 to 2014.

Besides Coach Brown and Riley, Anderson and Esiason, such players as receiver Chris Collinsworth, defensive lineman Tim Krumrie, tackle Anthony Munoz, and wide receiver Isaac Curtis are in the Bengals.com Hall of Fame. More significantly, Brown, Munoz, and wide receiver Charlie Joiner have been inducted into the pro football Hall of Fame. Also, the club retired center Bob Johnson's number while quarterback Carson Palmer was the pro bowl Most Valuable Player (MVP) in 2007. In short, Brown and these different players were honored because of their outstanding contributions to various Bengals teams.

Performance Highlights

Since 1970, the club's most productive periods consecutively were in 1981 to 1982 and the 2011 to 2015 NFL seasons. In seven other years, the Bengals appeared in playoffs including a Super Bowl in 1988. Those accomplishments occurred because of such coaches as Gregg and Lewis, quarterbacks Ken Anderson and Andy Dalton, and receivers Chris Collinsworth and A.J. Green. Although they lost both their Super Bowls by respectively five and four points to the NFC's 49ers, Cincinnati football fans were proud of and supported their hometown team. Alternatively, the franchise failed to win enough games and play in consecutive postseasons in other years including 1976–1980, 1983–1987, and 1991–2004.

The Bengals played their home games at Riverfront Stadium from 1970 to 1999. One year later, the 65,515-seat Paul Brown Stadium opened for the team. Covering approximately forty acres, the facility is 157 feet high with three levels, and contains 7,600 club seats and 114 private suites. Along with Louisiana's Mercedes-Benz Superdome and Minnesota's Hubert H. Humphrey Metrodome, it features the new UBU Sports' Speed Series S5-M synthetic turf system. Also, the new playing surface displays an inlaid Bengals center logo and a branded end-zone design.

Among thirty-one NFL venues, Paul Brown Stadium ranked twenty-third in a recent study. According to an article about it in an edition of the *Sporting News*, the author wrote:

> The Tigers Den is one of multiple middle-aged NFL stadiums in need of a refresh. For the season, new and bigger video boards will be installed at a cost of $10 million. Improved Wi-Fi coverage, concession stand upgrades and new furniture in the clubs are other improvements. The Banks, a mixed-use development along the Ohio River near the stadium, has several bars and restaurants to congregate before the game.[7]

Based on such things as their winning percentage in the ND and premium ticket prices at home games, and also Cincinnati's weather conditions, market size, population growth, and household per capita income, the Bengals occasionally struggle to attract enough fans to their home games. Historically, for example, total attendances in regular seasons ranged from 321,586 to 414,859 in the 1970s; 216,233 to 440,906 in the 1980s; 353,273 to 473,228 in the 1990s; 464,678 to 526,467 in the early 2000s; and at least 568,000 each year from 2010 to 2014. However, if the club continues to compete in its division and qualify for the playoffs even as a wild card, Paul Brown Stadium will be filled to capacity at all home games and increase the franchise's gate receipts, revenue, and operating income.

Cleveland Browns

Frustrated about Cleveland's other two professional teams getting new venues and also about stadiums being built in cities throughout the NFL, Browns owner Art Modell announced in 1995 his intention to move his club to Baltimore, Maryland. Besides needing a new stadium with luxury boxes to offset losses in nonfootball investments, his franchise was not making enough money in Cleveland despite selling out every home game for two decades.[8]

Immediately after Modell's announcement, the city of Cleveland tried to keep the Browns there. Although the NFL has battled team owners who attempted to relocate their franchises but nevertheless lost to them in court, the league wanted the Browns to remain in Cleveland and eventually get a new stadium. However, as a result of negotiations, a compromise was made which permitted Modell to move his team but not allowed to take the Browns' history with him. The deal also stipulated that Cleveland would get a new NFL franchise in 1999 and also own the history of the Browns. Finally, the league decided Modell's team in Baltimore was an expansion franchise.

While work on Cleveland Browns Stadium was being completed, the team's front office organized in 1998. After multimillionaire Al Lerner won a bidding war for ownership of the Browns for $750 million, he decided to get administrative staff for the office by raiding the San Francisco 49ers who had been one of the most successful teams in pro sports for several years. In fact, Learner hired the 49ers' Carmen Policy and Dwight Clark to serve respectively as the Browns' president and vice president. One year later, Cleveland joined five other clubs to play in the AFC's CD.

Historical Results

A member of the conference's CD from 1999 to 2001 and then of the ND during the league's 2002–2015 seasons, the Browns played 271 regular-season games and won approximately 32 percent of them. For various reasons but particularly performances of their coaches and players, Browns teams appeared in only one playoff game (2002) and had zero division and conference titles and failed to compete in a Super Bowl. Compared to other AFC teams, Cleveland ranked sixteenth in number of victories, winning percentage, division titles, and total playoffs, tied for twelfth with four other clubs in conference titles, and tied for eighth with eight teams in number of Super Bowl championships. Among their ND rivals the Browns had the fewest wins, lowest winning percentage, and least number of total titles and playoff appearances (Table A.1).

In comparison to performances of thirty-one other teams as of the league's 2015 season, the seventeen-year-old Browns ranked thirty-second in total wins, winning percentage, division titles, and playoff appearances, tied for twenty-eighth with four other clubs in winning their conference, and tied for eighteenth with several teams in number of championships. These and other results prove that, except for the 2002 and 2007 seasons, Cleveland's NFL team has been at or near the bottom of the group competitively while playing games in their division and across the conference (Table A.2).

The club's two most successful seasons were 2002 and 2007. In the former year, Cleveland finished with a 9–7 record and second in its division. As a wild card qualifier, the team was seeded sixth in the playoffs but lost to the Steelers 36–33. In 2007, the Browns were 10–6 in the regular season yet failed to make the playoffs because the Tennessee Titans had a better record against common opponents. During fourteen other years Cleveland had more losses, which ranged from nine to twelve, than wins.

From the 1999 to 2015 NFL season, there were no Browns coaches with winning records during their career with the club. Ranked from most to least in wins, Butch Davis and Romeo Crennel each had 24, then Eric Mangini 10, Pat Shurmur 9, Mike Pettine 7, Chris Palmer 5, Rob Chudzinski 4, and Terry Robiskie 1. Interestingly, the New England Patriots' Bill Belichick coached the previous Cleveland Browns franchise for five seasons in the early 1990s and his teams played, but lost, in only one conference playoff game.

As of 2015, some Browns players established new or tied former records for the franchise. The two career record holders were Dave Zastudil with a 44-yard punting average from 2006 to 2010, and Phil Dawson with 305 field goals during 1999–2012. For a single season, Kellen Winslow had 89 receptions in 2006; Josh Gordon 1,646 receiving yards in 2013; Anthony Henry 10 interceptions in 2001; and Dawson 30 field goals in 2008. In a single game, records include Jerome Harrison's 286 rushing yards; Kelly Holcomb's 5 passing touchdowns; Gordon's 14 receptions and 261 receiving yards; Henry's 3 interceptions; Dawson's 6 field goals; and Andra Davis's 4 sacks. In short, these players had outstanding performances for Browns teams.

Performance Highlights

In 1999, the 68,000-seat—now 73,000-seat—FirstEnergy Stadium opened for the team. A crown jewel of the North Coast Harbor, the facility is located next to the Rock and Roll Hall of Fame Museum and Great Lakes Science Center. The columns, beams, and notches in its seating bowl have a distinctive architectural design. In addition to 8,754 club seats and 147 luxury suites, there are also 10,644 bleacher seats in the stadium's "Dawg Pound." Along with annual events such as the team's Draft Party, Family Night, and Ladies Chalk Talk, this venue has hosted Ohio State University football games, men's and women's national soccer matches, and music concerts.

Among thirty-one NFL venues, Cleveland's FirstEnergy Stadium ranked eleventh in a recent study. According to an article in an edition of *Sporting News*:

> [Quarterback] Johnny Manziel may have retired his "money" gesture, but the team and the city invested $125 million to bring the building up to par with newer facilities. The new fan decks in the end zones provide trendy hangouts for people more interested in communicating through their mobile devices. The renovation's second phase, to be completed for this season, includes more concession and concourse upgrades. For premium patrons, the new Club 46 at event level gives them a peek at players coming to and from the locker room.[9]

Based on such things as their winning percentage in the ND and ticket prices at home games, and also Cleveland's weather conditions, market size, population growth, and household per capita income, the Browns struggle to attract fans to their home games. Throughout its regular seasons, the club's home attendances each year averaged from 89 to 94 percent of the stadium's capacity. Famed for their "Dawg Pound," fans tend to show up pretty well for a team who has not performed in a similar manner. For sure, better performance from the Browns in future years will get the stadium's seats filled to at least 95 percent.

At a press conference in August 2015, third-year owner Jimmy Haslam praised the work of Coach Mike Pettine and general manager Ray Farmer and also expressed his commitment to them as integral members of the organization. He said:

> "They're [Pettine and Farmer] quality people, smart, work hard and have been around football all of their lives," remarked Haslam. "If I had said this time last year we were going to be 7–9, you all would have said that's pretty good. The problem is, we lost our last five [in the 2014 season] and we get that and understand that. We're not pleased with it; I don't want to say that. At the same time, I think it's unfair to say you have to win X amount of games because injuries happen, schedules are harder-easier than you think. It's a tough league. You have to look at the body of work over a period of time. I feel good about where we are versus two years ago or even a year ago."[10]

In sum, the Browns have disappointed their fans for losing too many games since joining the league in 1999. With one of the smallest payrolls in the AFC, it will be a challenge for the team to consistently defeat the Bengals, Ravens, and Steelers, and thus win the ND or even qualify for the playoffs as a wild card. Consequently, it will take a group effort that jointly includes owner Haslam and his front office, and the coaching staff and players to convert the Browns into a more popular, successful, and well-respected organization in the NFL.

Pittsburgh Steelers

Although football was a popular sport in northeast Pennsylvania during the late 1920s to early 1930s, Pittsburgh had no full-time professional team due, in part, to the state's puritanical blue laws, which prohibited athletic competition on Sundays. Nevertheless, NFL teams had to play primarily on Sundays to avoid conflict with college football games on Saturdays.[11]

Anticipating the repeal of some of Pennsylvania's restrictive laws in 1933, sports promoter Art Rooney applied to the NFL for a new franchise. After the league granted his request, the Pittsburgh Professional Football Club joined teams from Boston, Brooklyn, New York, and Philadelphia in the league's ED in exchange for a $2,500 franchise fee.

The new team, co-owned by Rooney and A. McCool, was nicknamed Pirates in reference to their MLB landlords at Forbes Field. The NFL Pirates' first uniforms were gold with black stripes and adorned with the city crest. This color scheme was inspired by Pittsburgh's city flag. The stripes were created with felt overlays and had functional as well as aesthetic value because they allowed players to hold the football more securely in games.

Renamed Steelers in 1940, the club played in the Eastern Division from 1933 to 1949. One year later, Pittsburgh was assigned to the AFC and then Eastern Conference (EC) in 1953 for fifteen seasons. In 1967, the Steelers joined the EC's Century Division for three years and then the AFC's Central Division through 2001. From 2002 to 2014, Pittsburgh has played in the AFC's ND along with the Ravens, Bengals, and Browns.

Historical Results

Since joining the NFL and playing games for eighty-three years, the Steelers accumulated 590 victories and established a 51-percent winning percentage through the league's 2015 season. In addition they won twenty-one division titles, eight conference titles, and six Super Bowls in twenty-nine playoff appearances. When compared to other teams in the AFC as of the league's 2015 season, Pittsburgh ranked first in both number of wins and division titles, sixth in winning percentage, tied for first with the Patriots and Broncos in being conference champions, and also first in winning Super Bowls and participating in playoffs (Table A.1).

Among only clubs in the ND, the Steelers had the most victories, titles and championships, but a lower proportion of wins than the Ravens' 54 percent. Based on these results, Pittsburgh has been a very competitive, well-prepared, and superior club in the league for many seasons and postseasons but especially since the early 1970s.

In comparison to performances of thirty-one other teams as of the NFL's 2015 season, the eighty-three-year-old Steelers ranked fourth in both number of wins and division titles, twelfth in winning percentage, tied for third with the Patriots, Broncos, and Cowboys in winning their conference, and fourth in total championships and also playoff appearances. These and other results indicate that Pittsburgh's NFL team has been competitive with excellent performances during many of its seasons and postseasons while playing against opponents in the AFC's ND and across the league (Table A.2).

To become popular and successful, Steelers teams had excellent coaches and an abundant number of exceptional players. Within the former group Coach Chuck Noll won 209 total games, Bill Cowher 161, Mike Tomlin 87, and Raymond (Buddy) Parker 51. For their leadership role, Noll was AFC coach of the year in 1972 and Cowher AP coach of the year in 1992. Alternatively, Pittsburgh coaches with few wins each include Forrest Douds, Luby DiMelio, Johnny McNally, Walt Kiesling, Bert Bell, Aldo Donelli, Jim Leonard, and Mike Nixon.

Some of the club's players set records at their positions for the franchise. Career milestones, for example, were 11,950 rushing yards by Franco Harris; 219 passing touchdowns by Ben Roethlisberger; 12,083 receiving yards by Hines Ward; 57 interceptions by Mel Blount; and 77 sacks by Jason Gildon. Among single season records, Barry Foster rushed for 1,690 yards in 1992; Bobby Joe Green averaged 47 yards per punt in 1961; Norm Johnson scored 141 points and kicked 34 field goals in 1995; and Antonio Brown had 1,499 receiving yards in 2013. For a single game in a season, Terry Bradshaw and two other quarterbacks each passed 5 touchdowns; Jack Butler had 4 interceptions; Chad Brown recorded more than 4 sacks; and Ray Matthews and Roy Jefferson each had the most touchdowns and total points. As a group, these were outstanding performances by Steelers' players.

The following athletes were given AP awards by a nationwide panel of media. As of 2015, Terry Bradshaw was the NFL's MVP in 1978; Jimmy Orr the offensive rookie of the year in 1958, Louis Lipps in 1984 and Roethlisberger in 2004; Joe Greene the defensive player of the year in 1972 and 1974, Mel Blount in 1975, Jack Lambert in 1976, Rod Woodsen in 1993, James Harrison in 2008 and Troy Polamalu in 2010; and Greene the defensive rookie of the year in 1969, Lambert in 1974, and Kindrell Bell in 2001. Including owners Art and his son Dan Rooney, and coaches Chuck Noll and John McNally, twenty-six Steelers have been inducted into the pro football Hall of Fame.

Performance Highlights

After appearing in only one playoff game from 1933 to 1971, Pittsburgh's most productive periods were the 1972–1979, 1982–1984, 1992–1997, and 2014–2015 NFL seasons, and also winning consecutive titles four times since 2000. A majority of the aforementioned Steelers' coaches and players made important contributions in different ways to successful Steelers' teams during these years.

Following home games at Forbes Field for thirty-one years, the team moved to Pitt Stadium in 1958 and then Three Rivers Stadium in 1970 and finally to Heinz Field in 2001. As a result, its attendances increased from the high 200,000s in the late 1960s to 300,000s in the 1970s and from the high 300,000s/low 400,000s in the 1980s to mid- to high 400,000s in the 1990s. However, because of more night games, there have been numerous no-shows at Heinz Field since 2000 causing less than full-capacity crowds at the stadium.

Among thirty-one NFL venues, Heinz Field ranked eleventh in a recent study. According to an article about it in an edition of the *Sporting News*, the author stated:

> [There are] no models in hot pink bikinis in the Steel City. It's all about football, cloaked in glorious black and gold. The field takes a beating in Pennsylvania's rough winter climate, but the plaza in the south end provides great views of the Ohio River. The open-air museum on the main concourse takes Steelers fans on a nostalgic trip down memory lane. Nearby bars and restaurants on the North Shore, as well as Clemente Bridge in downtown, includes Jerome Bettis' Grille 36, branded for the Steelers' Hall of Fame running back.[12]

FRANCHISE BUSINESS

Besides performing as teams in regular season and postseason games, NFL franchises are also commercial enterprises. To that end, their economic objective is to earn maximum revenue and obtain the greatest amount of profit on a fiscal basis from their operations. Although they share revenues with each other from such sources as national television contracts and other deals, it is important for them to efficiently allocate resources, determine and distribute payrolls, set nonpremium and premium ticket prices, and schedule investments in short- and long-term assets. To reveal and manage these activities, this section focuses on different parts of four AFC franchise's business and how these organizations rank and succeed or not succeed from a financial perspective.

Baltimore Ravens

Born in Philadelphia in 1960, Stephen Bisciotti moved with his family to Baltimore during 1961, and years later, his father Bernard, took him to MLB Orioles and also NFL Colts games. After Bernard died of leukemia when Steve was eight, his mother Patricia, a huge Ravens fan, raised the children.[13]

After graduating from Salisbury (Maryland) State University in 1982 with a degree in liberal arts, Bisciotti worked in the temporary help industry. In 1983, he started Aerotek with his cousin Jim Davis and provided aerospace and technology companies with skilled but temporary employees. Aerotek grew into the Allegis Group, which currently is the largest staffing firm in America and privately held talent management firm in the world. With its headquarters outside Baltimore, it has offices throughout North America, Europe, the Middle East, Africa, and Asia Pacific, and more than 15,000 internal employees and 130,000 high-end contract workers who perform in positions from engineers to cable installers, computer programmers, and marketing specialists.

Bisciotti, who is the third-youngest owner in the NFL following Kansas City's Clark Hunt and Washington's Daniel Snyder, bought a minority interest in the Ravens from owner Art Modell in 2000. Four years later, he completed his purchase of the franchise. Steve's initial investment in the team provided funds to secure free agents for its 2000 Super Bowl XXXV championship. While his influence in the league continues to rise, he serves as a member of the Broadcast and Digital Media committees. Demanding consistency from his coaches and players, Bisciotti's goal is to put the Ravens in the AFC playoffs every season and avoid dips in performances that plague some NFL franchises.

Team Financials

According to data and other financial information published in *Forbes* for sixteen franchises in the AFC as of the league's 2015 season, the Ravens ranked fifth in both estimated market value at $1.93 billion and total revenue at $345 million. For its other amounts, the team was fourth in gate receipts at $68 million, eighth in operating income at $59 million, first in player expenses at $184 million, and tied for third with the Bills and Raiders each with a debt-to-value ratio of 14 percent. Based on these results, Baltimore had the largest amounts of all teams in the ND and also the highest debt ratio. From a financial perspective, the Ravens are a relatively rich and prosperous business enterprise compared to rivals in their division and conference (Table A.3).

With respect to the data of thirty-one other NFL clubs as their 2015 season, the Ravens were twelfth in both estimated market value and total revenue, ninth in gate receipts, seventeenth in operating income, second in player expenses, and tied for third with the Bills and Raiders in percent of debt-to-value. Consequently, Baltimore ranks above-average based on this financial information and with respect to other franchises in the league although its debt is significantly higher than most of them and should concern majority owner Bisciotti and other investors in the franchise (Table A.4).

For several years a Chicago-based company named Team Marketing Report (TMR) has prepared and published a Fan Cost Index (FCI) for the home games of teams in professional sports leagues. To attend a game for a typical family with two kids, an FCI includes the costs of four average-priced tickets, two cheapest-priced draft beers and four each cheapest-priced soft drinks and hot dogs, and also parking for one vehicle, and two each game programs and least-expensive, adult-size adjustable caps. Costs are determined by telephone calls with team representatives, venues and concessionaires, and from questions asked during interviews.[14]

For the 2015 NFL season, the Ravens' FCI was approximately $538 or eighth highest in the league but less by 1.6 percent than in 2014. Listed from most to least amounts by item for one person, the club's nonpremium ticket price averaged about $100, parking per vehicle $40, $15 for a cap, more than $8 for a beer and $7 a soft drink, and $5 for a hot dog. Among three other ND teams, the Ravens had the highest FCI and then the Steelers at $481 (fourteenth), Browns at $401 (twenty-sixth), and Bengals at $398 (twenty-seventh). While the Patriots' index was first in the AFC at $624, the Jaguars' FCI placed last at $347.

According to this data, Ravens games are relatively expensive to attend for fans at M&T Bank Stadium in Baltimore. During sellouts, however, this results in more revenue, gate receipts, and operating income for the franchise from its home games compared to any lower prices charged spectators especially for nonpremium and premium ($258 each) tickets.

Business Highlights

Using fifteen years of data on such things as NFL team performances, home-game ticket prices, and market populations and their median incomes, Emory University researchers created an equity index to determine which clubs had the most avid, engaged, passionate, and supportive fans as of 2015 but before the NFL season. Among the conference's ND teams, the Ravens ranked fourth and above the Steelers at fourteenth, Bengals at twenty-fourth, and Browns at thirty-first. Meanwhile the AFC's Patriots were second in the index and Dolphins thirty-second. For various reasons, the Ravens' avid and passionate fans are very engaged and enthusiastic about their football team and similar to those of the NFC's New York Giants and Jets.[15]

In another index at Emory University titled NFL Social Media Equity, the Ravens ranked tenth and ahead of the Browns in thirteenth and Bengals in thirty-first but behind the Patriots in first. While this index measured which teams over- or underperform with respect to their Twitter following, the Ravens had a more dedicated fan base than twenty-two other NFL clubs including twelve in the AFC.

During July 2015 Constellation, a leading retail energy supplier, and the Ravens announced an agreement to construct a 375-kilowatt solar generation project at the team's headquarters and training facility in Owings Mills, Maryland. A longtime sponsor of the club, Constellation provides energy services to the team and is the "Official Energy Services Sponsor of the Baltimore Ravens." In fact, the roof-mounted solar power system expanded their current energy services relationship. Constellation owns and operates the solar power system while the Ravens purchase the electricity generated by the solar panels from the company under a twenty-year power purchase agreement.[16]

For other news, Baltimore finished 10–6 and won a wild card playoff game despite a rocky start to the 2014 season highlighted by the release and indefinite suspension of running back Ray Rice after a video emerged of Rice hitting his fiancée. He filed a wrongful termination grievance and settled for $1.6 million of his $3.5 million base salary. Previously, Rice had received a $15 million signing bonus for his deal with the club in July 2012. It was the largest signing bonus ever for a running back. While six playoff appearances in seven seasons kept ticket demand high, the franchise expects to improve its financial status by playing consistently and winning more games, titles, and championships before larger crowds in 2016 and thereafter.[17]

Cincinnati Bengals

One of two living sons of legendary football coach/team co-founder Paul Brown, Mike Brown was born in 1935 in Massillon, Ohio. He graduated from Dartmouth College in 1957 where he played quarterback on their football team, and two years later graduated from Harvard Law School. In a meeting between future sports owners, the New York Yankees' George Steinbrenner hired him for a summer job as a deckhand for Kinsman Marine Transit Company.[18]

Eventually Mike followed his father into pro football management and began his executive duties with the Bengals as assistant general manager. Along with personnel decisions, he was a spokesman for the team on issues of league rules and team policy. When his father Paul died in August 1991, Brown assumed ownership responsibilities of the franchise and since then has remained in that position. His first significant decision as owner was to fire popular coach Sam Wyche after the club's 1991 season. Shortly thereafter Brown hired Dave Shula to be head coach, which made him the second youngest NFL head coach in history. As a result, he and his father Don Shula became the first father-son members to lead different NFL teams in the same year.

Historically Brown has been a controversial owner regarding such things as negotiating a new lease with Cincinnati officials to keep the franchise in the city, lack of on-the-field success of his team, being too tolerant of players' off-the-field misconduct, loyalty issues involving Bengals coaches, for maintaining a small scouting staff, overreliance on the team's quarterback, and being too frugal in compensating players. Despite fan protests and media criticism since the late 1990s, some football officials consider Brown to be a fair owner who passionately and thoughtfully cares about the Bengals and the franchise's competitiveness and future in the league.

Team Financials

According to data and other financial information published in *Forbes* for sixteen franchises in the AFC as of the league's 2015 season, the Bengals ranked fifteenth in market value at $1.445 billion, tied for fourteenth with the Bills each with $296 million in revenue and $49 million in gate receipts, eighth in operating income at $55 million, and tied for tenth with the Raiders in player expenses each at $166 million. In addition the franchise tied for ninth with the Patriots, Texans, Jaguars, and Chargers each with a debt-to-value ratio of 10 percent (Table A.3).

Among only ND teams in the AFC as of their 2015 season, Cincinnati had the smallest market value, total revenue, gate receipts, and players' expenses but also the second highest operating income and lowest debt ratio. These amounts were below-average results in the conference for this Cincinnati-based NFL franchise. The data denote the Bengals' risky financial status and struggle to be a profitable and successful business enterprise given what competitors earn in operating their teams while playing within a division and across the conference.

Based on the financials of thirty-one other clubs as of the NFL's 2014–2015 season, the Bengals were tied for thirtieth in market value, tied for twenty-eight in total revenue, tied for twenty-seventh in gate receipts, tied for nineteenth in operating income, tied for twenty-second in player expenses, and tied for nineteenth with several teams in their debt-to-value percentage. Thus, Cincinnati ranks below average based on the financial data of all franchises in the league although the club's debt ratio is significantly smaller than most of them. This, in part, reflects owner Brown's decision to be exceptionally frugal but also indicates how effectively he operates and spends money to improve, or not to invest, in his organization (Table A.4).

For several years a Chicago-based company named Team Marketing Report (TMR) has prepared and published a Fan Cost Index (FCI) for the home games of teams in professional sports leagues. To attend a game for a typical family with two kids, an FCI includes the costs of four average-priced tickets, two cheapest-priced draft beers and four each cheapest-priced soft drinks and hot dogs, parking for one vehicle, and two each game programs and least-expensive, adult-size adjustable caps. Costs are determined by telephone calls with team representatives, venues, and concessionaires, and from questions asked during interviews.

For the 2015 NFL season, the Bengals' FCI was approximately $398 or twenty-seventh highest in the league and 3.1 percent less than in 2014. Listed from most to least amounts by item for one person, the club's nonpremium ticket prices averaged about $71, parking $22, cap $15, and a beer, hot dog, soft drink, and program each at least $5. Among three other ND teams in the league, the Ravens' FCI ranked eighth at $538, Steelers fourteenth at $481, and Browns twenty-sixth at $401. While the 49ers' index of $640 was highest for teams in the NFL, the Jaguars placed thirty-second at $347.[19]

In short, Bengals' home games are relatively inexpensive to attend for fans at Paul Brown Stadium. Because of its lack of success in seasons particularly in the 1990s and early 2000s and other factors such as location, market size, and demographics, the team is compelled to set low prices for nonpremium and premium ($193 each) tickets and also for other items sold to spectators at games in order to boost attendances and likely its gate receipts, revenue, and operating income.

Business Highlights

Using fifteen years of data on such things as NFL team performances, home-game ticket prices, and market populations and their median incomes, Emory University researchers created an equity index to determine which of thirty-two clubs had the most avid, engaged, passionate, and supportive fans before the NFL's 2015 season. Among the AFC's ND teams, the Bengals ranked twenty-fourth and ahead of the Browns at thirty-first but far behind the Ravens at fourth and Steelers at fourteenth. For various reasons including franchise owner Brown and his decisions, the index suggests that Bengals' fans are not very engaged or passionate about their football team. Instead, many of them prefer to support MLB's Reds in addition to sports programs provided by local colleges and universities.[20]

In another index at Emory University titled NFL Social Media Equity, the Ravens ranked tenth and ahead of the Browns in thirteenth and Bengals in thirty-first but behind the Patriots in first. While this index measured which teams over- or underperform with respect to their Twitter following, the Ravens had a more dedicated fan base than twenty-two other NFL clubs including twelve in the AFC.

For a new $10 million Daktronics scoreboard at Paul Brown Stadium in Cincinnati, Hamilton County taxpayers are covering $7.5 million of the cost, which is part of a broader deal the county and Bengals reached whereby the team pays about $4 million toward stadium improvements. Meanwhile, local taxpayers will likely get used to such subsidies as the team's lease requires the county to cover renovations for years through a county-wide sales tax. In 2014, the Bengals took advantage of the NFL's 85 percent rule regarding blackouts. The rule allows teams to declare a sellout and broadcast a game on local television if only 85 percent of nonpremium tickets are sold. Although the NFL relaxed its previous 100 percent tickets-sold policy of 2012, teams must declare before their season if they want the rule to apply to them.[21]

Cleveland Browns

Cleveland Browns owner Randy Lerner, whose family has owned the franchise since it returned to the NFL in 1999, announced negotiations to sell the club during the summer of 2012. The late Al Lerner, Randy's father, purchased the franchise from the NFL in 1998 for $530 million after the original Browns team moved from Cleveland to Baltimore in 1996 and then was nicknamed the Ravens.

A few weeks after his announcement, Randy agreed to sell his club for about $1.05 billion to Tennessee truck-stop magnate Jimmy Haslam III, a minority stockholder in the rival Pittsburgh Steelers and the president and chief executive officer of the Pilot Flying J travel centers and plazas in North America. Lerner sold 70 percent of the Browns to Haslam then, with the other 30 percent reverting to him no later than four years after the closing date. In October 2012, Jimmy completed his purchase of the Browns. The franchise value paid by Haslam, discounting for the three-year term of the deal, was approximately $987 million.[22]

According to a 2010 profile on the website www.steelers.com, Haslam had been a Dallas Cowboys and then an Indianapolis Colts fan. However, because of his Pittsburgh investment, Haslam became a Steelers fan in 2008. The Haslam brothers, Jimmy and Bill, financially support the University of Tennessee where their father Jim played tackle on the 1951 national championship football team under Robert Neyland, who had built the Volunteers into a football powerhouse.

Team Financials

According to data and other financial information published in *Forbes* for sixteen franchises in the AFC as of the league's 2015 season, the Browns ranked eleventh both in market value at $1.5 billion and total revenue at $313 million. In addition the team was thirteenth in gate receipts at $50 million, sixteenth in operating income at $34 million, fifth in player expenses at $167 million, and sixth with a debt-to-value ratio of 13 percent. Among only ND teams, the Browns' results were neither the highest nor lowest except for their operating income. This data, in part, reveals that the franchise had about average amounts in its division but below-average among teams within the conference from a financial perspective (Table A.3).

Based on the financials of thirty-one other NFL clubs as of their 2015 season, the Browns were twenty-fifth highest in market value, tied for twenty-first with the Buccaneers in total revenue, twenty-sixth in gate receipts, tied for twenty-ninth with the Rams in operating income, tied for tenth with the Eagles and Rams in player expenses, and eleventh in percent of debt-to-value. Similar to the Bengals and a few other clubs, Cleveland ranks below-average based on the financial data of all franchises in the league although the team's player expenses are relatively high but debt ratio lower percentage-wise than most of them. For the most part, this reflects the Browns' small market size and such other factors as its win-loss record in the ND since 1999 and also how owner Jimmy Haslam operates and spends money to improve his organization including the amount for athletes' payroll (Table A.4).

Based on several years of information, a Chicago-based company named Team Marketing Report (TMR) has prepared and published a Fan Cost Index (FCI) for the home games of teams in professional sports leagues. To attend a game for a typical family with two kids, an FCI includes the costs of four average-priced tickets, two cheapest-priced draft beers and four each cheapest-priced soft drinks and hot dogs, parking for one vehicle, and two each game programs and least-expensive, adult-size adjustable caps. Costs are determined by telephone calls with team representatives, venues, and concessionaires, and from questions asked during interviews.

For the league's 2015 season, the Browns' FCI was approximately $401 or twenty-sixth highest in the league and 15.1 percent greater than in 2014. Listed from most to least amounts by item for one person, the club's non-premium ticket prices averaged approximately $69, parking $25 and a cap $20, hot dog $6, and a beer and soft drink each $5, and a program $3. Among its rival ND teams, the Ravens' FCI ranked eighth at $538, Steelers fourteenth at $481, and Bengals twenty-seventh at $398. While the 49ers' index of $640 was first in the league, the Jaguars placed thirty-second at $347.

In short, Browns' home games are relatively inexpensive to attend for fans at FirstEnergy Stadium. Because of the team's lack of success in regular seasons particularly in the 2000s and such other factors as location, market size and demographics, Cleveland must set affordable ticket prices for non-premium and premium ($229 each) seats and any items sold to spectators at games in order to increase its attendance and also gate receipts, revenue, and operating income.

Business Highlights

Using information about NFL teams' fans and their enthusiasm, passion, and support but excluding market size, ticket prices, and stadium capacity, Emory University researchers published a Social Media Equity index. Essentially, it measured which clubs over- or underperform with respect to their Twitter following.

According to the study, the Browns ranked thirteenth and below the Steelers at first and Ravens at tenth but far above the Bengals at thirty-first. In other words, Browns fans are about average with respect to following and supporting their team on social media but actually more engaged and passionate than those of nineteen other clubs in the league. Furthermore, Cleveland neither over- nor underperforms based on its fans expectations despite only two winning seasons in nineteen years including eleven of them with significant losses since 2003.[23]

To highlight the franchise's other business topics, the Browns are feeling the effects of seven consecutive losing seasons since 2008. Six years later, they had one of the cheapest average ticket prices in the NFL and also ranked twentieth in the league in average attendance at home games (67,425). Because of this recent and troublesome decline in attendances, the club needs better coaching and more production from its players to attract fans from the region and win additional games against the ND's Ravens, Bengals, and Steelers, besides those in other divisions.

Pittsburgh Steelers

According to Pittsburgh Steelers history, sports entrepreneur Art Rooney paid the NFL a $2,500 franchise fee and founded the team in 1933. Forty-two years later, he officially turned over day-to-day operations of the club to his oldest son, Dan, who became its president. After Art died in 1988, the Steelers were transferred to his five sons—who each inherited an 18-percent share—with the McGinley family owning the other 10 percent.[24]

A former quarterback at Dartmouth University and America's ambassador to Ireland, Dan Rooney continued to operate the team as president, and two decades after his father's death kept the Steelers in the only family that ever owned them. In 2008, however, the NFL ordered the organization to restructure its ownership to comply with league rules. These, in turn, do not allow owners to have ties to the gaming industry and require majority owners to have at least a 30 percent stake in a team or a 20/10 split if the 10 percent holder of the ownership stake is a member of the immediate family.

In response to the requirements, Dan and his son Art II raised enough money to buy sufficient shares of the Steelers for them to have a 20/10 ownership split. Also, they put together an ownership group that bought enough shares for the Rooney's to maintain continuous control of the organization.[25]

Besides serving on the board of directors of the NFL trust fund, NFL Films, and a scheduling committee, Dan was appointed chairman of the expansion committee in 1973, which directed the addition of Seattle and Tampa Bay as new teams in 1976. Art II, meanwhile, has been chairman of the NFL's stadium committee and on numerous boards including the legislative committee, management council executive committee, international committee, NFL Foundation, and the digital media committee.

Team Financials

According to data and other financial information published in *Forbes* for sixteen franchises in the AFC as of the league's 2015 season, the Steelers ranked sixth in market value at $1.9 billion, total revenue at $334 million, and gate receipts at $61 million. Furthermore the club's operating income was tenth in the conference at $54 million, and also its player expenses tied for second with the Broncos at $170 million, and debt-to-value ratio seventh at 11 percent. Compared to other ND teams in the conference, Pittsburgh had the second-highest amounts to the Ravens except for operating income, and also for its debt percentage to the Ravens and Browns. According to these results, the Steelers are a mediocre to above-average franchise from a financial perspective although they have won more titles and championships than their competitors (Table A.3).

Based on financials of thirty-one other NFL clubs as of 2015, the Steelers were thirteenth in market value, tied for thirteenth with the Seahawks in total revenue, fifteenth in gate receipts, twenty-first in operating income, tied for fourth with the Broncos and Redskins in player expenses, and sixteenth in their debt-to-value percentage. Similar to results for teams only in their conference, Pittsburgh ranked average to above-average based on the financial data of all franchises in the league although the club's operating income was below average and player expenses above-average compared to amounts for most other franchises. This, in part, reflects the Steelers' small market size and such factors as their recent and historical win-loss records in the ND, attendances at home games, and how efficiently majority owners Art II and Dan Rooney operate their franchise financially and also how they allocate resources to improve its organization (Table A.4).

For the 2015 NFL season, the Steelers' FCI was approximately $481 or fourteenth highest in the league but 6.1 percent less than in 2014. Listed from most to least amounts by item for one person, the club's nonpremium tickets averaged about $84, parking for one vehicle $40 and a cap $20, and also $8 for a beer, more than $5 for a hot dog, and almost $5 each for a soft drink and program. Among other ND teams in the AFC, the Ravens' FCI ranked eighth at $538, Browns twenty-sixth at $401, and Bengals twenty-seventh at $398. While the Patriots' index of $624 was highest in the conference but fourth from being top in the league, the Jaguars placed thirty-second at $347.[26]

Given these amounts, Steelers' home games are relatively inexpensive to attend for fans at Heinz Field. Because of the team's success in seasons and postseasons especially since the early 1970s and such other factors as location, market size, and local demographics, Pittsburgh is able to set fair ticket prices for nonpremium and premium ($217 each) seats and other items sold to spectators at games in order to maximize the franchise's gate receipts and total revenue.

Business Highlights

Using fifteen years of data on such things as NFL team performances, home-game ticket prices, and market populations and their median incomes, Emory University researchers created an equity index to determine which clubs had the most avid, engaged, passionate, and supportive fans before the NFL's 2015 season. Among the AFC's ND teams, the Steelers ranked fourteenth and ahead of the Bengals at twenty-fourth and Browns at thirty-first but far behind the Ravens at fourth.

For various reasons including the owners and their decisions, the index suggests that Steelers' fans, on average, are moderately engaged or enthusiastic about their football team. However, they also support MLB's Pirates in addition to sports programs provided by local colleges and universities. In another index titled Social Media Equity, the Steelers had the league's best fan base according to people on Twitter followed by the ND's Ravens at tenth, Browns at thirteenth, and Bengals at thirty-first. Despite differences in these indexes, this Pittsburgh-based NFL team has been popular and successful for decades.[27]

Regarding other business news topics, the Steelers added 2,400 seats, including 837 of them premium, to Heinz Field ahead of their 2015 season and will pay Pittsburgh's Sports and Exhibition Authority $2.1 million per year to cover the cost through the end of their lease, which expires in 2030. In addition, the team expected to impose a $1 ticket surcharge to pay for the stadium's renovation, which also includes a new scoreboard and other improvements. The Steelers are one of the NFL's model franchises for (a) winning several championships including six Super Bowls since the early 1970s, (b) hiring smart coaches, (c) playing groups of dedicated and talented players, and (d) finishing with only one losing season during the past fifteen years.

NOTES

1. Two books about NFL history and the league's teams, players, seasons, and postseasons are Frank P. Jozsa Jr., *Football Fortunes: The Business, Organization and Strategy of the NFL* (Jefferson, NC: McFarland, 2010), and James Quirk and Rodney D. Fort, *Pay Dirt: The Business of Professional Team Sports* (Princeton, NJ: Princeton University Press, 1992).

2. References for team performances including the Ravens, Bengals, Browns, and Steelers include the *NFL Record & Fact Book 2014* (New York, NY: NFL, 2014), "NFL Links," http://www.sportsecyclopdia.com, cited August 25, 2015, and "Teams," http://www.pro-football-reference.com, cited August 25, 2015.

3. See "Teams," http://www.profootballhof.com, cited September 1, 2015, and the league's website at http://www.nfl.com for Hall of Fame coaches and players of the Ravens, Bengals, Browns, and Steelers.

4. Three sources of information are Michael Potts, "Ranking All NFL Stadiums for 2015—From Worst to Best," http://www.whatculture.com, cited September 2, 2015; "Ranking All 31 NFL Stadiums." http://www.sportingnews.com, cited August 31, 2015; "Ranking the Best and Worst NFL Stadiums," http://www.athlonsports.com, cited August 31, 2015.

5. NFL teams' attendances are available on pages 488–94 of *Pay Dirt* and also in "Rod Fort's Sports Business Data," http://www.sites.google.com cited September 1, 2015.

6. For data and other information regarding Cincinnati Bengals' performances, see notes 1–4.

7. The article to read is "Ranking All 31 NFL Stadiums," http://www.sportingnews.com, cited August 31, 2015.

8. The history and performances of the Browns franchise and its specific teams and their seasons are in the articles, books, Internet sources, and media guide mentioned in notes 1–5.

9. "Ranking All 31 NFL Stadiums," http://www.sportingnews.com, cited August 31, 2015.

10. For the full press conference, see Andrew Gribble, "Owner Jimmy Haslam Focused on Cleveland Browns' Ultimate Goal," www.clevelandbrowns.com, cited September 18, 2015. For his other strategies since becoming owner, see Don Muret's following articles: (a)"Browns' New Fan Decks Raise Branding Profile for Sponsors," *SportsBusiness Journal* (August 18, 2014): 13 and (b) "Browns Sell Out Ticket Inventory for Event-Level Club," *SportsBusiness* Journal (August 3, 2015): 15. Another reading about him is Daniel Kaplan, "Haslam, NFL Develop Plan B," *SportsBusiness Journal* (August 5, 2013): 4.

11. The references in notes 1–5, as a group, contain historical performances of the Pittsburgh Steelers franchise including owners, coaches and players, and seasons, stadiums, and home-game attendances.

12. Results of the study on the quality of teams' venues were reported in "Ranking All 31 NFL Stadiums," http://www.sportingnews.com, cited August 31, 2015.

13. To research NFL team owners including Stephen Biscotti, read about them from a business perspective on such websites as http://www.forbes.com, http://www.bleacherreport.com, and http://www.profootballhof.com.

14. For how the Ravens, Bengals, Browns, and Steelers ranked in the index, see "2015 NFL Fan Cost Index," http://www.teammarketing.com, cited November 20, 2015. To compare the change in FCIs from 2014 to 2015, use the "2015 NFL Fan Cost Index" and "2014 NFL Fan Cost Index," https://www.teammarketing.com, cited August 26, 2015.

15. Manish Tripathi, "2015 NFL Fan Equity Rankings," https://scholarblogs.emory.edu, cited September 4, 2015. These rankings also apply to other teams in divisions of the AFC.

16. "Baltimore Ravens Go Solar with Constellation," http://www.baltimoreravens.com cited September 23, 2015.

17. For other news about the Ravens, see John Ourand, "Roll Out Small-Town Feel," *SportsBusiness Journal* (September 20, 2013): 39.

18. See note 12 for information about the Bengals' owner and also for those of the Browns and Steelers.

19. "2015 NFL Fan Cost Index."

20. See the reading in note 14 for the club's ranking in the index.

21. Other business news for this franchise is "Bengals, 49ers Stakes Change Hands," *Sports-Business Journal* (December 19, 2011): 4.
22. For the personal and business careers of Jimmy Haslem, see "NFL Team Owners," http://www.biography.yourdictionary.com, cited December 24, 2015.
23. Michael Lewis, "2015 NFL Social Media Equity Rankings," https://scholarblogs.emory.edu, cited September 4, 2015. The Ravens, Bengals, and Steelers are also ranked in the index.
24. Besides "NFL Team Owners," other information about them is available on the club's website at http://www.nfl.com.
25. The team's co-owners stated their views for the franchise in Bill King, "Rooney Rule: Just Do the Right Thing," *SportsBusiness Journal* (May 19, 2014): 28 and "The Sit-Down: Art Rooney II, Pittsburgh Steelers," *SportsBusiness Journal* (August 4, 2014): 54.
26. "2015 NFL Fan Cost Index."
27. See the reading in note 13 for the Steelers' rank in the Fan Equity Index and the article in note 16 for the club's results in the Social Media Equity Index.

Chapter Three

South Division

Before the 2015 National Football League (NFL) season, which team or teams in the South Division (SD) of the American Football Conference (AFC) had the highest all-time winning percentage, least number of wins, fewest division titles and championships, and appeared in the most playoffs? Were the Houston Texans more valuable as a franchise than the Indianapolis Colts, and did the Jacksonville Jaguars earn less revenue, gate receipts, and operating income from their home games than did the Tennessee Titans?

To answer these and other questions, next are some interesting but important, practical, and relevant facts that highlight the historical performances of four teams in the AFC's South Division as of the league's 2014–2015, or simply 2014, season. Besides their winning percentage and number of seasons, wins and also titles and championships, this information includes special coaches, players, and events regarding each of them while competing in the NFL's regular seasons and any playoffs. In the chapter's final section—labelled Franchise Business—are these franchises' success or failure as business enterprises both individually and in comparison to each other from a financial perspective.[1]

TEAM PERFORMANCES

Houston Texans

In mid-1997, franchise owner Bud Adams received approval from the NFL to move his Oilers team from Houston, Texas, to Nashville, Tennessee. Because of that relocation and being blocked from entry into the National Hockey League (NHL), wealthy businessman Bob McNair turned his focus to bringing an expansion professional football team to Houston. That year,

NFL Commissioner Paul Tagliabue praised McNair's plans at an owners' meeting.[2]

Six months after NFL owners unanimously voted to award the thirty-second franchise to Houston, and McNair and his syndicate, for a record $700 million in October 2000, the city celebrated the official groundbreaking of a new 69,000-seat, state-of-the-art, retractable-roof stadium that would host the team when it began play in 2002 and to share the facility with the Houston Livestock Show and Rodeo.

During late 2000, majority owner NcNair unveiled his team's nick-name—Texans—and also its colors and logo. In addition, Reliant Energy acquired the naming rights for the new stadium and also the sports, entertainment, and convention complex known as the Astrodomain Complex. The energy company's thirty-two-year agreement for five different buildings and the Complex was supposedly the most comprehensive naming rights deal in sports history.

In May 2001, the league announced its realignment plan for the 2002 season at meetings in Chicago, Illinois. Within each conference there would be four, four-team divisions with the Texans joining the Indianapolis Colts, Jacksonville Jaguars, and Tennessee Titans in the AFC South Division (SD). Shortly thereafter, the Texans revealed their team uniforms and introduced the club's cheerleading squad.

Historical Results

While competing in the AFC's SD from the 2002 to 2015 seasons, the Texans played 224 games and won approximately 43 percent of them. Among clubs in their conference as of the league's 2015 season, Houston ranked fifteenth in both wins and winning percentage, and also tied for twelfth with the Titans each with two division titles, tied for twelfth with four other teams each with zero conference titles, tied for eighth with eight other teams each with zero NFL and Super Bowl championships, and placed fifteenth with three playoff appearances (Table A.1).

Compared to teams in their division, the Texans had much worse results than the Colts in championships but won more total titles than the Jaguars and fewer than the Colts and Titans, and also qualified for the lowest number of playoffs. As of their 2015 season, the Texans had below-average performances historically because of different problems with their draft choices and not signing enough free agents and veterans, lack of talent at such positions as quarterback, running back, offensive guard and tackle, and also due to the Colts' on-the-field success since 1999.

In contrast to the performances of thirty-one other NFL teams as of their 2015 season, the fourteen-year-old Texans ranked thirty-first in total wins and playoffs, twenty-eighth in winning percentage, tied for twenty-sixth with the Titans, Cardinals, and Rams in number of division titles, tied for twenty-eighth with several other teams in winning their conference, and tied for eighteenth with zero Super Bowl victories. These and other results prove that, except for a few regular seasons including 2011, 2012, and 2015, Houston's NFL team has been below-average competitively while playing clubs in their division, conference, and across the league (Table A.2).

Despite these issues, Houston had some memorable coaches and players who established milestones for the franchise. In the former group, Gary Kubiak coached more than seven seasons and won 63 games. Alternatively, Dom Capers had 18 victories in four seasons while Wade Phillips won 0 games and former New England Patriots' offensive coordinator Bill O'Brien 9 in the 2014 season. Given the Texans' relatively brief history in the NFL, someone will become the club's coach of the year and eventually get his team into a conference final and perhaps win a Super Bowl.

Thus far, some prominent players were talented enough to hold career, single-season, and single-game records for the franchise. Career marks were set, for example, by Arian Foster in rushing yards; Andre Johnson in number of catches; Matt Turk in punting; J. J. Watt in sacks; and Kris Brown in field goals and total points. In a single season, quarterback Matt Schaub passed for 4,770 yards and twenty-nine touchdowns in 2009; Marcus Coleman intercepted seven passes in 2003; and Shayne Graham scored 138 points in 2012. Besides Foster, Johnson, Brown, and Schaub, such players as Glover Quin in interceptions, Ryan Moats and Ben Tate in touchdowns, and Connor Barwin in sacks established records in individual games. As such, these athletes had remarkable performances in seasons and games for the Texans.

Although Houston has no players in the pro football Hall of Fame as of 2014, three have received awards from the Associated Press (AP). These include defensive player of the year J. J. Watt in 2012, 2014, and 2015, and defensive rookies of the year DeMeco Ryans in 2006 and Brian Cushing in 2009. Also, quarterback Schaub and defensive end Watt each won a pro bowl Most Valuable Player (MVP) award for their outstanding performances in these postseason games.

Among their years in the league, the Texans most successful periods consecutively were 2011 and 2012. Respectively, they won ten and twelve games and SD titles but lost to the Ravens and Patriots in the playoffs. Led by Coach Kubiak, the teams' top players were quarterback Schaub, running back Foster, and receiver Johnson. Except for 9–7 records in 2009 and 2014, the club had more losses than wins in seven regular seasons and finished 8–8 in two other years. With Watt and Jadeveon Clowney playing tough on defense, the Texans have talent but need to score more touchdowns and field goals to win games. Unfortunately such first-round selections as quarterback David Carr, defensive end Travis Johnson, and linebacker Whitney Marcilus failed to perform as expected for the team.

Performance Highlights

At its home games in NRG Stadium—formerly known as Reliant Stadium—the club's attendances have been above the league's average. For example, the number of spectators was actually between 550,000 and 560,000 yearly from 2002 to 2005; 561,000 and 569,000 annually from 2006 to 2010; and 573,000 to 575,000 each year during 2011–2015. Not surprisingly, sports fans in southeast Texas love football and consider the Texans games to be fun, popular, and entertaining events for them and their families and friends on Sundays.[3]

Among other NFL venues, NRG Stadium ranked thirteenth in a recent study. According to an article about it in *Sporting News*, the author wrote:

> Since the NFL returned to Houston thirteen years ago with an expansion team in a brand new stadium, the Texans have made considerable upgrades in tandem with the Houston Livestock Show & Rodeo, their co-tenant. Many improvements revolve around premium seat retrofits and new video boards. Amid a sprawling sports and entertainment complex, football-crazy Texas fans, poised for tailgating, lines up several hours before the parking lots open at 8 a.m.[4]

In the Entertainment Sports Programming Network's (ESPN) future power rankings, the network asked three experts to rate each NFL team for three seasons (2015–2017) on a scale of 0 to 100 percent in five categories including roster (excluding quarterback), quarterback, draft, front office, and coaching. To conclude their analysis of the Texans, the experts admitted a glaring question mark at quarterback and also were not sure how that alone could mathematically influence the team with the ninth least promising future in the league, especially since its quarterbacks' contracts had no long-term or far-reaching effects on the team's salary cap going forward.[5]

Given other strengths within the organization, particularly at head coach and elsewhere on the players roster, the experts wondered whether the quarterback situation and the uncertainty surrounding defensive end/linebacker Jadeveon Clowney's ability were enough to think that twenty-three other teams have a brighter future in the NFL for these three seasons than the Texans.

Although Houston was 9–7 in the conference's 2014 and 2015 seasons but played in a weak division, the club should be competitive in 2016–2017 to 2017–2018. According to the ESPN troika responsible for the future power rankings, this might or might not be realistic. In other words, because of problems at quarterback and the team's youth movement, the Texans scored only 64 percent in the rating yet finished in second place of their division and ahead of the Jaguars and Titans, but behind the Colts led by quarterback Andrew Luck.

Indianapolis Colts

From 1978 to 1981 and in 1983, the Baltimore Colts finished fourth or fifth in their division. In addition the club's attendances at its home games in the city's 53,200-seat Memorial Stadium were among the lowest in the NFL. In order to compete and win more games against such rivals in their conference as the Miami Dolphins and Buffalo Bills and also to improve economically, Colts owner Robert Irsay became frustrated and demanded that the city build a new stadium for his franchise.[6]

After negotiating but failing to reach an agreement with public officials from Baltimore and the municipality during the early 1980s, Irsay realized it would be years or perhaps a decade before the city approved funds to finance the construction of a modern football stadium with enough amenities to substantially increase revenue. The city of Indianapolis, meanwhile, had built a new facility to attract an existing or expansion NFL team and also to bring more sports games and other events to entertain people in central Indiana.

Based on financial problems and his club's series of poor performances in the AFC, Irsay secretly and without public announcements moved the Colts' assets in several Mayflower tractor-trailer trucks from Baltimore to Indianapolis in March 1984 in order to play their home games in the 60,100-seat Hoosier Dome. In fact the relocation occurred at night when these large trucks were loaded with Colts equipment and other property, and then driven six-hundred miles west on Interstate highways to Indiana's capital city.

For moving his team this way, Irsay was immediately criticized by the media and politicians in Baltimore and also despised by thousands of sports fans within the community. In contrast to them, most Indianapolis residents and others throughout the state praised him for being an aggressive, passionate, and smart team owner and a clever and ambitious businessman.

Historical Results

While competing in the AFC's Eastern Division from 1984 to 2001 and then in the SD during the league's 2002–2014 seasons, the Colts played 510 games and won approximately 53 percent of them. In addition the club won eleven division and two conference titles, and also one Super Bowl in seventeen playoff appearances. Compared to results of other teams in its conference, Indianapolis ranked tenth in total victories, fifth in both winning percentage and number of division titles, tied for seventh with the Ravens and Bengals in conference titles, seventh in total championships, and fifth in playoff appearances (Table A.1).

With respect to only SD teams as of their 2014 season, the thirty-one-year-old Colts had the highest winning percentage and more wins, titles, and championships including Super Bowls than the thirteen-year-old Texans, twenty-year-old Jaguars, and seventeen-year-old Titans. Based on these results, Indianapolis has been superior against teams within its division but only above-average in performances across the conference.

Compared to the performances of thirty-one other NFL teams as of their 2014 season, the thirty-two-year-old Colts ranked twenty-second in total number of wins, tenth in winning percentage, thirteenth in division titles, tied for seventeenth with four other clubs in winning their conference, tied for twelfth with five teams in winning one Super Bowl, and thirteenth in playoff appearances. These and other results prove that, except for a few seasons during the mid to late 1980s and early 1990s, Indianapolis's NFL team has been above average competitively while playing against rivals in its division and conference but simply average in performances when compared to teams across the league (Table A.2).

During regular seasons and postseasons totaling more than three decades while located in Indianapolis, Colts teams had some successful coaches and outstanding players as of the league's 2015 season. The former group includes Tony Dungy with 92 wins while Ron Meyer had 36, Chuck Pagano 34, and Ted Marchibroda and Jim Mora each 32. For his achievements as offensive coordinator/interim head coach, the Associated Press (AP) rewarded Bruce Arians with the NFL coach of the year award in 2012.

Since 1984, some players have established career, single season, and single game records for the franchise. Among career record holders, the most significant are Edgerrin James in rushing yards; Peyton Manning in passing yards and touchdowns; Marvin Harrison in number of receptions and total yards; and Mike Vanderjagt in field goals and total points. Single season records, for example, were set by punter Pat McAfee, punt returner T. J. Rushing, and defensive linemen Robert Mathis. For a single game, James rushed for 219 yards in 2000, and Manning passed for 472 yards in 2004. Furthermore, Reggie Wayne had 15 catches in 2010, while Johnie Cooks recorded more than 4 sacks in 1984. In short, these were truly unforgettable performances by outstanding athletes during various NFL games and seasons.

Besides Coach Arians, other AP award winners for the Colts include MVP Manning in 2003 (shared with Titans quarterback Steve McNair), 2004, 2008–2009, and 2013; offensive player of the year Manning in 2004 and 2013; offensive rookie of the year Marshall Faulk in 1994 and James in 1999; defensive player of the year Bob Sanders in 2007; and defensive rookie of the year Duane Bickett in 1985. As of 2014, no Colts players had won the AP comeback player of the year award. Nevertheless, Manning and the other players were spectacular at their positions during these seasons.

For their great careers in the sport, former Indianapolis Colts inducted into the pro football Hall of Fame include running back Eric Dickerson in 1999, defensive end Richard Dent and running back Marshall Faulk in 2011, and general manager Bill Polian in 2015. Each of them made major contributions to the franchise for many seasons and deserve being honored as Hall of Famers.

While located in Indianapolis since 1984, Colts teams' most successful periods consecutively were their 1995–1996, 1999–2000, 2002–2010, and 2012–2014 seasons. Some of these victories occurred, in part, because of coaches Mora and Dungy, quarterbacks Jim Harbaugh and Manning, running backs Faulk and James, and receivers Harrison and Wayne. Alternatively, the club's worst periods in not qualifying for the conference playoffs included seasons 1984–1986, 1988–1994, and 1997–1998.

Performance Highlights

At its home games in the Hoosier Dome from 1984 to 2007 and then in Lucas Oil Stadium since 2008, the team's attendances varied according to its performances. From the mid to late 1980s to early 2000s, for example, the club averaged about 450,000 per season. When the Colts won consecutive titles beginning in 2002 and a Super Bowl four years later, their attendances per-season increased into the low 500,000s with the majority of tickets being sold each year despite the departure of Peyton Manning to the Denver Broncos following the league's 2011 postseason.[7]

Among other NFL venues, Lucas Oil Stadium ranked fourteenth in a recent study. According to an article published about it in *Sporting News*, the author stated:

> Flexibility is the key word for this building, originally designed for NFL games and the Final Four in the NCAA's hometown. The brick exterior [area] calls to mind the retro-fieldhouse theme in the state that made 'Hoosiers' famous. Indoors, there are plenty of sponsor zones, and at one time, you could order appliances from H.H. Gregg, a hometown brand. The downtown stadium is in the thick of a bar and restaurant scene, making it convenient for fans to grab a bite to eat before heading to the game.[8]

In ESPN's future power rankings, the Colts placed sixteenth or in the middle of the league when looking at the outlook for their 2016 to 2017 seasons. Overall the club had a raw score of 69, which was highest in the conference's SD. The five areas, scores, and where it ranked in the league were the roster/ 59.7/twenty-seventh; quarterback/96.3/second; draft/65.0/twenty-first; front office/62.3/twenty-eighth; and coaching/ 63.7/twenty-fifth.

Except for quarterback Andrew Luck's high score, these rankings do not reflect a team capable of competing for a Super Bowl. In reality, however, they are probably closer to being accurate than admitted by many football officials. There are plenty of questions about general manager Ryan Grigson and Coach Chuck Pagano, while the team's signing of veteran players during the offseason certainly did not prepare it for the future. Although they might be a bit low, the scores seem neither high nor low for this franchise.

Jacksonville Jaguars

During August 1989, a nine-member partnership—titled Touchdown Jacksonville, Ltd.—formed to seek and then acquire an NFL expansion franchise for the city. Filing an application with the league, the group, which included shoe magnate J. Wayne Weaver and who nicknamed their prospective football club the Jaguars, represented one of eleven cities and thus unlikely to be awarded a new team.[9]

At the league's winter meeting in March 1992, the application list was reduced from eleven to seven cities and two months later, to five. But in October, the league delayed its expansion vote until fall 1993 because of problems with the players' union. However, when the league and union signed a seven-year collective bargaining agreement in March 1993, expansion again became a priority project.

After NFL officials toured Jacksonville's 80,000-seat Gator Bowl, which needed significant improvement to host a new pro team, the city council and Touchdown Jacksonville failed to agree on how to finance the stadium's renovation and thus discontinued their discussions. Because of this dispute, Touchdown Jacksonville withdrew its application for the city to become a potential site for an expansion team.

Less than a month after negotiations about financing ended, Weaver and Jacksonville community leaders proposed a new plan that capped renovation costs at $121 million whereby the city contributed $53 million while the team and team-related sources paid $68 million. In addition, civic and business leaders agreed to help the new team sell 9,000 tickets for club seats.

Based on this private/public effort and the successful sale of tickets for stadium seats, the NFL awarded Jacksonville its thirtieth franchise in November 1993. Two years later more than 50,000 tickets were sold within a few weeks, which occurred before the club's first season in the AFC's Central Division (CD) where it joined other teams from Cincinnati, Cleveland, Houston, and Pittsburgh.

Historical Results

A member of the conference's CD from 1995 to 2001 and then the SD during the NFL's 2002–2015 seasons, the Jaguars played 336 games and won approximately 45 percent of them with six playoff appearances. As of the league's 2015 season, they won their division twice but zero conference titles and therefore no opportunity to compete in a Super Bowl. Among other AFC teams, Jacksonville ranked thirteenth in both number of wins and winning percentage, tied for thirteenth with the Jets in division titles, tied for twelfth with four other clubs in conference titles, tied for eighth with eight teams in Super Bowl victories, and tied for thirteenth with the Titans in qualifying for AFC playoffs (Table A.1).

In comparison to its ED rivals as of their 2015 season, Jacksonville ranked second in wins and third in winning percentage, but had won fewer division and conference titles and also Super Bowl championships than the Colts. Based on these results and other reasons, Jaguars teams have performed below-average in games against division rivals while playing more than two decades in the AFC.

With respect to the performances of thirty-one other NFL teams as of their 2015 season, the twenty-one-year-old Jaguars ranked twenty-eighth in total wins, twenty-fourth in winning percentage, tied for thirtieth with the Jets in division titles, tied for twenty-eighth with four other clubs in winning zero conference titles, tied for eighteenth with fourteen other teams in winning zero Super Bowls, and tied for twenty-seventh with the Titans in number of playoffs. These and other results reveal that, except for six years when they appeared in postseasons, Jacksonville's NFL team has been below-average competitively while competing against rivals in its division, conference, and across the league (Table A.2).

Despite its dismal record in most regular seasons and during two postseasons, the club featured one winning coach and several talented players as of the league's 2015 season. Among the former group, Coach Tom Coughlin won 72 games from 1995 to 2002 and following him in later seasons was Jack Del Rio with 69, Gus Bradley 7, and Mel Tucker and Mike Mularkey 2 each. In 1996, Coughlin was AFC coach of the year when his team finished second to the Steelers in the CD, won the wild card and divisional playoffs, but then lost the conference game to the Patriots.

Since 1995, some Jacksonville players have established career, single season, and single game records for the franchise. During their career with the team, for example, Fred Taylor rushed for 11,271 yards; Mark Brunell completed 144 touchdown passes; Rashean Mathis intercepted 30 passes; and Tony Brackens tackled quarterbacks for 55 sacks.

Within a single season, Jimmy Smith caught 116 passes for 1,636 yards; Bryan Anger punted 47 times; and Mike Hollis kicked 31 field goals and scored 134 points. In a single game, four record holders were Keenan McCardell with 16 receptions; James Stewart with 5 touchdowns and 30 points; and Taylor with 234 rushing yards and Brunell 432 from throwing to his receivers. Between 1995 and 2014, these were exceptional performances by Jaguars players.

Besides Brunell being MVP in the 1997 pro bowl, Jaguars' players have not won any AP awards for their performances such as offensive and defensive player and rookie of the year or comeback player of the year. Interestingly when Jacksonville's players have very good to outstanding seasons, others in the conference or league have better games defensively or they score more touchdowns and points, and/or receive, rush, and pass for more yards.

While located in northeast Florida for two decades, Jaguars teams most successful seasons were from 1996 to 1999 and in 2005 and 2007. Alternatively, their worst years included the 1995, 2000–2004, 2006, and 2008–2014 seasons. More specifically, they won fourteen games in 1999 but also lost an equal number in 2012. Since 2000 this franchise has qualified for only two playoffs which, in turn, indicate its coaching problems and lack of talented players especially at positions in the offensive and defensive lines.

Performance Highlights

At home games played in the city's EverBank Field—known as Alltel Stadium from 1997 to 2006 and Jacksonville Municipal Stadium during 2007–2009—the team's attendances per season have been below the league's average and fluctuate according to its performances. To illustrate, four specific results were 482,510 in 2000 and 555,464 in 2004, and 521,388 in 2012 and 504,704 in 2014. Among SD teams in the AFC, the Jaguars have smaller attendances at home than games of the Texans in Houston and Colts in Indianapolis but more spectators than the Titans in Nashville during the majority of their NFL seasons.[10]

Among other NFL venues, EverBank Field ranked sixth in a recent study. According to an article published about it in *Sporting News*:

> The Jags continue to struggle on the field, but they're building lots of buzz for improving the fans experience at EverBank Field. Over the past two years, the building has added the biggest video boards in sports, swimming pools and cabanas and bikini-clad girls fronting the Cleveland Deck, another sports spin-off of the famous South Beach establishment. Outside the stadium, Jacksonville Landing, a dining/entertainment district sits less than two miles from EverBank Field. In February [2015], the team laid out its plan to develop the Shipyards' mixed-use project to fill vacant space around the stadium.[11]

In ESPN's future power rankings, the Jaguars ranked thirty-second in the NFL when looking at their outlook for the 2015 to 2017 seasons. Overall the club had a raw score of 53.2, which was lowest in the conference's SD. The categories and where it placed among members of the league included the roster and coaching each at thirty-first; quarterback at twenty-seventh; drafting players at nineteenth; and front office at twenty-seventh. While the club had only seven wins in head coach Gus Bradley's first two seasons, some losses occurred because of an unprecedented roster overhaul and a historic number of youth at many positions on defense and offense.[12]

Most importantly, while team quarterback Blake Bortles is clearly a question mark moving into the future, it is hard to fault general manager David Caldwell for other players on the roster. The Jaguars are better at essentially every position from when he took over in 2011, so it is a matter of knowing how much better or worse the club's young players develop athletically and compete in games at their position. While disappointing to see the Jaguars ranked last in ESPN's analysis of NFL teams, they may surprise everyone with more wins than in any regular season since 2007.

If everything goes right, the Jaguars might improve enough to challenge an 8–8 record soon and then improve enough to be a potential playoff contender in 2016 or 2017. That is a legitimate expectation under Caldwell and Bradley, especially since the team will have two first-round picks including its normal one and another one for former defensive end Dante Fowler, who was selected third in the 2015 draft.

Tennessee Titans

After playing ten seasons in the AFL and another twenty-seven in the NFL, the Oilers relocated from Houston, Texas, to Memphis, Tennessee, after their 1996 season in order to play their home games in the city's 61,000-seat Liberty Bowl Memorial Stadium. For various reasons, however, the renamed Tennessee Oilers failed to establish a strong fan base in Memphis despite winning eight games and finishing third in the AFC's CD behind the Steelers and Jaguars. In fact, when Oilers owner Bud Adams announced his club would move from Memphis to Nashville following the club's 1997 season, many local fans rooted for the opposing team.[13]

Following their move to Nashville, the Oilers played home games before small crowds during their 1998 season at 40,500-seat Vanderbilt Stadium on the campus of Vanderbilt University. Although the Oilers competed for a wild card in the AFC, they finished second to the Jaguars in their division.

Since the university's stadium was too small to permanently host an NFL team, the Oilers shifted from Vanderbilt Stadium to 67,000-seat Adelphia Coliseum before its next season. Built in 1999 and owned by the metropolitan government of Nashville and Davidson County, the facility is also the home field of college football's Tennessee State Tigers, site of the Franklin American Mortgage Music Bowl, and a venue for soccer matches and large concerts.

Before his club's 1999 season, Adams appointed an advisory committee to decide on a new nickname that reflected power, strength, leadership, and other heroic qualities. The team's new nickname, Titans, met Adams' requirements and also served as a nod to Nashville's recognition as "The Athens of the South" because of the city's large number of higher-learning institutions, classical architecture, and full-scale replica of the Parthenon.

Historical Results

While in the conference's CD from 1998 to 2001 at home in Nashville and then a member of the SD during 2002–2015 in the same city—nicknamed Oilers for one season and Titans for another sixteen—the team had a total of 288 games and won approximately 50 percent of them. As of the league's 2015 season, these years included winning three divisions and one conference title but zero Super Bowls. In comparison to fifteen other AFC clubs, Tennessee ranked fourteenth in number of victories, seventh in winning percentage, tied for twelfth in division titles, tied for tenth with the Chargers in conference titles, tied for eighth with eight other teams in Super Bowl championships, and tied for thirteenth with the Jaguars in playoff appearances (Table A.1).

Among only SD clubs the Titans had fewer wins and less division and conference titles and also championships than the Colts, the second highest winning percentage of the group, and appeared in more playoffs than the Texans but not the Colts or Jaguars. Based on these results, Tennessee's NFL team has performed average to below-average in games during its eighteen-year history among rivals in its division and the AFC.

Compared to the performances of thirty-one other NFL teams as of their 2015 season, the Titans ranked twenty-ninth in total wins, thirteenth in winning percentage, tied for twenty-sixth with the Texans, Cardinals, and Rams in number of division titles, tied for twenty-second with five other clubs in winning their conference, tied for twentieth with twelve other teams in failing to win a championship including a Super Bowl, and tied for twenty-seventh with the Jaguars in number of playoff appearances. These and other results prove that, except for six seasons when they appeared in playoffs, Nashville's NFL team has been average to below-average competitively while playing against rivals in each conference of the league (Table A.2).

To establish its record since 1997, the team had some successful and unsuccessful coaches and several talented players. In the former group was Jeff Fisher with 147 wins, Mike Munchak 22, and in 2014, Ken Whisenhunt 2. While coaching for thirteen years Fisher's teams were in six playoffs and in one of them, when competing as a wild card, the Titans lost to the St. Louis Rams in Super Bowl XXXIV at the Georgia Dome in Atlanta.

Some of Tennessee's players were good enough at their positions to set or tie career, single season, and/or single game records for the franchise during 1997–2015. For example, Brett Kern established a career record by punting an average of 44.4 yards while playing from 2009 to 2013. In a single season, Chris Johnson rushed for 2,006 yards in 2009, and Kern's average punts covered 47.6 yards in 2012. For single game records, Johnson rushed for 228 yards; Drew Bennett caught 13 passes; Keith Bulluck intercepted 3 passes;

and Rob Bironas kicked 8 field goals (an NFL record). As a group, these were dedicated and exceptionally skilled athletes for the Titans.

Through 2015, Tennessee players had won various AP awards for their accomplishment in different NFL seasons. These athletes were offensive player of the year Chris Johnson in 2009; offensive rookie of the year Vince Young in 2006; and defensive rookie of the year Jevon Kearse in 1999. In addition to them, quarterback Steve McNair was co-MVP in 2003 for having an NFL-best 100.4 passer rating and throwing for 3,215 yards with 24 touchdowns against seven interceptions.

A center/guard/tackle, Bruce Matthews performed for the Tennessee Oilers/Titans from 1997 to 2001. Six years later he was inducted into the pro football Hall of Fame for playing in 296 games during his career with Houston and Tennessee Oilers and then Titans teams, for being in fourteen consecutive pro bowls and a nine-time all-pro, and an all-AFC selection in twelve seasons.

While located in Nashville for seventeen years, the Titans' most successful consecutive periods were the NFL's 1999–2000, 2002–2003, and 2007–2008 seasons. Alternatively, they lost ten or more games each season during 2004–2005 and also in 2010, 2012, and 2014. Based on its six postseason appearances, Tennessee has been in the AFC's playoffs every third year.

Despite inconsistent performances, failure to win more titles and playing in a demographically small to mid-sized sports market, attendances at the team's home games have surprisingly been average compared to other clubs in the league but below the attendances of such rivals as the Texans. Typically Titans' attendances ranked between tenth and twentieth in the league each season from 1998 to 2014. Thus, Nashville's football fans support their hometown team in both winning and losing seasons especially when competing against rival clubs from Houston, Indianapolis, and Jacksonville.

Performance Highlights

Among other NFL venues, Nissan Stadium ranked twentieth in a recent study. According to an article about it in an edition of *Sporting News*, the author stated:

> The 16-year-old building just got a new name after Nissan took over naming rights from Louisiana-Pacific. A few years ago, the stadium underwent $27 million in renovations, covering among other upgrades, two new monster video boards in the end zones and a dozen high speed elevators, music to the ears of Titans fans in Music City. Unfortunately, the Cumberland River separates the stadium from downtown Nashville and its bustling, honky-tonk scene, so fans are pretty much on their own for tailgating before the game.[14]

In ESPN's future power rankings, the Jaguars ranked thirty-first in the NFL when looking at their outlook for the 2015 to 2017 seasons. Evaluated by insiders Mike Sando, Louis Riddick, and John Clayton, they rated each team on a scale of 0 to 100 in five categories that included rosters (but not quarterback), quarterbacks, draft, front office, and coaching. The polls weighted each category, giving the roster 30 percent, quarterback 20 percent, draft and front office each 15 percent, and 20 percent for the coaching staff.

According to Mike Sando the ranking seemed low for a team excited about selecting quarterback Marcus Mariota with the second overall pick, but a disastrous 2–14 record in 2014 affected how voters perceived the Titans' future. Thanks to Mariota, however, Tennessee improved from thirty-second in 2014 to twenty-first in quarterback outlook, the second-largest gain in that category behind the fourteen-spot improvement of the NFC Vikings. But the Titans fell six spots overall after suffering double-digit drops in drafting (thirty-second), front office (thirty-first), coaching (twenty-ninth), and non-quarterback roster (thirty-second).[15]

In Riddick's view, Mariota is adapting more quickly than his critics had expected, which should not be a surprise if you scouted him in the proper context at the University of Oregon. The real question is: can Coach Ken Whisenhunt and his offensive staff extract the maximum performance out of Mariota, given what he did in college? If coached right, Mariota could change the fate of the franchise.

Regarding its youth movement, Clayton thinks the Titans have been playing catch-up after three subpar drafts from 2011 to 2013. While Mariota is trying to fix the failure of Jake Locker from the 2011 draft, the continued development of players at wide receiver and the guard and center positions should help Mariota succeed at quarterback.

FRANCHISE BUSINESS

Besides performing as teams in regular season and postseason games, NFL franchises are also commercial enterprises. To that end, their economic objective is to earn maximum revenue and obtain the greatest amount of profit on a fiscal basis from their operations. Although they share revenue with each other from such sources as national television contracts and other deals, it is important for them to efficiently allocate resources, determine and distribute payrolls, set nonpremium and premium ticket prices, and schedule profitable investments in short- and long-term assets. To reveal and manage these activities, this section focuses on different parts of four AFC franchises' business and how these organizations rank and succeed or not succeed from a financial perspective.

Houston Texans

A native of Forest City, North Carolina, the Texans' longtime majority owner Robert McNair graduated from the University of South Carolina in 1958 with a Bachelor of Science degree. After moving to Houston, Texas he founded the cogeneration company Cogen Technologies, which was sold in 1999 to Enron Inc. for $1.5 billion. Besides owning power plants in New York and West Virginia, McNair serves as chairman and chief executive officer of the McNair Group, a financial and real estate firm headquartered in Houston. In June 2000, he formed a biotechnology investment firm, Cogene Biotech Ventures, for which he is the company's chairman.[16]

After discovering he had two kinds of cancer, seventy-seven-year-old McNair received treatment and his health has improved in recent years. He attends every Texans game and learned to stop worrying about things and enjoy the sport. While owning the team, multibillionaire McNair has been actively involved in NFL affairs by serving as chairman of the league's finance committee and being a member of the audit committee.

Team Financials

According to data and other financial information published in *Forbes* for sixteen franchises in the AFC as of their 2015–2016 season, the Texans ranked third in market value at $2.5 billion, tied for second with the Jets in revenue at $383 million, fifth in gate receipts at $65 million, third in operating income at $114 million, thirteenth in player expenses at $151 million, and tied for ninth with the Patriots, Bengals, and Chargers each with a 7 percent debt-to-value ratio. Compared to only teams in the SD of the conference, Houston had the highest amounts except for the Titans' $164 million in player expenses and Titans' 10 percent debt ratio. From a financial perspective, this NFL franchise is above-average and a relatively rich and prosperous business organization compared to rivals in its division and conference (Table A.3).

Based on data of the other thirty-one NFL clubs as of their 2015 season, the Texans were seventh in estimated market value, tied for sixth with the Jets in total revenue, tied for eleventh with the Packers and Panthers in gate receipts, sixth in operating income, twenty-seventh in player expenses, and tied for seventeenth with several teams in their percent of debt-to-value. Except for its relatively low amount of player expenses, Houston ranks above-average in market value, total revenue, gate receipts, and operating income with respect to other franchises in the league (Table A.4)

Because of a relatively low payroll for its players and such other things as the club's large receipts from home-game attendances and earnings from operations, this is a very profitable commercial enterprise that provides plenty of cash and wealth for owner Robert McNair and his syndicate. In fact the only NFL teams with better or comparable financial results than the Texans are the AFC's Patriots and Jets, and NFC's Cowboys, Giants, and Redskins.

For several years a Chicago-based company named Team Marketing Report (TMR) has prepared and published a Fan Cost Index (FCI) for the home games of teams in professional sports leagues. To attend a game for a typical family with two kids, an FCI includes the costs of four average-priced tickets, two cheapest-priced draft beers and four each cheapest-priced soft drinks and hot dogs, parking for one vehicle, and two each game programs and least-expensive, adult-size adjustable caps. Costs are determined by telephone calls with team representatives, venues, and concessionaires, and from asking questions during interviews.[17]

For their 2015 season, the Texans' FCI was approximately $491 or twelfth highest in the league but the same amount as in 2014. Listed from most to least in amount by item for one person, the club's nonpremium tickets averaged about $89, parking $33, a cap $20 and hot dog $6, and almost $5 each a beer, soft drink, and program. Among three other SD teams, the Colts' FCI ranked eighteenth at $462, Titans' twenty-fifth at $404, and Jaguars' thirty-second at $347. While the 49ers' index of $640 placed first in the league, $480 was the average for all teams.

Given these amounts, Texans' home games are neither ultra-expensive nor cheap to attend for fans at NRG Stadium. Because of the team's lack of success in most regular seasons and postseasons especially from 2002 to 2010 and during 2013–2014, and other social and economic factors, Houston sets competitive ticket prices for seats and other items sold to spectators at its games in order to increase attendances and, in part, to maximize the franchise's revenue from gate receipts.

Business Highlights

Using fifteen years of data on such things as NFL team performances, home-game ticket prices, and market populations and their median incomes, Emory University researchers created an equity index to determine which clubs had the most avid, engaged, passionate, and/or supportive fans before the NFL's 2015 season. Among the AFC's SD teams, the Texans ranked twelfth in the index and ahead of the Titans at sixteenth and Jaguars at twenty-ninth but behind the Colts at ninth.[18]

For various reasons, including owner Robert McNair and his decisions to support the team, the index suggests that Texans fans, on average, are engaged or passionate about their football team partly because of the sport's popularity in their home state and Houston's economy and large market size. In another index titled Social Media Equity, the Texans had the league's fifteenth best fan base followed by the SD's Titans at twenty-second, Jaguars at twenty-fifth, and Colts at twenty-ninth. This index reflected whether teams over- or underperform with respect to their Twitter following.[19]

Because they recently opened their privately-financed $1.2 billion stadium in Santa Clara and booked more than $1 billion in ticket and sponsorship revenue, the NFC's 49ers surpassed the Texans in estimated market value. Despite the 49ers' 8–8 record in the 2014 season and departure of Coach Jim Harbaugh, their financial status considerably improved due to the club's potentially higher attendances, gate receipts, and operating income at newly constructed Levi's Stadium.

To highlight this franchise in southeast Texas, the Texans are among the most profitable in the NFL. This enabled owner Robert McNair to gradually pay down the huge debt he used to buy the team in 1999, including the portion of his purchase price that was deferred. At the end of 2014, credit rating agency Fitch noted that the Texans average earnings before interest, taxes, depreciation, amortization (EBITDA), and lease payments since the fiscal year ending in March 2009 have been above ten times the team's stadium lease payments of $4 million and well above five times when combined with other debt service payments. According to Fitch, the Texans' EBITDA margins are projected to be between 20 percent and 30 percent in 2015 and 2016.[20]

Indianapolis Colts

Born in 1959 in Lincolnwood, Illinois, to Robert and Harriet Irsay, James Irsay attended high school at Loyola Academy in Wilmette, a suburb just north of Chicago, and at Mercersburg Academy in Pennsylvania. After finishing high school, he graduated from Southern Methodist University in 1982 with a degree in broadcast journalism. While there he played linebacker for the school's football team as a walk-on, but an ankle injury ended his playing career.[21]

Following college, Irsay joined the NFL Baltimore Colts' executive staff. He was vice president and general manager of the organization in 1984, just one month after the team relocated from Baltimore to Indianapolis. After his father suffered a stroke in 1995, Jim assumed day-to-day management of the Colts franchise being its senior executive vice president, general manager, and then chief operating officer in April 1996. When his father died in 1997, Irsay engaged in a legal battle with his stepmother over ownership of the team. Later, at thirty-seven-years-old, he became the league's youngest team owner and currently controls the franchise.

Regarding Irsay's actions following the team's dismal 2011 season, he stunned his players and cemented his reputation as a shrewd but decisive owner when he axed its longtime president, Bill Polian, removed Polian's son Chris as general manager, and dismissed head coach Jim Caldwell. In a sweeping reorganization, Irsay hired youthful Ryan Grigson from the Philadelphia Eagles to replace Chris and recruited Chuck Pagano, then the defensive coordinator of the Baltimore Ravens, as his club's new head coach. He also drafted former Stanford University quarterback Andrew Luck instead of Robert Griffin III. Irsay impressed Pagano for being passionate about his team and direct about what he expected from it in the near future.

Team Financials

According to data and other financial information published in *Forbes* for sixteen franchises in the AFC as of their 2015 season, the Colts ranked seventh in both market value at $1.875 billion and gate receipts at $58 million, eighth in revenue at $321 million, fourth in operating income at $90 million, and fourteenth in player expenses at $141 million. Compared to those of three other clubs in the conference's SD, the Colts' value, revenue, gate receipts, and operating income were second following amounts for the Texans while its player expenses were third and percentage of debt fourth. Based on these results, owner Irsay's Indianapolis NFL franchise is above-average from a financial perspective within its division and among fifteen other AFC teams (Table A.3).

Based on data of thirty-one other NFL clubs, the Colts were fourteenth in market value, eighteenth in revenue, tied for sixteenth with the Seahawks in gate receipts, eighth in operating income, twenty-ninth in player expenses, and thirty-second in their debt-to-value ratio. While the club's operating income was relatively high and its debt ratio extremely low, the Colts ranked about average as a commercial enterprise relative to different franchises across the league. Indeed they have a profitable business model based, in part, on owner Irsay's leadership and wealth (Table A.4).

As previously discussed for the Texans, a Chicago-based company named Team Marketing Report prepares and publishes an annual Fan Cost Index (FCI) for the home games of teams in professional sports leagues. For the NFL's 2015 season, the Colts' FCI was approximately $462 or ranked eighteenth for a four-person family. Listed from most to least expensive to purchase for one individual at a regular-season home game at 63,000-seat Lucas Oil Stadium was a nonpremium ticket at about $87, parking for one vehicle $20, a team cap $18 and beer $7, and a soft drink and hot dog each between $5 and $6. In addition, there was no cost reported for a program.[22]

For FCI's of other clubs in the SD, the Texans ranked twelfth at $491, Titans twenty-fifth at $404, and Jaguars thirty-second at $347. Compared to the league average FCI of $480, it cost $18 or about 4 percent less for spectators to watch the Colts play at home than tickets and expenses at the stadium of a typical NFL team. Besides these amounts, the Colts' average premium ticket at games cost $166 or thirtieth lowest in the league and considerably less than the average of $255. By setting competitive ticket prices for premium and nonpremium seats, Colts teams get higher attendances and earn more gate receipts and also revenue from sales of beverages, clothing, food, and memorabilia.

Business Highlights

Using fifteen years of data on such things as NFL team performances, home-game ticket prices, and market populations and their median incomes, Emory University researchers created an equity index to determine which clubs had the most avid, engaged, and/or supportive fans before the NFL's 2015 season. Among the AFC's SD teams, the Colts ranked ninth and ahead of the Texans at twelfth and Titans at sixteenth and the Jaguars at twenty-ninth. For various reasons, including owner Jim Irsay and his policies to finance the team and its operations, the index suggests that Colts fans, on average, are very engaged or highly enthusiastic about their football team partly because of the sport's popularity in the Midwest and the National Collegiate Athletic Association's home site in Indianapolis.[23]

In another but unique index titled Social Media Equity, the Colts had the league's twenty-ninth best fan base and fourth in the SD but behind the Texans at fifteenth, Titans at twenty-second, and Jaguars at twenty-fifth. These results were different than the equity index because they reflected whether teams over- or underperform with respect to their Twitter following and fans' comments on other social media.

Although the Colts played in the AFC championship game in their 2014 season, they were blown out by the eventual Super Bowl winners, the New England Patriots. The important element in measuring the Colts' value is their great lease at Lucas Oil Stadium, where the team pays annual rent of just $250,000, and also the franchise's rock-solid balance sheet that has a small amount of debt. For their 2015–2016 season, the Colts went from six to eleven price points for nonpremium seating. In addition they lowered some ticket prices, but increased others to reflect demand from the secondary market. For the NFL, the changes in ticket prices amounted to an overall increase of about 1 percent, placing the average nonpremium ticket at about $87.

For the Colts to significantly increase in market value and receive more revenue at games during and after its 2016 season, it needs quarterback Andrew Luck to lead offensively and consistently defeat such rivals as the Texans in the AFC's weakest division. Although his four-year, $22 million contract expired in 2015 and includes a team option for 2016, the club may or may not sign him again because of his demand for a huge salary increase including bonuses and incentives, and/or injury. Nevertheless, for this Indianapolis-based team to financially succeed in its small to mid-sized market, franchise owner Irsay must re-sign Luck to a lucrative but multiyear contract and recruit enough players to help him win more titles.[24]

Jacksonville Jaguars

Born in Lahore, Pakistan, to a middle-class family, sixteen-year-old Shahid Khan moved to the United States to attend the University of Illinois and while there, worked at automotive manufacturing company named Flex-N-Gate in Urbana, Illinois. After graduating from the university with an industrial engineering degree in 1971, he became the company's engineering director. Seven years later Khan started Bumper Works, which manufactured bumpers for customized pickup trucks and body shop repairs. In 1980, he bought Flex-N-Gate from his former employer and brought Bumper Works into the business.[25]

In 1984, Khan began supplying a small number of bumpers for Toyota pickups and within a few years became the only supplier for that vehicle. Five years later, Flex-N-Gate was the sole supplier for Toyota in America. Since then the company has grown from $17 million in sales to an estimated $2 billion by 2010. In 2011, Flex-N-Gate had 12,450 employees and forty-eight manufacturing plants in the nation and several other countries, and earned $3 billion in revenue.

Khan attempted to purchase an NFL team in February 2010 when he entered into an agreement to acquire 60 percent of the St. Louis Rams from Chip Rosenbloom and Lucia Rodriguez, subject to the approval of other franchise owners. However, the minority shareholder of the Rams, Stan Kroenke, ultimately exercised a clause in his ownership agreement to match any proposed bid and thus completed the deal.

Despite failing to buy the Rams, Khan purchased the league's Jacksonville Jaguars for $760 million from J. Wayne Weaver and his ownership group during November 2011. Subject to NFL approval, the deal was finalized two months later. Then in July 2012, Khan acquired the London soccer club Fulham of the English Premier League from its previous owner, Mohamed Al Fayed. Those deals, in turn, increased Khan's net worth to an estimated $2 billion.

Team Financials

According to data and other financial information published in *Forbes* for sixteen franchises in the AFC as of their 2015 season, the Jaguars ranked thirteenth in market value at $1.48 billion, tenth in total revenue at $315 million, eleventh in gate receipts at $54 million, fifth in operating income at $67 million, fifteenth in player expenses at $140 million, and tied for ninth with the Patriots, Bengals, Texans, and Chargers each with a debt-to-value ratio of 7 percent (Table A.3).

Among clubs in only the SD, Jacksonville had the lowest amounts in market value, revenue, and player expenses, also was third in gate receipts and operating income, and tied for second with the Texans in their debt-to-value percent. Based on these results, the Jaguars are inferior financially in the conference and their division, in part, because of the team's dismal performances, small market size, and ownership problems.

In comparison to financials of thirty-one other NFL teams as of their 2015–2016 season, the Jaguars ranked twenty-seventh in market value, twentieth in revenue, twenty-third in gate receipts, thirteenth in operating income, thirtieth in player expenses, and tied for nineteenth with several other clubs in their debt-to-value ratio. Other than its operating, this Jacksonville-based team ranks below the league's averages from a financial perspective, and also it commercially struggles as a business operation (Table A.4)

As explained for the Texans and Colts, a company in Chicago named Team Marketing Report prepares and publishes an annual Fan Cost Index (FCI) for the home games of teams in professional sports leagues. For its 2015–2016 season, the Jaguars' FCI was approximately $347 or thirty-second in the NFL for a four-person family. Listed from most to least expensive to purchase for one person at a typical home game in 76,800-seat EverBank Field was a nonpremium ticket at about $57, parking for one vehicle $25, a team cap $20 and beer $6, and a hot dog and soft drink each $5. In addition, the cost for a program was not reported in TMR's calculations.

For FCI's of other clubs in the SD, the Texans ranked twelfth at $491, Colts eighteenth at $462, and Titans twenty-fifth at $404. Compared to the league's FCI of $480, it cost $133 or approximately 28 percent less for a family to watch the Jaguars play at home than spent by them at the stadium of a typical NFL team. Besides these amounts the team's average premium ticket at its games cost $38 or 15 percent lower than the league average. By setting relatively low ticket prices for nonpremium and premium seats, Jaguars teams get higher attendances and therefore earn more gate receipts and also revenue from the sale of beverages, clothing, food, and other items.

Business Highlights

Using fifteen years of data on such things as NFL team performances, home-game ticket prices, and market populations and their median incomes, Emory University researchers created an equity index to determine which clubs had the most avid, engaged, and/or supportive fans before the NFL's 2015 season. Among the AFC's SD teams, the Jaguars ranked twenty-ninth and below the Colts at ninth, Texans twelfth, and Titans sixteenth. For various reasons, including new owner Shahid Khan and his policies to fund the team and its operations, the index suggests that Jacksonville fans, on average, are not really engaged nor highly enthusiastic about their football team partly because of its failure to win more games and availability of other entertainment opportunities in the metropolitan area besides professional sports.

In another index from Emory University titled Social Media Equity, the Jaguars had the league's twenty-fifth best fan base and third highest in the SD following the Texans at fifteenth and Titans at twenty-second but ahead of the Colts at twenty-ninth. These results were different than the Fan Equity Index because they measured whether teams over- or underperform with respect to their Twitter following and fans' comments on other social media.

During July 2015, the Jaguars and a website jointly launched the "Small Business Breakthrough powered by Web.com" to provide small businesses in North/Central Florida and South Georgia an opportunity to compete and win a comprehensive NFL sponsorship with the team and a full digital makeover from Web.com. Valued at more than $250,000, the competition challenges entrants to answer to a detailed questionnaire about their business, create an optional video discussing what they would do to grow their business if they won the money, and also convince a panel of judges featuring owner Khan, team president Mark Lamping, and Web.com chief executive officer David Brown that they deserve the prize.

To highlight this Florida-based franchise's success, the Jaguars racked up the worst record in the NFL over three seasons (2012–2014) with only nine wins against thirty-nine losses. The local but small corporate base and poor results on the field make selling tickets in Jacksonville difficult for the team. The club's 45,000 season ticket base was one of the lowest in the NFL in 2014, and the season ticket renewal rate equaled only 83 percent, while most other teams' exceeded 90 percent. Even so, owner Khan has spent more than $100 million since 2013 to improve EverBank Field in order to attract more fans from the area to Jaguars home games.[26]

Tennessee Titans

After the Titans' founder/majority owner Bud Adams died in July 2013, members of his family inherited the franchise. In a 2008 interview with *USA Today*, Adams said the club's ownership would be split in thirds between his two daughters, Susie Smith and Amy Strunk, and the family of his deceased son. At the time, grandson Kenneth S. Adams IV was being groomed to eventually control and also to operate the team.[27]

Since graduating from the University of the South in 2006, Kenneth has been employed by the Titans. At one point, he was an administrative assistant to Steve Underwood, who served as Nashville-based senior executive vice president and general counsel during 2006–2010. Tommy Smith, Bud's son-in-law, was offered an opportunity to move to Nashville and help operate the franchise when, as the Oilers, it landed on Tennessee turf in 1997. Nevertheless, he declined the offer.

More specifically, Kenneth has rotated from department to department and handled various assignments with the Titans for more than seven years. He worked in the front office, and on some Sundays, was visible on the sideline at LP Field prior to games and often visiting with his grandfather. While only in his early thirties, Kenneth is supposedly a smart and sensible guy with good communication skills. However, despite knowledge of and experience with the Titans' operations, his age may prevent him from being the controlling owner of the franchise at this time of his life.

Team Financials

According to data and other financial information published in *Forbes* for sixteen franchises in the AFC as of their 2015–2016 season, the Titans ranked twelfth in both market value at $1.49 billion and gate receipts at $52 million, and also ninth in total revenue at $318 million, eleventh in operating income at $50 million, sixth in player expenses at $164 million, and eighth with a debt-to-value ratio of 10 percent (Table A.3).

Among SD clubs in the conference, Tennessee had the most player expenses, third highest market value and total revenue, and the lowest gate receipts and operating income. Except for the club's player's expenses and debt ratio, these amounts were below average compared to other teams in the conference and, in part, reflected the Titans' disadvantages and problems from a financial perspective.

With respect to financials of thirty-one other NFL teams as of their 2015–16 season, Tennessee was twenty-sixth in market value, nineteenth in total revenue, tied for twenty-fourth with the Lions in gate receipts, twenty-second in operating income, fifteenth in player expenses, and tied for fourteenth with the Cardinals in their debt-to-value ratio. Based on these results, the Titans rank below the majority of NFL clubs financially and also as a business enterprise that operates in the professional sports industry (Table A.4).

As described before for the Texans, Colts, and Jaguars, a Chicago-based company named Team Marketing Report prepares and publishes an annual Fan Cost Index (FCI) for the home games of teams in professional sports leagues. For the 2015 NFL season, the Titans' FCI was approximately $404 or twenty-fifth in the NFL for a four-person family. Listed from most to least expensive to purchase for one person at a typical home game in 69,100-seat Nissan Stadium was a nonpremium ticket at about $67, parking for one vehicle $30, a team cap $25 and beer $7, program at $5, and a hot dog and soft drink each $4.[28]

For FCI's of other clubs in the conference's SD, the Texans ranked twelfth at $491, Colts eighteenth at $462, and Jaguars thirty-second at $347. Compared to the league's FCI of $480, it cost $76 or approximately 16 percent less for a four-person family to watch the Titans play at home than spent at the stadium of a typical NFL team. Besides these amounts, the team's premium ticket price at games cost $87 or 35 percent lower than the league's average. By setting realistic but competitive ticket prices for seats, Titans teams play home games before larger audiences and earn more gate receipts and also revenue from the sale of beverages, clothing, food, and other items.

Business Highlights

Using fifteen years of data on such things as NFL team performances, home-game ticket prices, and market populations and their median incomes, Emory University researchers created an equity index to determine which clubs had the most avid, engaged, and/or supportive fans before the NFL's 2015 season. Among the AFC's SD teams, the Titans ranked sixteenth following the Colts at ninth and Texans twelfth, but ahead of the Jaguars at twenty-ninth. For various reasons, including the death of Bud Adams in 2013 and new owners of the franchise, the index indicates that Tennessee fans, on average, are moderately engaged or somewhat enthusiastic about their football team partly because of its record in winning and losing games and also other entertainment opportunities in the Nashville metropolitan area besides professional sports.[29]

In another but unique index from Emory University titled Social Media Equity, the Titans had the league's twenty-second best fan base and second highest in the SD following the Texans at fifteenth but ahead of the Jaguars at twenty-fifth and Colts at twenty-ninth. These results were different than the Fan Equity Index because they reflected whether teams over- or underperform with respect to their Twitter following and fans' comments on other social media.

For other business news, the Titans and Nissan North America recently announced a twenty-year, exclusive naming-rights partnership that rebrands Nashville's downtown football stadium as Nissan Stadium. One component of the partnership will be assisting charitable organizations throughout the region in an array of community outreach programs. A centerpiece of this is the annual "Taste of Titans" charitable event, for which Nissan will serve as presenting sponsor and benefit the Wounded Warrior Project. During the course of the multiyear relationship, a total of more than $1 million resulting from these events will be distributed to local nonprofit organizations.

Aside from Titans games the stadium also has hosted Tennessee State University football games, the Music City Bowl and annual CMA Music Festival, a U.S. Soccer match, and various concerts during recent periods. Thus, the deal is a good fit for the auto maker. The Nissan facility in Smyrna, Tennessee, opened more than thirty years ago, and the impact of the company and its employees continues to be felt throughout Nashville and Middle Tennessee. Regarding the Titans, co-owner Amy Adams Strunk remarked, "This partnership sends a strong message about the positive future on the horizon for the Titans franchise, Nissan, the City of Nashville, and Middle Tennessee."[30]

NOTES

1. Two prominent books about the NFL and its teams and their seasons and postseasons are Frank P. Jozsa Jr., *Football Fortunes: The Business, Organization and Strategy of the NFL* (Jefferson, NC: McFarland, 2010), and James Quirk and Rodney D. Fort, *Pay Dirt: The Business of Professional Team Sports* (Princeton, NJ: Princeton University Press, 1992).
2. For information regarding the Houston Texans and other NFL teams and their performances see the *NFL Record & Fact Book 2014* (New York, NY: NFL, 2014) and also the website "Teams," http://www.pro-football-reference.com, cited August 25, 2015.
3. Home attendances of teams in the NFL and other professional sports leagues are reported in "Rod Fort's Sports Business Data," http://www.sites.google.com, cited September 1, 2015 and on pages 488–94 of *Pay Dirt*.
4. See "Ranking All 31 NFL Stadiums," http://www.sportingnews.com cited August 31, 2015 and "Ranking the Best and Worst NFL Stadiums," http://www.athlonsports.com cited August 31, 2015.
5. Tim Battle, "ESPN's NFL Future Power Rankings Bode Poorly for Houston Texans," http://www.battleblog.com, cited September 24, 2015.
6. Notes 1–4 contain the Colts' performances each season and their home attendances at the former Hoosier Dome and current Lucas Oil Stadium in Indianapolis.
7. See "Rod Fort's Sports Business Data" and attendance data on http://www.espn.go.com.
8. "Ranking All 31 NFL Stadiums," http://www.sportingnews.com, cited August 31, 2015.
9. See previous references for the Texans and Colts to research the historical performances of Jaguars teams and their coaches and players, and the club's attendances at its home games.
10. Besides *Pay Dirt*, the sources are "Rod Fort's Sports Business Data" and attendance data reported on http://www.espn.go.com.
11. This quote appeared in "Ranking the Best and Worst NFL Stadiums," http://www.athlonsports.com, cited August 31, 2015.
12. For more information about the club's future, see "2015 NFL Future Power Rankings." http://www.insider.espn.go.com, cited October 10, 2015.
13. Sources for the Titans' performances were those used to research the Texans, Colts, and Jaguars in this chapter.
14. "Ranking All 31 NFL Stadiums," http://www.sportingnews.com, cited August 31, 2015.
15. As stated in note 12, the reading is "2015 NFL Future Power Rankings."
16. To research NFL franchise owners and their business history online, beside teams on http://www.nfl.com, such websites as http://www.forbes.com, http://www.bleacherreport.com, and http://www.profootballhof.com are recommended.
17. For FCIs of the Texans, Colts, Jaguars, and Titans, see "2015 NFL Fan Cost Index," http://www.teammarketing.com, cited November 20, 2015.
18. Indexes for SD teams and their ranking are contained in the following article: Manish Tripathi, "2015 NFL Fan Equity Rankings," https://scholarblogs.emory.edu, cited September 4, 2015.
19. Michael Lewis, "2015 NFL Social Media Equity Rankings," https://scholarblogs.emory.edu, cited September 4, 2015.
20. Other business news about the Texans includes these readings: Joshua Brustein, "Houston Running Back Arian Foster Is Going Public at the Perfect Time," *Business Week* (October 14–20, 2013): 1; Eric Chemi, "Why Arian Foster Has Zero Chance of Making $50 Million on

the Field," *Business Week* (October 28–November 3, 2013): 1; Daniel Kaplan, "Focus Group Helps Texans Program New Video Boards," *SportsBusiness Journal* (July 29, 2013): 6.

21. See the websites in note 16 for information about the Irsay family and especially current Indianapolis Colts owner James Irsay.

22. For more details about these costs, read and contrast the data in the "2015 NFL Fan Cost Index" to amounts in the "2014 NFL Fan Cost Index," https://www.teammarketing.com, cited August 26, 2015.

23. See the articles in notes 17 and 18 for indexes regarding the Colts and where the club ranked among NFL teams.

24. Two articles about this franchise are Don Muret, "Post-Manning Colts Get Some Help Selling Season Tickets," *SportsBusiness Journal* (May 28, 2012): 14, and Michael Salfino, "The Count: Luck is on Colts' Side," *Wall Street Journal* (September 15, 2014): B8.

25. One source is "NFL Team Owners," http://www.biography.yourdictionary.com, cited December 24, 2015.

26. One reading about this team's business is "Shahid Khan: The New Face of the NFL and the American Dream," *Forbes* (September 24, 2012): 1.

27. See the website in note 24 above for more information about the franchise owners of the Texans, Colts, Jaguars, and Titans.

28. To compare specific costs of the Texans' games to those of other teams in the league from their 2014 to 2015 seasons, review changes in amounts from the "2014 NFL Fan Cost Index" to the "2015 NFL Fan Cost Index."

29. See notes 17 and 18 for where the Titans and other teams ranked in each index.

30. Mike Ramsey, "Nissan Buys 20-Year Naming Rights to NFL's Tennessee Titans' Stadium," *Wall Street Journal* (June 25, 2015): 1. Besides naming rights, other marketing/public relations deals of the franchise are discussed by Don Muret in "Titans Sign 10-Year Deal with ANC for Boards," *SportsBusiness Journal* (June 11, 2012): 8, and "Jaguars Create New Category of Poolside Seating," *SportsBusiness Journal* (June 9, 2014): 17.

Chapter Four

West Division

When the National Football League (NFL) postseason ended after Super Bowl XLIX in early 2015, which team or teams in the West Division (WD) of the American Football Conference (AFC) had the most all-time victories and playoff appearances, worst winning percentage, and least number of titles and championships? Did the Denver Broncos rank higher than the Oakland Raider in their gate receipts and player expenses, and were the Kansas City Chiefs more valuable as a franchise than the San Diego Chargers?

In response to these and other questions, next are some interesting but important, practical, and relevant facts that highlight the historical performances of four teams in the AFC's WD as of the league's 2015–2016, or simply, 2015 season. Besides their winning percentage and number of wins, titles, championships, and postseason, this information includes special coaches, players, and events regarding each of them while competing in the league's regular seasons and any playoffs. In the chapter's final section—labelled Franchise Business—have these franchises succeeded or failed as business enterprises both individually and in comparison to each other from a financial perspective?[1]

TEAM PERFORMANCES

Denver Broncos

The majority owner of minor league baseball's Denver Bears—sports entrepreneur Bob Howsam—was awarded an AFL charter franchise for $25,000 in August 1959. Several months later, his Denver Broncos team joined seven others to play their first season in the new league. While competing against such opponents as the Dallas Texans, Los Angeles Chargers—renamed San Diego Chargers in 1961—and Oakland Raiders in the AFL's Western Division from 1960 to 1969, the Broncos compiled a 39–97–4 record and finished second once, but third or fourth during its other nine seasons.[2]

After a disastrous 4–9–1 regular season in 1960, Howsam sold controlling interest of his Bears and Broncos teams to businessmen Calvin Kunz and Gerald and Allan Phipps in May 1961. Four years later, the club almost lost its franchise because of financial problems. However, a local ownership group took control and rebuilt the team.

The Bronco's first superstar, running back Floyd Little, was instrumental in keeping the team in Denver when he signed a contract in 1967 and also when he played well enough to appear in AFL pro bowls and later enter into the pro football Hall of Fame. Despite Little's ability in games and popularity among fans, the Broncos were the only original AFL team that failed to play in the league's title game or to have a winning season. When the AFL and NFL actually merged, the Broncos joined the Chargers, Raiders, and also Kansas City Chiefs as members of the combined league's AFC in 1970.

In May 2001, the NFL announced its realignment plan for the 2002 season at meetings in Chicago, Illinois. In each conference there would be four each four-team divisions with the Broncos being with the Chargers, Chiefs, and Raiders in the AFC WD. These teams continue to co-exist in that division and challenge each other to win a title.

Historical Results

While competing in the AFC's Western Division from 1970 to 2001 and then the WD during the league's 2002–2015 seasons, the Broncos played 712 games and won approximately 58 percent of them. In addition they succeeded to win fifteen division and eight conference titles, and two Super Bowl championships in twenty-two playoffs. Compared to the performances of fifteen different AFC teams, Denver ranked second in total wins, first in winning percentage, third in division titles, tied for first with the Patriots and Steelers in conference titles, third winning Super Bowls following the Steelers and Patriots, and tied for third with the Patriots in qualifying for the playoffs (Table A.1).

Compared to three other clubs in the WD as of the league's 2014 season, the Broncos had the most wins and also number of division and conference titles and postseasons, highest winning percentage, and more Super Bowl victories than the Chiefs, Raiders, and Chargers. Based on these statistics, the Broncos have been a superior competitor and one of the best performing teams in its division and conference during forty-six years in the NFL.

In analyzing and contrasting the performances of thirty-one other NFL teams as of the league's 2015–2016 season, the forty-six-year-old Broncos ranked eleventh in total wins, first in winning percentage, ninth in division titles, tied for third in winning their conference, tied for seventh in championships including three Super Bowls, and tied for eleventh in number of playoff appearances. These and other results prove that, except for its losing seasons, Denver's NFL team has been above-average and very competitive while playing games against clubs in the WD, other divisions of the AFC, and across the league since 1970 (Table A.2).

To accomplish results during their regular seasons and postseasons, Broncos teams had some outstanding and mediocre coaches and also talented players. Among the former group were Mike Shanahan who won 146 games, Dan Reeves 117, John Fox 46, Robert (Red) Miller 42, and John Ralston 34. Because of their leadership Ralston was AFC coach of the year in 1973, Miller in 1977, and Reeves in 1989 and 1991. Also, the NFL rewarded Miller with coach of the year in 1977. Alternatively, less successful leaders of the team included Jerry Smith, Wade Phillips, Josh McDaniels, and Eric Studesville, although Phillips was Associated Press (AP) assistant coach of the year for the 2015 season.

Since 1970 a few players set career, single season, and single games records for the franchise. For example, during their years with the club, Terrell Davis rushed for 7,607 yards; John Elway threw 300 passes for touchdowns; Steve Foley intercepted 44 passes; and Jason Elam kicked 395 field goals and scored 1,786 points. Season record-holders included quarterback Peyton Manning's 5,477 passing yards in 2013; Rod Smith's 113 receptions in 2001; Britton Colquitt's 47.4-yard punting average in 2011; and Von Miller's 18.5 sacks in 2012.

During a single game, Mike Anderson rushed for 251 yards and Jake Plummer passed for 499; Clinton Portis had 5 touchdowns and scored 30 points; and setting NFL records, Brandon Marshall had 21 receptions and Deltha O'Neal intercepted 4 passes. Historically, these players had great individual performances at their positions by establishing career, single season, and/or single game records for the Broncos.

After each NFL season, players earn AP awards for their performances on teams including the Broncos. Denver's John Elway was Most Valuable Player (MVP) in 1987 and Manning in 2013. Besides them, other award winners were Davis in 1996 and 1998 and Manning in 2013 for offensive player of the year; Anderson in 2000 and Portis in 2002 for being offensive rookie of the year; Randy Grandishar in 1978 for defensive player of the year; Mike Croel in 1991 and Von Miller in 2011 for defensive rookie of the year; and Manning in 2012 for comeback player of the year.

For their fabulous careers in the sport, six Broncos are in the pro football hall of fame. Chronologically, those inducted have been cornerback Willie Brown in 1984, running back Tony Dorsett in 1994, quarterback John Elway in 2004, offensive tackle Gary Zimmerman in 2008, running back Floyd

Little in 2010, and tight end Shannon Sharpe in 2011. Besides these stars several others are in the team's Ring of Fame. It was created in 1984 by franchise owner Pat Bowlen to honor former players and administrators who played significant roles in the franchise's history. In 1985, former co-owner Gerald H. Phipps became the first nonplayer to have his name placed in the Ring of Fame.

Performance Highlights

Among its years in the league, Denver's most successful periods consecutively were 1977–1979, 1996–1998, 2003–2005, and 2011–2015. In large part, these seasons of playoffs and winning titles occurred because of quarterbacks Elway and Manning and also Craig Morton and Jake Plummer. In contrast, the club had disappointing years during 1970–1976, 1980–1982, and 2006–2010. Various factors contributed to Broncos' losses in regular-season games including coaches making wrong decisions and players getting injured or simply performing poorly at their positions while on the field.

At its home games in 76,100-seat Sports Authority Field at Mile High—known as Invesco Field during 2001–2010—the club's attendances have been above the league's average. For example, the number of spectators there were actually between 340,763 to 597,503 in the 1970s; 369,555 to 598,402 in the 1980s; 560,703 to 590,808 in the 1990s; and 584,984 to 615,517 in the 2000s. Simply put, Bronco fans love their hometown team especially during seasons when they win enough games to compete for a conference title in the playoffs.[3]

Among other NFL venues, Sports Authority Field at Mile High ranked thirteenth in a recent study. According to an article about it in an edition of *Sporting News*, the author wrote:

> In the heart of the Rocky Mountains, NFL fans still have a reverence for the Mile High Stadium by keeping the old name in the title for the Broncos' newer facility. The defining feature is the seating bowl's wavy design. Two years ago [2013], the Broncos and their food provider, Centerplate, developed two open-end bars on the main concourse to draw fans in before kickoff to watch the early Sunday games on video walls with 55-inch TVs [televisions]. The stadium is not far from the bars and restaurants tied to Denver's LoDo neighborhood. The Broncos also run their own tailgate parties at the stadium.[4]

In the Entertainment Sports Programming Network's (ESPN) future power rankings, the network asked three experts to rate each NFL team for three seasons (2015–2017) on a scale of 0 to 100 percent in five categories including roster (excluding quarterback), quarterback, draft, front office, and coaching. In their analysis, the Broncos ranked fourteenth in the NFL despite a ten position tumble from a similar analysis in 2014. This placed them above the division's Raiders but below the Chiefs and Chargers who each improved because of free agents and the draft.[5]

Most interestingly, Denver fell from fourth to twenty-third in the quarterback category because of quarterback Peyton Manning's struggles at the end of the 2014 season. Although the Broncos appear confident in backup quarterback Brock Osweiler, he played in just thirteen games and attempted only thirty passes in three years. Also, the team dropped from eleventh to nineteenth in the coaching category, though first-year head coach Gary Kubiak had success in recent seasons and could again.

In addition to Manning's departure—he retired after his contract expired at the end of the NFL's 2015 season—the team allowed many of its best-drafted players to leave due to free agency. If the Broncos want to be successful in the next few years, they cannot afford to lose receiver Demaryius Thomas or have impact defenders like Von Miller and Malik Jackson walk away as free agents after 2015.

Kansas City Chiefs

Owned by twenty-six-year-old Lamar Hunt, who also founded the AFL in 1959, the Dallas Texans played in the league for three seasons and defeated the two-time champion Houston Oilers in a two-overtime game to win a championship in 1962 after finishing second in the WD in 1960 and 1961. Texans teams were led by coach Hank Stram and such players as quarterback Len Dawson, running back Abner Haynes, and receiver Chris Burford.[6]

The Texans and NFL Dallas Cowboys began their existence by sharing the Cotton Bowl as their home venue, and the teams' players closely monitored each other's progress in what became a fierce civic rivalry. Although the Texans went 25–17 in their three seasons and won the 1962 AFL title, Hunt ceded the Dallas market to the Cowboys, who struggled with a 9–28–3 record and were not in any postseasons between 1960 and 1962 although they claimed the title of being "America's Team."

Hunt, meanwhile, became more concerned about the AFL succeeding than challenging the Cowboys for football fans and business support in the local community. Rather than stay there, he moved his franchise from Dallas to Kansas City, Missouri, after its 1962 season even though his family's lucrative oil business gave him the financial means to keep the club in northeast Texas indefinitely. Then in 1963 Hunt renamed his team Kansas City Chiefs, who joined the Denver Broncos, Oakland Raiders, and San Diego Chargers in the league's WD.

During 1963–1969 the Chiefs won an AFL championship in 1966 and then after another league title in 1969, became the second AFL club (after the New York Jets) to defeat an NFL team in an AFL–NFL world championship game when they defeated the Minnesota Vikings in Super

Bowl IV held in New Orleans' Tulane Stadium. The Chiefs were the second team, after the Green Bay Packers, to appear in more than one Super Bowl and the first to appear in the championship game during two different decades. After the two leagues merged before the 1970 season, the Chiefs played in the NFL's AFC WD along with the Broncos, Chargers, and Raiders.

Historical Results

While competing in their division during the league's 1970–1971 to 2015–2016 seasons, the Chiefs played 712 games and won approximately 48 percent of them. Their postseasons included six division and zero conference titles without any Super Bowl championships in fourteen playoff appearances. Compared to fifteen other AFC teams during this period, Kansas City ranked fifth in total wins, eighth in winning percentage, tenth in division titles, tied for twelfth with four other clubs in conference titles, tied for eighth with eight other teams in number of Super Bowls victories, and tied for sixth with the Bengals and Chargers in qualifying for the playoffs (Table A.1).

Within the AFC's WD as of the league's 2015 season, the Chiefs had the second most wins but also less championships and playoffs than the Broncos, third highest winning percentage of the group, and the least number of division and conference titles combined. Based on these results, Kansas City has been below-average competitively in its division and also while performing against other teams in the AFC. These results occurred for various reasons including inferior coaching, lack of talented players, and rigorous competition especially from the WD's Broncos and Raiders since 1970.

Compared to the performances of thirty-one other NFL teams as of their 2015–16 season, the forty-six-year-old Chiefs ranked fourteenth in total wins, seventeenth in winning percentage, tied for twentieth with the Panthers and Buccaneers in division titles, tied for twenty-eighth with four other clubs in winning their conference, tied for eighteenth with zero championships, and tied for sixteenth in number of playoffs. These and other results prove that Kansas City's NFL team has performed below-average competitively while playing clubs in its division, conference, and across the league since 1970 (Table A.2).

Despite their many dismal regular seasons while in the league, the Chiefs had a few excellent coaches and some highly skilled players as of their 2015–16 season. In number of wins, coach Marty Schottenheimer had 104, Dick Vermeil 44, and Hank Stram 37 (1970–1974). When his team won a title but lost to the Colts in the 1995 divisional playoffs, Schottenheimer was AFC coach of the year. Beside that group, seven others each won less than 20 games while coaching for Kansas City.

Since 1970, a few players set career, single season, and single game records for the Chiefs franchise. For example, during their careers with the club, Priest Holmes rushed for 6,070 yards; Len Dawson passed for 237 touchdowns; Tony Gonzalez received 916 passes; and Nick Lowery kicked 329 field goals and scored 1,466 points. During a single season, Larry Johnson rushed for 1,789 yards in 2006; Trent Green passed for 4,591 yards in 2004; Emmitt Thomas had 12 interceptions in 1974 and Derrick Thomas 20 sacks in 1990; and Dustin Colquitt's punts travelled 46.8 yards in 2012.

For record-holders in a single game, Jamaal Charles rushed for 259 yards and Elvis Grbac passed for 504; Ryan Succop kicked six field goals; Stephone Page had 309 receiving yards; and Derrick Thomas set an NFL record with seven sacks. Individually, these were outstanding performances by players on Chiefs teams in one or more games of NFL seasons.

Earning AP awards, running back Holmes was offensive player of the year in 2002 while defensive rookies of the year included nose tackle Bill Maas in 1984, linebackers Derrick Thomas in 1989, Dale Carter in 1992 and cornerback Marcus Peters in 2016, and also safety Eric Berry as comeback player of the year in 2016. In addition to them, quarterback Dawson and placekicker Jan Stenerud and linebackers Willie Lanier and Derrick Johnson were each a pro bowl Most Valuable Player (MVP).

Beside several players the most prominent former Chiefs in the pro football Hall of Fame include founder/owner Lamar Hunt, inducted in 1972, and coaches Marv Levy in 2001 and Stram in 2003. Although he never won a conference title or Super Bowl, Schottenheimer may eventually be inducted into the league's Hall of Fame for winning two hundred games in regular seasons and another five in postseasons. In twenty-one years as head coach, only two of his Chiefs teams had more losses than wins, and from 1990 to 1995 they were in six consecutive playoffs.

Performance Highlights

At its home games in 34,200-seat Memorial Stadium during 1970–1971 and then 76,000–79,000-seat Arrowhead Stadium since 1972, the club's attendances have been above average among teams in the league. For example, the number of spectators there was actually between 342,863 to 459,249 in the 1970s; 123,042 to 487,056 in the 1980s; 560,193 to 629,545 in the 1990s; and 518,6 to 615,517 in the 2000s. Simply put, Chiefs fans love their hometown team especially during seasons when they win enough games to compete for a title in the playoffs.[7]

Among thirty other NFL venues, Arrowhead Stadium ranked thirteenth in a recent study. According to an article about it in an edition of *Sporting News*:

> Five years ago, one of the NFL's oldest stadiums completed a $375 million facelift, preserving a building that first opened in 1972. The seating bowl, featuring some of the league's best sightlines, was left untouched. The same held true for the iconic arrowhead—shaped video boards in both end zones. For baby boomer NFL fans, it's nice to still see some things we grew recognizing on TV haven't gone away. The strong tailgate experience in the parking lots enables fans to showcase their master recipes in a city known for its barbecue.[8]

Similar to the Broncos, Raiders, and Chargers in the conference's WD, three ESPN experts developed a future (2015–2017) power ranking for the Chiefs. Among NFL teams, the club ranked ninth and five positions higher than in 2014. They have improved in drafting players (nineteenth to thirteenth), front office (seventeenth to ninth), and the nonquarterback roster (eighteenth to thirteenth). Experts rated the Chiefs as best positioned to overtake Denver in their division now that the end appears very near for Broncos quarterback Peyton Manning.[9]

Based on these factors, the Chiefs should rank high in their conference. They have a strong nonquarterback roster because only one team drafted more pro bowlers in the last decade than Kansas City. That also indicates how well they drafted. The front office under general manager John Dorsey and coach Andy Reid seem strong, too. As for the quarterback position, the Chiefs are probably average or slightly above average. In other words, this team has the potential to compete for a title among rivals in its division.

Oakland Raiders

When a deal to put an original AFL franchise in Minneapolis, Minnesota, failed in late 1959/early 1960, an eight-man syndicate led by investors Chet Soda and Wayne Valley paid a $25,000 fee to sponsor a new team in Oakland, California, and nickname it the Raiders. Because the city did not have an adequate football stadium in 1960, the Raiders played their home games one year at 59,900-seat Kezar Stadium and another at 69,700-seat Candlestick Park both in San Francisco; four years at 22,000-seat Frank Youell Field in Oakland; and then in 1966 at the newly constructed, 56,600-seat Oakland Coliseum.[10]

During the 1960–1962 AFL seasons, the Raiders had a 9–33–0 record and finished third and then fourth twice in the league's four-team Western Division. Frustrated by poor performances and low attendances at home games, owners Valley and Ed McGah reorganized the franchise and hired San Diego Chargers' assistant coach Al Davis in 1963. That year, the Raiders improved to 10–4–0 and second in its division while Davis became AFL coach of the year.

After mediocre records the next three seasons, the team won an AFL championship in 1967 but lost to the NFL Green Bay Packers in Super Bowl II at the Orange Bowl in Miami. In 1968 and 1969, the club won its division again but was defeated in the championship game each year. When the two leagues merged in 1970, Oakland joined the Broncos, Chargers, and Chiefs in the AFC's Western Division.

Historical Results

While competing in their division from 1970 to 1981 and then during the league's 1995–2015 seasons, Oakland Raiders teams played 512 games and won approximately 48 percent of them. Their postseasons included nine division and three conference titles, and two Super Bowl victories in eleven playoff appearances. Among fifteen other teams in their conference, Oakland ranked eleventh in total victories and number of playoffs, ninth in winning percentage, tied for seventh with the Bengals in number of division titles, sixth in conference titles, and tied for fourth with the Dolphins and Ravens in Super Bowl championships (Table A.1).

Compared to only teams in the WD as of their 2015–2016 season, Raiders teams had won the fewest games but also ranked third in division titles, second in winning percentage and conference titles, tied with the Broncos for most championships, and qualified for the least number of playoffs. Except for division and conference titles and championships, these results denote that Raiders teams have performed about average in their division but below average among clubs in other divisions of the AFC.

Of thirty-one other clubs in the league as of their 2015–2016 season, the Raiders were twenty-third in total wins, eighteenth in winning percentage, tied for fifteenth with the Bengals and Seahawks in division titles, tied for fourteenth with the Eagles and Seahawks in winning their conference each three times, tied for eighth with the Dolphins and Ravens in number of Super Bowl victories, and ranked twenty-second from appearing in eleven playoffs. Based on these results, this Oakland-based club has been average across all teams in the league during the 1970–1981 plus 1995–2015 seasons. During their years in the league, the Raiders have been occasionally competitive against many clubs especially when they appeared in postseasons and won nine division and three conference titles and also two Super Bowls (Table A.2).

To achieve victories in seasons and postseasons since 1970, Oakland had at least two excellent coaches and many talented players during its thirty-two-year history in the NFL. In number of wins the former group included John Madden with 100 and Jon Gruden 38. Alternatively, such coaches as Joe Bugel, Norv Turner, Lane Kiffin, and Hue Jackson each won fewer than 10 games.

Because of their outstanding performances, some Raiders players set career, single season, and single game records for the franchise. Players and their career records, for example, included Ken Stabler's 19,078 passing yards and 150 touchdowns; Shane Lechler's 47.5-yard punting average; Greg Townsend's 107.5 sacks; and Sebastian Janikowski's 345 field goals and 1,489 total points. During a single season Rich Gannon passed for 4,689 yards in 2002; Tim Brown had 104 receptions and 1,408 receiving yards in 1997; Lester Hayes 13 interceptions in 1980; and Derrick Burgess 16 sacks in 2005.

In a single game Napoleon Kaufman rushed for 227 yards; Tim Brown and Brandon Myers each caught 14 passes; Janikowski kicked 6 field goals; Harvey Williams and Darren McFadden each scored 4 touchdowns; and Howie Long sacked quarterbacks 5 times. Unquestionably, these athletes contributed to their team and were responsible for many Raiders' wins during one or more regular seasons.

As recipients of AP awards, quarterback Ken Stabler was MVP and offensive player of the year in 1974 when he led the league with 26 touchdown passes and only 12 interceptions while his team finished with most wins at 12–2–0. Furthermore, quarterback Rich Gannon was NFL MVP in 2002 and also pro bowl MVP in 2001 and 2002; cornerback Lester Hayes defensive player of the year in 1980; and cornerback Charles Woodson defensive rookie of the year in 1998. Also, safety Charles Woodson won the Art Rooney award in 2016.

Besides those achievements a Raiders owner, one coach and a player/coach, and nine fulltime players who performed at least one season in Oakland have been inducted into the pro football Hall of Fame as of 2015. These were, respectively, owner Al Davis, Coach John Madden and player/coach Art Shell, and players Jim Otto, George Blanda, Willie Brown, Gene Upshaw, Fred Biletnikoff, Ted Hendricks, Howie Long, Dave Casper, and Ray Guy.

Performance Highlights

At its home games in 54,600-seat Oakland Alameda County Coliseum from 1970 to 1981 and then 63,100-seat O.co Coliseum during the 1995–2015 season—reduced to about 53,000 seats in 2013—the club's attendances have been below average and among the lowest for teams in the league. For example, the number of spectators at these facilities was actually between 345,782 and 423,838 during 1970–1981 and 375,499 to 433,732 during 1995–2012, and then 403,556 in 2013, 459,333 in 2014, and 436,910 in 2015. In short, local fans enthusiastically attended Raiders' games in Oakland when they won titles during the mid to late 1970s and early 2000s but not as much since 2003.

Among other NFL venues, O.co Coliseum ranked thirty-first in a recent study. According to an article about it in an edition of *Sporting News*, the author said:

> The stadium issue for the Silver and Black is just as muddled as San Diego's. An investment group stepped out of the shadows in Oakland to submit a proposal to keep the Raid-ahs in the Bay Area. To date [late 2015/early 2016], no deal has been signed. For the coliseum, yes it floods, but there are some positive views on the water front. The parking lots surrounding the stadium are where fans first encounter inhabitants of the Black Hole, dressed like castoffs from a Rob Zombie production.[11]

Similar to the Broncos, Chiefs, and Chargers in the WD, three ESPN experts developed a future (2015–2017) power ranking for the Raiders. To determine their power, each NFL team was rated in five categories including roster (excluding quarterback), quarterback, draft, front office, and coaching. For the final results, Oakland ranked twenty-ninth with an overall score of 56.5 out of 100.[12]

According to the experts' evaluation the Raiders climbed three spots in the league since 2014 after increasing from twenty-sixth to sixteenth in the quarterback category, which indicates a vote of confidence in Derek Carr. It seems surprising that the Raiders actually dropped two spots to thirty-first in drafting after signing Carr, Khalil Mack, Amari Cooper, and other talented college players. But it is also true that the team's promising young players are not yet proven difference makers. The Raiders remained thirty-second in front office outlook, which is fair given the franchise's organizational instability.

To clarify, football fans should not be shocked that Oakland received a low ranking. The key to the long-term future is the 2015 and 2016 seasons. The Raiders, who strengthened their overall roster during the offseason, must show improvement on the field after winning just eleven games from 2012 to 2014. Furthermore, they need to have another strong free agency and draft.

Although the Raiders are a building program, they must keep making progress. Perhaps in 2016 or later, experts may look at this organization and see a team ready to make a leap. In short, it is too early to be confident about them since a vast improvement may or may not occur in the future. There are some competitive and potentially outstanding players on the roster in Oakland, but they and their team are a work in progress.

Some developers claim a new stadium—designed by billionaire Floyd Kephart's New City Development Limited Liability Corporation (LLC)—could be ready by 2020 in Oakland. From the eternal flame to the Al Davis "Walk of Fame," the drawings of it are sure to be a hit with Silver and Black-clad fans. New City's proposal would pay for the construction of a $900 million to $1 billion stadium partly by using a $300 million, city-sponsored, twenty-five-year conduit bond that would not leave the city on the hook in the case of bond default. The bonds would be repaid by various stadium revenues including naming rights, non–game day revenue, and ticket or parking assessments.

During September 2015, however, Oakland and Alameda County blocked Kephart's attempt to develop a new stadium for the Raiders at the center of the $4 billion Coliseum City development. But Kephart is leaving the game with some pointed words for city and county officials. In an email to the *San Francisco Business Times*, Kephart said he's "not sure how one can function within such a process" as that set up around the exclusive negotiating agreement that his New City Development LLC inked earlier this year with the city and county.[13]

The Raiders, meanwhile, are also pursuing another stadium project with the San Diego Chargers in the Los Angeles suburb of Carson. The NFL is pressing Oakland officials to deliver a plan which is months ahead of an expected 2016 or 2017 league decision on where the team plays next season and beyond.

San Diego Chargers

For a $25,000 fee, the AFL awarded thirty-two-year-old hotel executive Barron Hilton a new franchise in 1959 to be located in Los Angeles. Nicknamed Chargers, the team played in the league's Western Division along with others from Dallas, Denver, and Oakland. Despite winning a division title in 1960, the Chargers had small attendances at their home games. Encouraged by California sports editor Jack Murphy, Hilton moved his club 120 miles south to San Diego in 1961 and played games there in 34,000-seat Balboa Stadium.[14]

Coached by Sid Gillman—whose teams emphasized the forward pass and scored many points in games—the Chargers won their division four times and an AFL championship in 1963. Led by such stars as wide receiver Lance Alworth, running backs Keith Lincoln and Paul Lowe, and quarterback John Hadl, the club provided image, impetus, and respect for the league as it struggled for fans and publicity with the established and well-financed NFL.

Although the Chargers moved into a new 60,835-seat stadium in 1967, they failed to win another division title in the AFL. In nine seasons, San Diego had a 76–44–6 record and a history of being a competitive, exciting, and glamorous team. When the two leagues actually merged in 1970, the Chargers joined the Broncos, Chiefs, and Raiders in the NFL's Western Division.

Historical Results

While competing as a member of its division from the league's 1970–1971 to 2015–2016 season, San Diego played 712 games and won approximately 47 percent of them with thirteen playoff appearances. Compared to the performances of other clubs in the AFC, the Chargers ranked sixth in number of wins and division titles, tenth in winning percentage, tied for tenth with the Titans in conference titles, tied for eighth with eight other teams each with zero Super Bowls, and tied for sixth with the Bills in qualifying for the conference's playoffs (Table A.1).

Among only WD teams as of their 2015–2016 season, the Chargers had the third most number of wins, lowest winning percentage, second highest division and third most conference titles, tied for third with the Chiefs each with zero NFL and Super Bowl championships, and second in total playoffs. Based on these results, San Diego has been average to below-average in performances within its division and the AFC. This occurred because of such things as the club's lack of enough talented players, wrong decisions and mistakes by coaches in games, different ownership problems, and other factors.

Compared to thirty-one other NFL clubs as of their 2015–2016 season, the Chargers were fifteenth in number of wins, twentieth in winning percentage, fourteenth in division titles, tied for twenty-second with the Titans and four NFC teams in winning their conference, tied for eighteenth with fourteen other clubs in number of Super Bowl victories and with the Bills from appearing in thirteen playoffs. Based on these results, Chargers teams have been average to below-average in their performances in the league. However, from 1979 to 1982 and during 2006–2009, this San Diego-based club was competitive in consecutive seasons than in other years (Table A.2).

Despite failing to win more titles including a Super Bowl, Chargers teams had a few good coaches and several excellent players. In number of wins the former group included Don Coryell with 72 victories, Norv Turner 59, Bobby Ross 50, and Marty Schottenheimer 47. Ross was AFC coach of the year in 1992 and Schottenheimer AP coach of the year in 2004. Alternatively, coaches with less success were Harland Svare, Ron Waller, Kevin Gilbride, and June Jones.

Between 1970 and 2015, some of San Diego's players set career, single season, and single game records for the franchise in various NFL games and seasons. For example, five career performances were LaDainian Tomlinson's 12,490 rushing yards; Dan Fouts's 43,040 passing yards; Gil Byrd's 42 interceptions; John Carney's 261 field goals; and Mike Scifres's 45.1-yard punting average. In a single season Philip Rivers passed for 34 touchdowns in 2008; Leslie O'Neal sacked quarterbacks 17 times in 1992 as Shawne Merriman did in 2006; and Tomlinson scored 31 touchdowns and 186 points in 2006.

Within a single game Kellen Winslow caught 15 passes and scored 5 touchdowns and 30 points; Wes Chandler had 260 receiving yards; Rivers passed for 455 yards and Fouts 6 touchdowns; and several players each intercepted 3 passes. For sure these athletes were outstanding for Chargers teams while setting career, single season, and/or single game records during their years in the league.

Each year the AP rewards players for their different performances. In 2006, Tomlinson was the league's MVP because of his number of touchdowns, points scored, and rushing yards. Beside him, Fouts was offensive player of the year in 1982 and Tomlinson in 2006; Don Woods won offensive rookie of the year in 1974; Merriman earned defensive rookie of the year in 2005; and quarterback Drew Brees became comeback player of the year in 2004 and Rivers in 2013. Also significant were pro bowl MVPs, which included quarterback Hadl in 1970, tight end Winslow in 1982, and quarterback Fouts in 1983.

For their great careers in the sport, several San Diego Chargers have been inducted into the pro football Hall of Fame. Besides Fouts and Winslow, they are defensive ends Fred Dean and David (Deacon) Jones; wide receivers Charlie Joiner and Lance Alworth; tight end John Mackey; linebacker Junior Seau; and quarterback Johnny Unitas. Sid Gillman entered in 1983 because of his 123–104–7 record and being the first coach to win titles in both the AFL and NFL.

Performance Highlights

At its home games in 70,000-seat Qualcomm Stadium, the club's attendances usually rank in the bottom one-third of the league. Since 2003, for example, the number of seats sold was about 90 to 95 percent of the stadium's capacity. Besides the team's performances, fans are also disappointed in the franchise and its failure to finance and build a new facility in the San Diego area.

Among other NFL venues, Qualcomm Stadium ranked thirtieth in a recent study. According to an article about it in an edition of *Sporting News*, the author wrote:

> Who knows where the Chargers will call home in the next few years. The stadium situation is a mess in one of the most beautiful cities in North America. Will the Bolts stay put in San Diego or build a two-team stadium with the Raiders in Carson, a suburb of Los Angeles? Qualcomm Stadium, meanwhile, gets older and greyer. At least, there's a new concessionaire on board to breathe some new life and a few million bucks into the aging lady. Similar to Oakland, the stadium is surrounded by parking lots. Given the stadium's age,

there are worse things in life than tailgating in beautiful San Diego on an NFL Sunday morning.[15]

Similar to the Broncos, Chiefs, and Raiders in the conference's WD, three ESPN experts developed a future (2015–2017) power ranking for the Chargers. To estimate their power, each NFL team was rated in five categories including roster (excluding quarterback), quarterback, draft, front office, and coaching. For the results, San Diego ranked thirteenth and behind Kansas City but ahead of Denver and Oakland. Although the Chargers dropped from fifth to fifteenth in the quarterback category from 2014 and fifth to seventeenth in drafting, they had few changes in their roster, front office, and coaching.

FRANCHISE BUSINESS

Besides performing as teams in regular season and postseason games, NFL franchises are also commercial enterprises. To that end, their economic objective is to earn maximum revenue and obtain the greatest amount of profit on a fiscal basis from their operations. Although they share revenue with each other from such sources as national television contracts and other deals, it is important for them to efficiently allocate resources, determine and distribute payrolls, set nonpremium and premium ticket prices, and schedule investments in short- and long-term assets. To reveal and manage these activities, this section focuses on different parts of four AFC franchise's business and how these organizations rank and succeed or not succeed from a financial perspective.

Denver Broncos

Born in February 1944 in Prairie du Chien, Wisconsin, Patrick "Pat" Bowlen attended Campion Jesuit Catholic High School and later earned degrees in business and law from the University of Oklahoma. He became a successful and wealthy lawyer in Edmonton, Alberta, and also worked as an executive for his father's company. As a real estate developer, Pat made major investments in the mining industry.[16]

The Bowlen family, including Pat's two brothers John and Bill and his sister Marybeth, purchased the NFL Denver Broncos from Edgar Kaiser in 1984 for approximately $71 million and thus saved it from potential bankruptcy. While Pat served as the organization's chief executive officer, he took steps to build a sense of pride and an attitude of success for the team. In his first year of ownership, for example, he created both an annual Broncos alumni reunion and the Ring of Fame, which graces the team's home stadium. During the early 2000s, Pat also became majority owner of the Arena

Football League's Orange Crush and Major League Lacrosse's Denver Outlaws.

During the summer of 2014, Pat relinquished control of the Broncos because of his Alzheimer's disease. More specifically he placed his Broncos' ownership in the Pat Bowlen Trust, which is controlled by non–family members with final authority delegated to team President Joe Ellis. Bowlen's long-term goal is for one of his seven children to operate it. Despite this change within the franchise, the club will not be offered for sale.

Team Financials

According to data and other financial information published in *Forbes* for sixteen franchises in the AFC as of their 2015–2016 season, the Broncos ranked fourth in both market value at $1.94 billion and revenue at $346 million, and also third in gate receipts at $70 million, sixth in operating income at $65 million, tied for second with the Steelers in player expenses each at $170 million, and fourteenth with a debt-to-value ratio of 6 percent. Except for its debt ratio, Denver's amounts were first compared to those of the Chiefs, Raiders, and Chargers in the conference's WD. From a financial perspective, the Broncos are a profitable and high-valued franchise with plenty of cash to spend on contracts of such players as linebacker Von Miller and wide receiver Demaryius Thomas (Table A.3).

Based on data of the other thirty-one NFL clubs as of their 2015–2016 season, the Broncos were eleventh in both market value and total revenue, seventh in gate receipts, fourteenth in operating income, tied for fourth with the Steelers and Redskins in player expenses, and tied for twenty-fourth with the Packers and Seahawks in their debt-to-value percent. Based on this information, Denver ranks above average as a current business, although its payments to players seem relatively low and so do operating income and revenue. Among teams in its division and conference, however, the Broncos organization has a financial advantage from being a valuable and successful enterprise (Table A.4).

For several years a Chicago-based company named Team Marketing Report (TMR) has prepared and published a Fan Cost Index (FCI) for the home games of teams in professional sports leagues. To attend a game for a typical family with two kids, an FCI includes the costs of four average-priced tickets, two cheapest-priced draft beers, four each cheapest-priced soft drinks and hot dogs, parking for one vehicle, and two each game programs and least-expensive, adult-size adjustable caps. Costs are determined by telephone calls with team representatives, venues, and concessionaires, and from asking questions during interviews.[17]

For the league's 2015 season, the Broncos' FCI was approximately $482 or thirteenth highest in the league but the same as in 2014. Listed from most to least in amount by item for one person, the club's nonpremium tickets averaged about $88, parking $30, a cap almost $20, beer near $7 and a cap $5, and between $4 and $5 each for a soft drink and hot dog. Among three other WD teams, the Chargers ranked fifteenth at $478, Raiders twenty-third at $420, and the Chiefs twenty-ninth at $396. While the San Francisco 49ers' index of $640 placed first in the league, $480 was the average for all teams.

Given these costs, Denver's home games are slightly above average among teams in the league and neither ultra-expensive nor cheap to attend for fans at Sports Authority Field at Mile High. Because of the team's success especially from 2003 to 2005 and during the 2011–2015 seasons, and due to other social and economic factors in their market area, the franchise sets competitive ticket prices for nonpremium seats and other items sold to spectators at games in order to maintain attendances and, in part, to maximize the franchise's revenue from gate receipts. For die-hard fans and corporations premium tickets average $311, which is $55 or 22 percent more than the league amount.

Business Highlights

Using fifteen years of data on such things as NFL team performances, home-game ticket prices, and market populations and their median incomes, Emory University researchers created an equity index to determine which clubs had the most avid, engaged, passionate, and/or supportive fans before the NFL's 2015 season. Among the AFC's WD teams, the Broncos ranked thirteenth and ahead of the Chargers at seventeenth, Chiefs at twenty-seventh, and Raiders at thirtieth.[18]

For various reasons, including the decision by former owner Pat Bowlen to financially support his team, the index suggests that Broncos fans are, on average, engaged or passionate about their football team partly because of the sport's popularity in their home state and the team's performances especially since Peyton Manning joined it in 2012. Meanwhile, in another index titled Social Media Equity, the Broncos had the league's eighteenth best fan base followed by the WD's Chargers at twenty-fourth and Chiefs at twenty-six, but below the Raiders at eighth. Although this index reflected whether teams over- or underperform with respect to their Twitter following, Denver fans were much less involved with the team on social media than those of the AFC Steelers, Patriots, and Jets, and NFC Cowboys, Packers, and Saints.

Since the AFL-NFL merger took effect in 1970, the Broncos have been one of the NFL's biggest winners. Their on-the-field success is more than matched by a spectacular attendance record of sellout crowds except for their strike-replacement games. In fact, the team's 74,000 season ticket sales are backed by a waiting list in the tens of thousands. In addition, the franchise's value has increased for several years because of dedicated fans, excitement and fun for them at home games, the team's recent seasons with a winning record, and the growth of Denver's metropolitan area population and household per capita income.

To highlight Denver's NFL franchise, the 2014 season was a transition period for the Broncos as longtime owner Pat Bowlen stepped away from operating it to continue his battle with Alzheimer's disease. Coach John Fox and the team mutually parted ways in January after a disappointing playoff exit in the AFC's divisional round against the Colts. Quarterback Manning set the all-time record for touchdown passes during the season, but struggled at the end of it with only five in his last five games including the playoff loss. As a result, Manning took a $4 million pay cut for the 2015 season. Since he retired in early 2016, he cannot earn the amount back in addition to his $15 million base salary.

Kansas City Chiefs

Following the death of his father Lamar in 2006, Clark Hunt and his sister and their brothers inherited ownership of the Kansas City Chiefs. As the most active, prominent, and well-known owner of the franchise, Clark is the organization's ultimate authority while serving as its chairman and chief executive officer. He also is chairman of Hunt Sports Group, where he oversees the operations of Major League Soccer's FC Dallas and, previously, the Columbus Crew.[19]

After graduating from St. Mark's School in Texas, Clark finished first in his class at Southern Methodist University (SMU) in 1987. He was captain of SMU's nationally ranked soccer team and a two-time academic All-American while earning a degree in business administration with a concentration in finance. A two-time recipient of the university's highest academic honor—Provost Award for outstanding scholar—Hunt began his business career as an analyst with investment bank Goldman Sachs.

During January 2013, Clark ushered in a new era of Chiefs leadership when he hired head coach Andy Reid on January 7, and a week later, general manager John Dorsey. He also modified the leadership structure of the organization announcing that for the first time in franchise history, its head coach, general manager, and team president would report directly to him.

In their 2013 regular season, the Chiefs enjoyed a record-setting resurgence under the direction of Reid and Dorsey and returned to the AFC postseason. Kansas City set a franchise record for the best single-season turnaround in the organization's history—a nine-win improvement over the 2012 season. Because of the team's dramatic turnaround, Hunt was named the 2014 Waddell & Reed Executive of the Year by the Kansas City Sports Commission for his outstanding leadership in the local sports community. His proven business acumen, coupled with two decades of experience working side-by-side with his father, helped shape his vision for the franchise's success.

Team Financials

According to data and other financial information published in *Forbes* for sixteen franchises in the AFC as of their 2015–2016 season, the Chiefs ranked ninth in market value at $1.53 billion, twelfth in both revenue at $307 million and operating income at $48 million, tied for ninth with the Chargers in gate receipts at $55 million, ninth in player expenses at $159 million, and fifteenth with a debt-to-value ratio of only 5 percent. Compared to only WD clubs, Kansas City had the smallest operating income and debt ratio, second highest market value, revenue, and gate receipts (with the Chargers), but lower amounts than the Broncos. Except for their percent of debt, the Chiefs' financial results were average to below-average among teams in its conference (Table A.3).

Based on data of the other thirty-one NFL clubs as of their 2015 season, the Chiefs were twenty-first in market value, twenty-fourth in revenue, tied for twentieth with the Chargers and Cardinals in gate receipts, twenty-third in operating income, tied for twentieth with the Packers in player expenses, and tied for twenty-seventh with the Cowboys and Saints in their debt-to-value ratio. Thus, Kansas City's data reflect its lack of power and success from a financial perspective compared to a group of fifteen other AFC teams and sixteen in the NFC (A.4).

As developed by the TMR company, an FCI includes the costs of four average-priced tickets, two cheapest-priced draft beers, four each cheapest-priced soft drinks and hot dogs, parking for one vehicle, and two each game programs and least-expensive, adult-size adjustable caps. Costs are determined by telephone calls with team representatives, venues, and concessionaires, and from asking questions during interviews.[20]

For the league's 2015 season, the Chiefs' FCI was approximately $396 or twenty-ninth highest in the league but 5.6 percent less than in 2014. Listed from most to least in amount by item for one person, the club's nonpremium tickets averaged about $68, parking $27 and a cap $20, a beer almost $8 and hot dog $6, and a soft drink between $4 and $5. Compared to FCIs of other clubs in the AFC's WD, the Broncos ranked thirteenth at $482, Chargers fifteenth at $478, and Raiders twenty-third at $420. While the 49ers had the highest cost at $640, the NFL averaged $480.

Given these amounts, Kansas City's home games are relatively inexpensive for fans to attend at 76,400-seat Arrowhead Stadium. Because of only four playoff appearances since 1988 and other social and economic factors within the team's market area, the franchise sets competitive ticket prices for seats and other items sold to spectators at games in order to maintain attendances and, in part, to maximize the franchise's revenue from gate receipts. In addition the Chiefs' premium tickets cost $202, which is $53 or 26 percent less than the league average.

Business Highlights

Using fifteen years of data on such things as NFL team performances, home-game ticket prices, and market populations and their median incomes, Emory University researchers created an equity index to determine which of the league clubs had the most avid, engaged, passionate, and/or supportive fans before their 2015 season. Among the AFC's WD teams, the Chiefs ranked twenty-seventh and ahead of the Raiders at thirtieth but following the Broncos at thirteenth and Chargers at seventeenth. For various reasons, including the franchise's new ownership and team performances, the index suggests that Chiefs fans are not, on average, very engaged or passionate about their pro football team even though the sport is popular across the Midwest.[21]

In another index titled Social Media Equity, the Chiefs had the league's twenty-sixth best fan base following the WD's Raiders at eighth, Broncos at eighteenth, and Chargers at twenty-fourth. Although this index reflected whether teams over- or underperform with respect to their Twitter following, Kansas City fans were much less interested in their team on social media than those, for example, of the AFC Steelers, Patriots, and Jets, and NFC Cowboys, Packers, and Saints.

From a marketing viewpoint the Chiefs have not really excited fans at their home games or renovated Arrowhead Stadium because, in part, they did not advance beyond a divisional playoff game in 2003 and wild card playoff games in 2006, 2010, and 2013. Nevertheless, the club expects to improve its performance in 2015 and thereafter.

During the league's recent offseason, Kansas City signed twenty-six-year-old Justin Houston to a six-year, $101 million deal. It is the richest contract in team history and the most lucrative ever given to a linebacker in NFL history. While ranking seventh on defense in the 2014 NFL season at 330.5 yards per game, they need to become more competitive and upgrade their offense.

For about a decade the Chiefs organized tailgate parties south of Arrowhead Stadium for group ticket buyers. Because of cramped space, however, the activity needed improvement. As a result, Overland Park-based Dimensional Innovations crafted a game-day experience with tailgate suites to replicate the essential Kansas City experience of a Chiefs tailgate in a premium environment.[22]

The suites are located in a fenced area with sturdy tents located on the grass and pavement on Lancer Lane, just steps away from the stadium's entrance. There are about twenty suites in the area which accommodate private gatherings sponsored by business customers. The area features tailgate games and a variety of setup and catering options. Although suite rental costs vary based on catering, beverage options, and other things, their average cost is about $100 per person.[23]

Oakland Raiders

When legendary Al Davis died in 2011, his wife Carol and son Mark—who graduated from California State University at Chico—became sole owners of the franchise. Worth an estimated $500 million, some people think Mark is fascinating but peculiar or even a lunatic and wildly out of touch with reality although he loves football. Unlike his dad, he has few responsibilities regarding the team. Yet when Mark makes decisions, he does so in curious fashion. Regarding his bowl haircut, for example, Davis travels many miles from his home in northern California to Palm Springs just to get it cut by the same barber.[24]

Since inheriting the Raiders franchise, Mark has a hands-off approach to the football side of operations but enjoys focusing on business aspects of the team. This type of management is in stark contrast to his father who, until his death, controlled both the business and football parts of the team. In 2013, Davis fired the Raiders public relations director after a *Sports Illustrated* article was critical of his dad. Indeed, Mark stated that the director's replacement needed to understand the importance of his father's legacy and to actively protect it.

Team Financials

According to data and other financial information published in *Forbes* for sixteen franchises in the AFC as of their 2015–2016 season, the Raiders ranked fourteenth in market value at $1.45 billion, sixteenth in both revenue at $285 million and gate receipts at $40 million, fifteenth in operating income at $39 million, tied for tenth with the Bengals in player expenses at $158 million, and tied for third with the Bills and Ravens each with a 14 percent debt-to-value ratio. Among teams in the conference's WD, Oakland had the lowest amounts except for its player expenses and debt percentage. Because the Raiders have appeared in only three playoffs since 1995 and experience such problems as an inferior stadium and ownership issues, this is the worst team in its division and conference from a financial perspective (Table A.3).

Based on data of the other thirty-one NFL clubs, Oakland was tied for twenty-eighth with the Rams in market value, thirty-first in total revenue, thirty-second in gate receipts, twenty-seventh in operating income, tied for twenty-second in player expenses, and tied for eighth in its debt-to-value ratio. As a business enterprise, the Raiders are near the bottom of the league and need to move to Los Angeles or build and co-finance a new stadium in the Oakland area with plenty of amenities that improves their gate receipts, total revenue, and market value (Table A.4).

As discussed before in this chapter for the Broncos and Chiefs and later for the Chargers, the Raiders' FCI in 2015 was $420 or twenty-third highest in the league but the same as in 2014. Listed from most to least in amount by item for one fan, the club's nonpremium tickets were approximately $65, parking for one vehicle $35, a cap $25 and one beer almost $11, a hot dog about $7, and a program and soft drink each $4 to $5. For FCIs of other WD teams, the Broncos ranked thirteenth at $482, Chargers fifteenth at $478, and Chiefs twenty-ninth at $396. Of thirty-two NFL teams, the 49ers had the highest cost at $640 and Jaguars lowest at $347.[25]

According to its amounts, Oakland's home games are relatively cheap for fans to attend at 53,300-seat O.co Coliseum. Because of only three playoff appearances since 1995 and social and economic factors within the team's market area, the franchise sets competitive ticket prices for nonpremium and premium (average $138 each) seats and other items sold to spectators at its home games. This, in turn, encourages them to buy food and other items and also maximizes the club's gate receipts and revenue from attendances.

Business Highlights

Using fifteen years of data on such things as NFL team performances, home-game ticket prices, and market populations and their median incomes, Emory University researchers created an equity index to determine which of the league's clubs had the most avid, engaged, passionate, and/or supportive fans before their 2015 season. Among the AFC's WD teams, the Raiders ranked thirtieth and below the Broncos at thirteenth, Chargers at seventeenth, and Chiefs at twenty-seventh. For various reasons, including the franchise's owners and team performances, the index suggests that Raiders fans are not, on average, very engaged or passionate about their football team even though the sport is popular in the Bay Area.

In another index titled Social Media Equity, the team had the league's eighth best fan base and superior to the Broncos at eighteenth, Chargers at twenty-fourth, and Chiefs at twenty-sixth. Although this index reflected whether teams over- or underperform with respect to their Twitter following, apparently Oakland fans are involved with the team on social media but less, however, than those of the AFC Steelers and Patriots, and NFC Cowboys and Packers.

If no agreement is reached in 2016 or soon thereafter regarding a new stadium in Oakland, the team could seek NFL permission to move to Los Angeles and jointly develop a new stadium there with the Chargers. Although the Raiders are hoping to construct an outdoor stadium but smaller than the 49ers' new home in Santa Clara—which was financed largely through the sale of personal seat licenses—there remains a significant funding gap, and city leaders refuse to pay for it. In May 2015, the Chargers and Raiders retained longtime NFL executive Carmen Policy to serve as the Director of Carson Holdings LLC, the joint venture in charge of the stadium project in Carson, California.

San Diego Chargers

Two years after he bought 10 percent of the Chargers from Barron Hilton for $4 million and acquired right of first refusal if majority owner Gene Klein decided to sell them, businessman Alex Spanos purchased the team from Klein in 1984 for $50 million. However, because of his age, health issues and family life, Alex transferred daily operations of the Chargers in 1994 to his oldest son Dean.[26]

During the spring of 2015, Dean announced his decision to permanently relinquish operations of the team to his sons' John and A. G. Going forward, John, 35-years-old, became president of football operations and A. G., thirty-six-years-old, the president of business operations. Each of them has final authority over their respective side of the company—whether it involves hiring and firing head coaches and general managers or the negotiation of sponsorship deals and setting ticket prices. Even so, Dean will probably continue as chairman of the board and oversee the franchise's push for a new stadium, whether built in San Diego, Los Angeles, or elsewhere.

Regarding their experiences with the Chargers, John spent years as executive vice president of football operations where his duties included representing the team at all league and management council meetings. Before that he worked in every phase of football operations including scouting, contract negotiations, and managing the salary cap. Meanwhile A. G. began working on the business side in 2003 as director of marketing programs and business development. He spent several years in that role before being promoted to executive vice president/executive officer in 2011.

Team Financials

According to data and other financial information published in *Forbes* for sixteen franchises in the AFC as of their 2015–2016 season, the Chargers ranked tenth in market value at $1.525 billion and thirteenth in revenue at $304 million, and also tied for ninth in gate receipts with the Chiefs at $55 million, seventh in operating income at $64 million, twelfth in player expenses at $155 million, and tied for ninth with the Patriots, Bengals, Texans, and Jaguars in their debt-to-value ratio of 7 percent. Among only WD teams in the conference, San Diego had the second or third highest amounts except for its player expenses. Given these results, the Chargers have been average in their division from a financial perspective but unfortunately below-average among all AFC franchises (Table A.3).

Based on data of thirty-one other NFL teams as of their 2015–2016 season, the Chargers were twenty-second in market value, twenty-fifth in total revenue, tied for twentieth with the Chiefs and Cardinals in gate receipts, fifteenth in operating income, twenty-sixth in player expenses, and tied for nineteenth with four other clubs in their percentage of debt-to-value. According to its rankings with all clubs, this San Diego-based franchise is inferior to the majority of them financially and as a business organization (Table A.4).

As discussed before in this chapter for the Broncos, Chiefs, and Raiders, the Chargers' FCI in 2015 was approximately $478 or fifteenth highest in the league but the same as in 2013. Listed from most to least in amount by item for one fan, the club's nonpremium ticket prices averaged about $84, parking $25 and a cap $20, one beer $9, a hot dog and soft drink each $6, and a program $5. For FCIs of the other WD teams, the Broncos were thirteenth at $482, Raiders twenty-third at $420, and Chiefs twenty-ninth at $396. Based on the league's FCI of $480, San Diego fans spend below-average amounts for their nonpremium and premium (average $170) tickets for seats and also for other items to attend Chargers home games at Qualcomm Stadium.[27]

Business Highlights

Using fifteen years of data on such things as NFL team performances, home-game ticket prices, and market populations and their median incomes, Emory University researchers created an equity index to determine which of the league's clubs had the most avid, engaged, passionate, and/or supportive fans before their 2015 season. Among the AFC's WD teams, the Chargers ranked seventeenth and below the Broncos at thirteenth but above the Chiefs at twenty-seventh and Raiders at thirtieth. For various reasons, including the franchise's owners and team performances, the index suggests that San Diego's sports fans are, on average, not extremely engaged or passionate about their football team because, in part, other outdoor sports are available, fun, and popular in southern California.[28]

In another index titled Social Media Equity, the team had the league's twenty-fourth best fan base and inferior to the Raiders at eighth and Broncos at eighteenth but superior to the Chiefs at twenty-sixth. Although this index reflected whether teams over- or underperform with respect to their Twitter following, apparently Chargers fans are not very involved with the team on social media and much less, for example, than those of the AFC Steelers, Patriots, and Jets, and NFC Cowboys, Packers, and Saints.

To highlight its role as a franchise, this San Diego team has appeared in six AFC playoffs since 1996 and financially ranks between ninth and twelfth in the conference. Led by owner Dean Spanos, the club needs to improve as an organization to increase attendances at its home games, successfully challenge and consistently defeat such division rivals as the Broncos and Chiefs, and prosper with more revenue, gate receipts, and operating income.

Recently the Chargers and Raiders hired a company named Legends, which is jointly owned by the New York Yankees and Dallas Cowboys, to market the clubs' proposed stadium in Carson, California. Legends marketed premium seating and season tickets for the San Francisco 49ers' Levi's Stadium in Santa Clara, which opened in 2014. The Chargers and Raiders are each using Carson as a fallback plan in case they are unable to negotiate stadium deals in their current home markets.[29]

Legends, meanwhile, has a challenge to sell an inventory of tickets for two teams in a new market. After being reimbursed by the city of San Diego for credits related to concession revenue at Qualcomm Stadium and property taxes at their headquarters, the Chargers effective rent is currently zero while they decide whether to depart from the area.

NOTES

1. Two books on the operations of teams in the NFL and the league's seasons and postseasons are Frank P. Jozsa Jr., *Football Fortunes: The Business, Organization and Strategy of the NFL* (Jefferson, NC: McFarland, 2010); and James Quirk and Rodney D. Fort, *Pay Dirt: The Business of Professional Team Sports* (Princeton, NJ: Princeton University Press, 1992).
2. For historical performances of the Denver Broncos and other NFL teams, see "Teams," http://www.pro-football-reference.com, cited August 25, 2015, and also the *NFL Record & Fact Book 2014* (New York: NFL, 2014).
3. Team attendances are available on pages 409 to 434 in *Pay Dirt* and in "Rod Fort's Sports Business Data," http://www.sites.google.com, cited September 1, 2015.
4. See, for example, the article "Ranking All 31 NFL Stadiums," http://www.sportingnews.com, cited August 31, 2015.
5. "2015 NFL Future Power Rankings," http://www.insider.espn.go.com, cited October 10, 2015.
6. The primary references for the Chiefs' performances are listed in note 2 and "NFL Links," http://www.sportsecyclopdia.com, cited August 25, 2015.
7. See "Rod Fort's Sports Business Data" and also NFL teams' home attendances on the website http://www.espn.go.com.
8. Beside the reading in note 4, there is Michael Potts, "Ranking All NFL Stadiums for 2015—From Worst to Best," http://www.whatculture.com, cited September 2, 2015.
9. The primary source is "2015 NFL Future Power Rankings."
10. For information about the Raiders and their performances in the NFL, see note 2 and "Teams," http://www.profootballhof.com, cited September 1, 2015.
11. Research the article in note 4 for the status of Oakland's stadium and its amenities for fans and the media.
12. Read "2015 NFL Future Power Rankings" for expectations of the Raiders competitiveness in future seasons.
13. Ron Leuty, "Ousted Oakland Raiders Stadium Developer Kephart Gets the Last Word (Video)," http://www.bizjournals.com, cited October 11, 2015.
14. Chargers teams' performances are in such readings as "History," http://www.nfl.com, cited August 25, 2015, and also in "History of National Football League Franchises, 1920–Present," http://www.profootballhof.com, cited August 25, 2015.

15. For information about Qualcomm Stadium, see "Ranking All 31 NFL Stadiums" and "Ranking All NFL Stadiums for 2015—From Worst to Best."

16. See the club's history at http://www.denverbroncos.com and read about the franchise's current owner on such other websites as http://www.profootballhof.com and http://www.nfl.com.

17. Specific cost data for home games of each NFL team is in such articles as "2014 NFL Fan Cost Index," https://www.teammarketing.com, cited August 26, 2015, and "2015 NFL Fan Cost Index," https://www.teammarketing.com, cited November 20, 2015.

18. The references for these indexes are (a) Michael Lewis, "2015 NFL Social Media Equity Rankings," https://scholarblogs.emory.edu, cited September 4, 2015; and (b) Manish Tripathi, "2015 NFL Fan Equity Rankings," https://scholarblogs.emory.edu, cited September 4, 2015.

19. One source to read is "NFL Team Owners." http://www.biography.yourdictionary.com, cited December 24, 2015.

20. To compare FCIs and costs per item for teams' games in 2014 and 2015, see the readings in note 17 above.

21. The articles for these indexes are listed in Note 18.

22. Austin Alonzo, "Chiefs Kick Corporate Tailgating Up a Notch," http://www.bizjournals.com, cited December 1, 2015.

23. For other business news about this club, see Terry Lefton, "In the Owner's Box, Listening, Learning," *SportsBusiness Journal* (April 22, 2013): 1, and Don Muret, "Chiefs Busy Checking Mobile Concessions Tech at Arrowhead," *SportsBusiness Journal* (October 20, 2013): 16.

24. Beside the team's website, see "NFL Team Owners" about the history and success of Al Davis and his family's role in owning the Raiders franchise.

25. Similar to researching costs and prices of other teams, two readings are "2015 NFL Fan Cost Index," http://www.teammarketing.com, cited November 20, 2015, and Ron Greenberg, "2014 NFL Fan Cost Index," http://www.teammarketing.com, cited August 26, 2015.

26. The Chargers' website at http://www.nfl.com and "NFL Team Owners" are sources to read about Alex Spanos's personal and business careers and also his family and their involvement with the franchise. For another perspective of these individuals, there is Dean Gomes, "Power Rankings: Rating NFL Owners from 1–32," http://www.cover32.com, cited August 31, 2015.

27. Rather than identify and repeat sources in the literature, the San Diego Chargers' attendances, FCI, and fan and social equity indexes are available in the same readings as for the Broncos, Chiefs, and Raiders as cited in various notes of this chapter.

28. The references for the Emory University researchers' fan equity index and Social Media Equity index are contained in note 18.

29. See Daniel Kaplan, "Chargers, Raiders Retain Legends for L.A. Bid," *SportsBusiness Journal* (June 15, 2015): 7; "NFL Move Could Cause Divisional Move," *Wall Street Journal* (August 18, 2015): 1; Darren Rovell, "Disney CEO Bob Iger Joins NFL Stadium Project in Carson, California," http://www.espn.go.com, cited November 12, 2015.

National Football Conference

Chapter Five

East Division

Prior to the 2015 National Football League (NFL) season, which team or teams in the East Division (ED) of the National Football Conference (NFC) had the most all-time wins, highest winning percentage, least number of division and conference titles, and largest number of championships and also playoff appearances? Did the Dallas Cowboys rank higher as a franchise than the New York Giants in market value, revenue, and gate receipts? Were the Philadelphia Eagles or Washington Redskins in the most debt with too much player expenses and not enough operating income?

To answer these and other questions about topics, next are some interesting but actual, important, and relevant facts that highlight the historical performances of four teams in the NFC's ED as of the league's 2015–2016, or simply 2015, season. Besides their winning percentage and number of wins, titles and championships, this information includes special coaches, players, and events regarding each of them while competing in the NFL's regular seasons and any playoffs. In the chapter's final section—labelled Franchise Business—is data about these franchises' success or failure as business enterprises both individually and in comparison to each other from a financial perspective.[1]

TEAM PERFORMANCES

Dallas Cowboys

Eight years after the NFL Dallas Texans failed, businessmen Clint Murchison Jr., and Bedford Wynne paid a $600,000 fee and then were awarded an expansion franchise in January 1960 at the league's annual meeting in Miami Beach, Florida. Although listed in the Western Division standings along with six others, it would exist as a "swing" team, playing every other club one time during its first season.[2]

The formation of an expansion team in Texas was met with strong opposition by Washington Redskins owner George Preston Marshall because, while located in the nation's capital, his Redskins enjoyed a monopoly as the only NFL team to represent the American south and southeast region for decades. After they purchased the rights to the Redskins fight song, a group of Texas investors threatened to not allow Marshall to play the song at Washington's home games. Since the song had become a staple for his so-called "professional football team of Dixie," Marshall changed his mind and agreed to expand the league into a southern state.

The new NFL team was initially but temporarily nicknamed the Steers and then Rangers. During March 1960, however, the organization renamed the team Cowboys to avoid confusion with the American Association's Dallas Rangers baseball team. Subsequently owners Clint Murchison and Bedford Wynne hired Tex Schramm as general manager, Gil Brandt as player personnel director, and Tom Landry as head coach. Beginning in the league's 1960 season and ten more, the Cowboys played their home games a few miles east of downtown Dallas at the 92,100-seat Cotton Bowl and shared it for three years with the AFL's Dallas Texans.

Historical Results

While playing in the league's Western Conference in 1960, Eastern Conference from 1961 to 1969, and NFC's Eastern Division during 1970–2001 and then in the East Division (ED) since 2002, the Cowboys played 850 total games and won approximately 56 percent of them. Among teams in the NFC as of the league's 2015–2016 season, Dallas ranked eighth in number of wins and first in winning percentage, and also third with twenty-two division and eight conference titles, tied for fourth with the Redskins and 49ers each with five championships including at least three to five Super Bowls, and tied for first with the Giants and Packers in qualifying for thirty-one playoffs (Table A.5).

With respect to only ED clubs as of their 2015 season, the Cowboys had the fewest wins, highest winning percentage, more total titles than the Eagles or Redskins but not the Giants, and less NFL plus Super Bowl championships than the Giants. Based on these results, Dallas's teams have been superior while performing within their division and also when competing against other clubs in the conference.

Compared to the performances of thirty-one other NFL teams as of their 2015–16 season, the fifty-six-year-old Cowboys ranked ninth in total wins, third in both winning percentage and number of division titles, tied for third with the AFC Patriots, Steelers, and Broncos in winning their conference, tied for fifth with the Redskins and 49ers each with five championships, and tied for first with the Giants in number of playoffs. These and other results prove that, except for periods in the early 1960s, late 1980s and early 2000s, and from 2010 to 2013, this Dallas-based NFL team has been an excellent competitor and also successful while playing clubs in its division and conference, and others in the AFC (Table A.6).

To be successful during various seasons and postseasons since 1960, the Cowboys had some outstanding and mediocre coaches and talented players. In number of wins the former group includes Coach Tom Landry with 270, Jimmy Johnson 51, and Barry Switzer 45. For their leadership, Landry in 1966 and Johnson in 1990 were each Associated Press (AP) coach of the year and also NFC coach of the year, respectively, in 1975 and 1990. Alternatively, coaches Dave Campo and Chan Gailey each won less than 20 games while Bill Parcells and Wade Phillips had more wins than losses.

Some Dallas players were remarkable by establishing individual career, single season, and single game records for the franchise in various years. Among career records, for example, were Emmitt Smith's 17,162 rushing yards; Troy Aikman's 32,942 passing yards; Mel Renfro's 52 interceptions; Rafael Septien's 162 field goals; and DeMarcus Ware's 117 sacks. During single seasons, Tony Romo passed for 4,903 yards in 2012; Michael Irvin received 111 passes for 1,603 yards in 1995; Mat McBriar averaged 48.2 yards on his punts in 2006; and Bob Hayes averaged 20.8 yards on punt returns in 1968.

In a single game, DeMarco Murray rushed for 253 yards; Jason Witten caught 18 passes; Miles Austin had 250 receiving yards; Chris Boniol and Billy Cundiff each kicked 7 field goals; and Jim Jeffcoat sacked the opposing quarterback 5 times. Because of these and other athletes' ability, determination, and performances, Cowboys teams were competitive and won many games in their regular seasons and postseasons.

Each year AP awards are earned by NFL players for their outstanding season at a position on offense and/or defense. In 1993 Emmitt Smith was Most Valuable Player (MVP) when he led the league in rushing yards (1,486) for the third consecutive year despite missing two games. Other award winners were DeMarco Murray (2014) for offensive player of the year; Calvin Hill (1969), Duane Thomas (1970), Tony Dorsett (1977), and Smith (1990) for offensive rookie of the year; Harvey Martin (1977) for defensive player of the year; and Greg Ellis (2007) for comeback player of the year.

For their excellent careers in the sport, one each executive and coach and several Cowboys players have been inducted into the pro football Hall of Fame. A few of them were former general manager/president Tex Schramm and coach Landry, quarterbacks Troy Aikman and Roger Staubach, defensive tackles Bob Lilly and Randy White, cornerback Deion Sanders, and offensive tackle Rayfield Wright. In short these men were important to the franchise in different ways, and particularly at their positions in many games of regular seasons and postseasons.

Performance Highlights

Among its years in the league, Dallas's most successful periods consecutively were 1966–1973, 1975–1983, and 1991–1996. In large part, these seasons of playoffs and winning titles occurred because of quarterbacks Don Meredith, Craig Morton, Troy Aikman, and Roger Staubach, and also running backs Duane Thomas, Tony Dorsett, and Emmitt Smith, and receivers Bob Hayes, Grant Hill, and Michael Irvin. In contrast, the club had disappointing years during 1960–1965, 1986–1990, and 2010–2013. Various factors contributed to the club's losses in games, including their coaches making wrong decisions and players getting injured or simply performing inefficiently at their positions while on the field.

At its home games in 80,000-seat AT&T Stadium, which opened in 2009, the club's attendances ranked first in the league. While the NFL's average each season was in the mid-500,000s, the number of spectators at Cowboys games ranged from 684,000 in 2011 to 731,600 in 2015. Simply put, Dallas fans adore their hometown team despite its appearance in only two playoffs and losing in divisional games against NFC rivals in 2009 and 2014.[3]

Among other NFL venues, AT&T Stadium was ranked second in a recent study. According to an article about it in an edition of the *Sporting News*:

> Jerry Jones takes criticism for many things. But this massive, three-million-square-foot facility is the NFL's crown jewel. The center-hung video board has influenced the design of monster screens at multiple NBA and NHL [National Hockey League] arenas. Everybody wants to experience Jerry World and the team's stadium tour business provides a major revenue stream for the Jones family. Tailgating is a mix between stadium parking and lots up the street at Globe Life Park, home of the Texas Rangers. At AT&T Stadium, the plazas just outside the building form another pregame party space with portable bars and smaller video boards.[4]

In the Entertainment Sports Programming Network's (ESPN) future power rankings, the network asked three experts to rate each NFL team for three seasons (2015–2017) on a scale of 0 to 100 percent in five categories including roster (excluding quarterback), quarterback, draft, front office, and coaching. In their analysis, the Cowboys ranked sixth in the league. After a 12–4 season in 2014, Dallas improved its average score from 68.1 to 76.9 heading into the 2015 season and beyond it.[5]

More specifically, the team's roster improved greatly with the addition of such players as defensive end Greg Hardy and the return of linebacker Sean Lee. The 2015 draft also helped with the selection of cornerback Byron

Jones and defensive end Randy Gregory. There was also the free-agent signing of first-round talent La'el Collins after the draft. With these athletes and the current roster, the Cowboys have young talent for several years.

The network gave Tony Romo and the Cowboys quarterback position a high score of near 80. In addition, the front office scored 78 due in large part to chief operating officer Stephen Jones taking charge. If the Cowboys decide to negotiate a favorable deal for wide receiver Dez Bryant, they will get an increase in score. In coaching, Jason Garrett proved his worth in 2014 after going 8–8 in each of the previous three regular seasons. For the Cowboys, winning more games in the future will continue to be a goal for them.

New York Giants

An expansion franchise in the twenty-one-team APFA in 1921, the New York Giants finished 0–2–0 but then folded before the league's 1922 season. Four years later, businessmen Tim Mara and Billy Gibson purchased an NFL franchise for $500 from Jimmy Jernail—who possibly owned the defunct 1921 APFA team—and named their new club New York Giants, or legally, New York Football Giants to distinguish them from the Major League Baseball (MLB) New York Giants team. With clubs in such small cities as Akron, Ohio, and Duluth, Minnesota, NFL officials needed to put a team in the large-market and prosperous New York City area.[6]

Although the Giants were successful on the field in their first season with an 8–4–0 record, their financial status was a problem. Overshadowed by baseball, boxing, college football, and horse racing, professional football was not a popular sport in the mid-1920s. In fact, the club had serious financial difficulties until the eleventh game of the season when it played the Chicago Bears before 73,000 fans. That event provided the Giants with enough revenue to continue operating as a member of the NFL.

Historical Results

While a member of the league from their 1925–1926 to 2015–2016 seasons, the Giants played 1,273 games and won approximately 53 percent of them. In addition, they won twenty-four division and eleven conference titles and also eight championships including four Super Bowls in thirty-one playoff appearances. Compared to fifteen other teams in the NFC as of their 2015 season, this New York-based club was third in number of wins and also total championships, and sixth in winning percentage, first in division and conference titles combined, and tied for first with the Cowboys in qualifying for thirty-one postseasons (Table A.5).

Among the conference's ED clubs as of their 2014 season, the ninety-one-year-old Giants had the most wins, total titles and championships, but also a lower winning percentage and same number of playoff appearances as the Cowboys. Based on these results, this New York-based team has been a top-notch, superior, and successful franchise because of outstanding performances in its division and conference during various seasons and in postseason games against rivals. In short, Giants teams have been among the best overall of any in the league during the twentieth and early twenty-first century.

Compared to the performances of thirty-one other NFL teams as of the league's 2015–2016 season, the Giants ranked third in total wins, eleventh in winning percentage, first in both number of division and conference titles, and third in total championships including four Super Bowl victories. These and other results prove that, except for some regular seasons in the late-1920s to early-1930s, early to mid-1950s, and mid-1960s to late-1970s, this New York team has frequently but not always been competitive while playing clubs in its conference and across the league (Table A.6).

Through the NFL's 2015–2016 season, some coaches and several players had memorable years while being on the rosters of Giants teams. In number of wins, the former group includes Steve Owen with 155 victories, Tom Coughlin 104, and Bill Parcells 85. Alex Webster was NFC coach of the year in 1970, Parcells in 1986, and Dan Reeves in 1993 while Allie Sherman became AP coach of the year in 1961 and 1962, Parcells in 1986, Reeves in 1993, and Jim Fassel in 1997. With fewer than 10 wins, however, were coaches Bob Folwell, Joe Alexander, and Bill Arnsparger. As a group, these have been the best and worst coaches in the history of the Giants franchise.

Some of the club's players established individual career, single season, and single game records at their positions as of the league's 2015 season. As examples of career records, Tiki Barber rushed for 10,449 yards, and Eli Manning passed for 35,345; Amani Toomer caught 668 passes for 9,497 yards; Frank Gifford scored 78 touchdowns and Pete Gogolak 646 points; and Michael Strahan recorded 141.5 sacks. During a single season, Y. A. Tittle passed for 36 touchdowns in 1963; Victor Cruz had 1,536 receiving yards in 2011; Don Chandler averaged 48.6 yards on his punts in 1959; and Joe Morris scored 21 touchdowns in 1985 and Jay Feely 148 points in 2005.

A sample of single-game records for Giants teams were Phil Simms's 513 passing yards; Del Shofner's 269 receiving yards; Joe Danelo's 6 field goals; Osi Umenyiora's 6 sacks; and several players each with 3 interceptions, 4 touchdowns, and 24 points. For sure these were remarkable career, single season, and single game performances in games and regular seasons by different Giants players.

Each year the AP awards players for being outstanding at their position while in games on the field. Besides quarterback Tittle in 1963, Giants linebacker Lawrence Taylor was the league's MVP in 1986 for his 20.5 sacks and led the team's second-ranked defense. Other award winners were offensive rookie of year Odell Beckham Jr. in 2014; defensive player of the year

Taylor in 1981, 1982, and 1986, and Strahan in 2001; and defensive rookie of the year Taylor in 1981. While playing in the pro bowl, players' Frank Gifford, Sam Huff, and Phil Simms were MVPs.

The most prestigious honor of all-time was the Giants inducted into the pro football Hall of Fame. Among many of them, the list included former owners Tim and Wellington Mara; defensive ends Red Badgro and Andy Robustelli; safety Emien Tunnell; quarterbacks Benny Friedman and Fran Tarkenton; and linebacker Harry Carson. Unquestionably these men had exceptional careers with the franchise and also made great contributions to the sport during their lifetime.

Performance Highlights

Since 1925, some Giants teams' most productive periods were when they appeared in at least three consecutive playoffs during their 1933–1935, 1961–1963, 1984–1986, and 2005–2008 seasons. In other years such as 1927, 1938, 1956, 1990, and 2011, they won NFL championships or Super Bowls. In contrast, the club's worst seasons consecutively included 1928–1932, 1951–1955, 1964–1980, and 2012–2015. However, because of its coaches' strategies and players' performances, the franchise has improved since 1997 with appearances in eight NFC playoffs and three Super Bowls.

At its home games in 82,500-seat MetLife Stadium, which opened in 2010, the club's attendances ranked among the top two in the league. While the NFL's average in each season was in the mid-500,000s, the number of spectators at Giants games ranged from 631,000 in 2014 to 643,000 in 2012 and 2013. Simply put, New York sports fans have supported this pro team especially when they won titles and championships coached by Tom Coughlin and featured such athletes as quarterback Eli Manning, receivers Plaxico Burress and Victor Cruz, and running backs Ahmad Bradshaw and Brandon Jacobs.[7]

Among other NFL venues, MetLife Stadium for the Giants (and Jets) was ranked seventeenth in a recent study. According to an article about it in an edition of *Sporting News*, the author stated:

> Some say the squabbles between the Jets and Giants resulted in a drab facility. But technology brings flexibility for branding the building green or blue depending on which team is playing a home game. The team can flip merchandise displays in minutes. As for special events, the stadium still does big business with concerts and truck shows just like its predecessor, old Giants Stadium. The light rail provides convenience for fans in New York traveling to New Jersey Meadowlands, and stadium officials over the years have created a "railgating" experience for those coming by train. Everyone else is tailgating in the lots surrounding the stadium.[8]

In ESPNs future power rankings, the network asked three experts to rate each NFL team for three seasons (2015–2017) on a scale of 0 to 100 percent in five categories including roster (excluding quarterback), quarterback, draft, front office, and coaching. In their analysis, the Giants ranked twentieth among all clubs. As Tom Coughlin became sixty-nine-years-old, the team fell from seventh to twenty-third in the coaching category. It also was between twentieth and twenty-second in every category but quarterback even though Eli Manning's contract expires soon.[9]

According to one expert, the Giants are still paying for their draft miscues from 2010 to 2012. Of those three drafts, the team has only three truly productive players—Jason Pierre-Paul, Prince Amukamara, and Rueben Randle. There are other factors, but this void is the biggest reason for the Giants' failure in recent years. The 2013 and 2014 drafts were better and if 2016 and/or 2017 continue that trend, this New York-based franchise could move up in rank a year or two from now.

To summarize the franchise's recent history following 6–10 records in 2014 and 2015, the Giants hired Steve Spagnuolo as their defensive coordinator, the position he held in 2007–2008. During his first tenure as coordinator, the Giants won Super Bowl XLII and ranked seventh and then fifth in the NFL in total defense. The team also ranked twenty-ninth in defense in 2014, and allowed 377 yards per game. Spagnuolo's return notwithstanding, the outlook for the defense is questionable due to Jason Pierre-Paul's fireworks accident in July, which resulted in the pass-rushing star having his right index finger amputated.

Philadelphia Eagles

An NFL expansion team based in Philadelphia, the Frankford Yellow Jackets played in the league from 1924 to 1931 and won one championship. After finishing 1–6–1 and in last place among ten clubs, the Yellow Jackets folded midway through the 1931 season with their ownership being transferred from founder Charles O'Brien to the league.

In 1933, a syndicate headed by businessman and former college coach Bert Bell and coach/administrator Lud Wray purchased Frankford's franchise from the NFL for approximately $3,000 and located it in Philadelphia. Owners Bell and Wray nicknamed the club "Eagles" in honor of the symbol of the New Deal's National Recovery Act. Coached by Wray, the team played in the Eastern Division along with the Boston Redskins, Brooklyn Dodgers, New York Giants, and Pittsburgh Steelers.[10]

Historical Results

While a member of the league's Eastern Division from 1933 to 1949, American Conference during 1950–1952, Eastern Conference from 1953 to

1966 and the conference's Capitol Division to 1969, and then the Eastern Division of the NFC until 2001 and finally the conference's ED, the Eagles played 1,156 games and won approximately 47 percent of them. Furthermore, they won thirteen division and three conference titles and also three NFL championships but zero Super Bowls in twenty-four playoff appearances. Among NFC teams, Philadelphia ranked fifth in number of wins, eleventh in winning percentage, seventh in division titles, tied for ninth with the Seahawks in conference titles, eighth in total championships, and seventh in qualifying for postseasons (Table A.5).

Compared to only ED clubs as of the NFL's 2015 season, the Eagles had the third most victories and lowest percentage of them, least number of conference titles and championships, but more playoff appearances than the Redskins. Based on these results, the eighty-three-year-old Eagles have been below-average while existing within their division but also average against other teams in the NFC. In all-time performances, this has been a competitive but mediocre franchise with sixteen total titles and three NFL championships during its history in the league.

With respect to the performances of thirty-one other NFL teams as of their 2015–2016 season, the Eagles ranked sixth in number of wins and also nineteenth in winning percentage, tied for tenth with the Dolphins in division titles, tied for fourteenth with the Seahawks and Raiders in conference titles, tenth in total championships with two losses in Super Bowl games, and eighth in qualifying for postseasons. Except for its relatively low proportion of victories, Philadelphia's results are above average compared to those of all clubs in the league. In other words, the team has been competitive during its history while in the NFC's ED but less so in performances than the Cowboys, Giants, and Redskins, and other division's Bears, Packers, and 49ers (Table A.6).

Since 1933, the club's coaches have ranged from superior to inferior as leaders in their careers with the franchise. In number of victories, the most successful were Andy Reid with 140, Earle Neal 66, Dick Vermeil 57, and Buddy Ryan 43. Vermeil was NFC coach of the year in 1978 and Ray Rhodes in 1995, while Buck Shaw won an AP award for being coach of the year in 1960, Rhodes in 1995, and Reid in 2002. Alternatively coaches Lud Wray, Alvin McMillin, Wayne Millner, Hugh Devore, Jerry Williams, Ed Khayat, and Fred Bruney each won less than 10 games.

Some Eagles players set career, single season, and single game records for the franchise. As of 2015, a few career records were Wilbert Montgomery's 6,538 rushing yards; Donovan McNabb's 32,873 passing yards and 216 touchdowns; Harold Carmichael's 589 catches for 8,978 yards; and David Akers's 294 field goals and 1,323 points. For a single season, some significant achievements include 1,607 rushing yards by LaSean McCoy in 2013 and 20 touchdowns in 2011; 32 passing touchdowns by Sonny Jurgensen in

1961; 11 interceptions by Bill Bradley in 1971; and 21 sacks by Reggie White in 1987.

In a single game, Adrian Burke and Nick Foles each passed for 7 touchdowns; Tommy McDonald had 237 receiving yards; Russ Craft intercepted 4 passes; and Tom Dempsey kicked 6 field goals. As a group, these were talented athletes who contributed in different ways to the success of their teams and won one or more games for the Eagles during seasons and in any postseasons.

Each year the AP honors NFL players for being great at their position in games. In 1960, quarterback Norm Van Brocklin was the NFL's most outstanding player because he guided Philadelphia to its first division title in eleven years by passing for 2,471 yards and 24 touchdowns. Besides Van Brocklin, Reggie White was defensive player of the year and pro bowl MVP in 1987. Other winners of the pro bowl award include linebacker Chuck Bednarik in 1954; defensive tackle Floyd Peters in 1967; and quarterbacks Randall Cunningham in 1989 and Nick Foles in 2014.

For their excellent careers in the sport, several former Eagles were inducted into the pro football Hall of Fame. Along with Bednarik in 1967, some of them were end Bill Hewitt in 1943; former owner Bert Bell in 1963; head coach Earl Neal in 1969; quarterback Sonny Jergensen in 1983; wide receiver Tommy McDonald in 1998; and tackle Bob Brown in 2004. In short, these men were important to the franchise in different ways including success at their positions in games during regular seasons and in any postseasons.

Performance Highlights

Among more than eight decades in the NFL, Philadelphia's most successful periods consecutively were the league's 1947–1949, 1978–1981, 1988–1990, 2000–2004, and 2008–2010 seasons. In large part, these periods of playoffs and winning titles occurred because of quarterbacks Tommy Thompson, Ron Jaworski, and Donovan McNabb, running backs Steve Van Buren, Wilbert Montgomery, and Brian Westbrook, and receivers Pete Pihos, Harold Carmichael, and DeSean Jackson. Alternatively, the club's worst periods included 1933–1946, 1950–1959, 1961–1977, and 1982–1987. Inferior coaching staffs, lack of enough talented players at key positions, and other franchise problems caused differences in Eagles' performances between the former and latter group of years.

At their home games in 69,144-seat Lincoln Financial Field, which opened in 2003, the Eagles had above average attendances in the league. For example, the club ranked twelfth or thirteenth from 2006 to 2012 with its total attendance each season at about 553,128 but then fell to fifteenth in 2014 at 556,000. During these years, however, the ED's Cowboys, Giants, and Redskins each had larger numbers of spectators at their home games. In short, the Eagles are not as popular at home as their division rivals are and also compared to games of the AFC Jets in New York and Ravens in Baltimore.

Among other NFL venues, Lincoln Financial Field placed twelfth in a recent study. According to an article about it in an edition of *Sporting News*:

> The bird's nest went under many of the same renovations as the Browns' building. In fact, both teams used the same architect and construction firm to complete their respective projects. In Philly, new video boards, a new team store, club renovations and 1,600 new seats were added for last [2014] season. The video boards stand out for their location midlevel in the end zones. The stadium, part of the South Philly Sports Complex, sits next to Citizens Bank Park and Wells Fargo Center. The opening of Xfinity Live a few years ago, an entertainment district with bars, restaurants and more at the complex, gives Eagles fans a pregame perch for those who don't want to mess with tailgating.[11]

In ESPNs future power rankings, the network asked three experts to rate each NFL team for three seasons (2015–2017) on a scale of 0 to 100 percent in five categories including roster (excluding quarterback), quarterback, draft, front office, and coaching. Unlike 2013 when they ranked seventeenth with a score of 62.71, the panel was more optimistic about Philadelphia's football franchise.[12]

Being eighth overall with a score of 79.75 as of 2015, only four NFC teams had finished above the Eagles. These were the Seahawks in first, Packers second, 49ers third, and Saints sixth. The Eagles were far and away the team with the best outlook in the NFC ED. In fact, the Giants placed eighteenth, Redskins twenty-fourth, and Cowboys twenty-eighth with each below the league average. The Cowboys and Raiders were the only two teams that ranked among the NFL's five worst in four of the five categories.

Regarding their analysis, the experts consider coach Chip Kelly to be a program-builder who made an important decision during the offseason by releasing DeSean Jackson. Indeed, that move could help define the team's success for a few years. Will there be addition by subtraction for the offense? Also, did the Eagles do enough defensively to make them a more explosive team in sacking the quarterback—ranked thirty-first in sacks per attempt in 2013—and defending the pass? First-round pick linebacker Marcus Smith will be observed each game to see whether he adjusts to Kelly's program in the future.

Washington Redskins

During July 1932, a syndicate led by businessman George Preston Marshall purchased an inactive NFL expansion franchise for approximately $7,500 and located it in Boston. After nicknamed the "Braves," the club was fourth that season among eight teams in the league. Renamed Boston Redskins for the next four years and playing their home games at the Boston Red Sox's Fenway Park, they won their division in 1936 but played and lost the NL championship game to the Green Bay Packers at the Polo Grounds in New York because Marshall was disappointed with fan support for his team in Boston. In other seasons of the Eastern Division, the Redskins were third in 1933, second in 1934, and fourth in 1935 but each year had a small fan base at, and low gate receipts from, their home games.[13]

Due to the club's problems with its poor attendances and financial situation, owner Marshall moved his franchise from Boston to Washington, D.C., before the league's 1937 season. Named Washington Redskins, the club played its local games at 32,000-seat Griffith Stadium. Within two years, Marshall created an official marching band and fight song, both first-time innovations for teams in the NFL. In retrospect, it was a smart decision for him to shift the franchise to our nation's capital city in 1937.

Historical Results

As a member of the league's Eastern Division from 1933 to 1949, American Conference during 1950–1952, Eastern Conference to 1966 and the conference's Capitol Division to 1969, and the NFC's Eastern Division from 1970 to 2001 and then the conference's ED through the 2015–16 season, the Redskins played 1,113 games and won approximately 49 percent of them. In addition they were successful in winning twelve division and five conference titles, and five championships including three Super Bowls. Among other conference teams as of their 2015 season, Washington ranked fourth in wins, eighth in both winning percentage and number of division titles, fifth in conference titles, tied for fourth with the Cowboys and 49ers in total number of championships, and eighth in qualifying for twenty-three postseasons (Table A.5).

Compared to only ED clubs as of the league's 2015–16 season, the Redskins had fewer all-time victories than the Giants and also the third highest winning percentage of the group, and they exceeded the Eagles in division plus conference titles but had more championships and fewer playoff appearances than they. Including its relatively high number of conference titles and championships, this seventy-nine-year-old franchise has been mostly average to above average in performances among teams in the conference. Since 1993, however, the Redskins have appeared in only four playoffs because of such things as their competitive schedule of regular season games, lack of leadership from coaches and players, and questionable decisions by the franchise's owners.

As to the performances of thirty-one other NFL teams as of their 2015–2016 season, the Redskins ranked fifth in number of wins, fifteenth in winning percentage, twelfth in division titles, tied for eighth with the Dolphins in conference titles, tied for fourth with the Cowboys and 49ers in number of championships, and tied for ninth with the Dolphins in qualifying for postseasons. Based on these results, Washington has been average—and in some rankings above average—while performing against teams throughout the league during its history (Table A.6).

Since 1937, some Redskins coaches were successful while others struggled to challenge and motivate their players in various NFL seasons. In number of wins, Joe Gibbs had 140, George Allen 69, Ray Flaherty 56, and Norv Turner 50. Allen was NFC and AP coach of the year in 1971 and Jack Pardee in 1979, while Gibbs earned the NFC award in 1982 and also AP in 1982 and 1983. Alternatively twelve Washington coaches each recorded less than 10 victories beginning with Lud Wray in 1932 and ending with Marty Schottenheimer in 2001. Interestingly former Cleveland Browns Hall of Fame quarterback Otto Graham had a 17–22–3 record as the Redskins head coach during the league's 1966–1968 seasons.

As of 2015, some Redskins players had exceptional years for the franchise by setting career, single season, and single game records. For example, a few career achievements were John Riggins's 7,472 rushing yards; Art Monk's 888 pass receptions and 12,026 yards; Sammy Baugh's 187 passing touchdowns and 45.1-yard punting average; and Mark Moseley's 1,206 points.

For single seasons Alfred Morris had 1,613 rushing yards in 2012; Jay Schroeder 4,109 passing yards in 1986; Dan Sandifer 13 interceptions in 1948; and Dexter Manley 18.5 sacks in 1986. In single games, Gerald Riggs rushed for 221 yards and Brad Johnson passed for 471; Dick James and Larry Brown each scored 4 touchdowns and 24 points; and several players each kicked 5 field goals. In short, these were very talented players because of their career, single season, and single game records for Redskins teams.

Since 1937, a few Washington players won AP awards at their positions in games of various NFL seasons. The league's MVPs were running back Larry Brown for leading the conference with 1,216 rushing yards in 1972; kicker Moseley for converting 20 of 21 field goals and setting a consecutive record of 23 in 1981; and quarterback Joe Theismann for leading an offense that scored an NFL record of 541 points in 1982. For another award, Washington's Charlie Taylor in 1964, Mike Thomas in 1975, and Robert Griffin III in 2012 each became an offensive rookie of the year. Besides quarterback Theismann in 1984, pro bowl MVPs were wide receiver Gino Brito in 1958 and running back DeAngelo Hall in 2011.

From when the pro football Hall of Fame opened its doors in Canton, Ohio, during September 1963, there have been twenty-six former Redskins coaches, players, and an owner inducted for their careers in the sport. Among the former group were coaches' George Allen, Ray Flaherty, and Joe Gibbs; such players as running backs Cliff Battles, Bill Dudley, and John Riggins; and team founder/owner George Preston Marshall. The first inducted was Marshall and quarterback Sammy Baugh in 1963 and latest linebacker Chris Hamburger in 2011. In short, these men were major figures for the franchise during its seventy-eight-year-old history.

Performance Highlights

Among its seven-plus decades in the league, Washington's most successful periods consecutively were 1942–1943, 1971–1974, 1982–1984, 1986–1987, and 1990–1992. Besides having its best win-loss records, the team won titles and championships including three Super Bowls. Alternatively, the Redskins' least productive periods were 1946–1970, 1977–1981, 1993–1998, 2000–2004, 2008–2011, and 2013–2015. During these years the club did not have the coaches or roster of players to be competitive enough while playing rivals primarily in its division.

At 85,000-seat FedEx Field in Landover, Maryland, which opened in 1997, Redskins' attendances were frequently in the top five of the league but less than the Cowboys in Dallas and Giants in New York. Washington sports fans really love professional football and support their team whether they win or lose in a season. These games attract businessmen who lease suites to entertain clients, and politicians who care about the sport and treat being there as a social event on a Sunday afternoon or evening.

Among other NFL venues, FedEx Field ranked twenty-eighth in a recent study. According to an article about it in an edition of the *Sporting News*, the author wrote:

> Redskins owner Daniel Snyder just can't sit still. He wants to move the team back to Washington and build a new stadium 18 years after the Skins moved to Maryland. FedEx Field has seen its fair share of improvements. Some worked, some didn't. The same can be said for the revolving door tied to FedEx Field's food providers. For this season [2014], the team unveils a new traffic plan to ease help congestion. Its welcome news for Skins fans familiar with 2-hour waits to exit the lots at games.[14]

In ESPNs future power rankings, the network assigned three experts to rate each NFL team for three seasons (2015–2017) on a scale of 0 to 100 in five categories including roster (excluding quarterback), quarterback, draft, front office, and coaching. The Redskins ranked third in the ED, fourteenth in the NFC, and twenty-seventh overall.

While coaching and the quarterback position were questionable and had dropped in the ratings from the previous year, the club's front office, draft, and roster improved and thus scored higher by the experts. After some transition, the front office stabilized following Mike Shanahan's departure. While many wanted to see a fresh general manager from outside the organization, Bruce Allen was given the title. Another change came with the departure of longtime director of pro personnel, Morocco Brown, who left for the Cleveland Browns and then replaced in-house by Alex Santos, a longtime scout for the Redskins.

Going forward, Washington's problems are defense, the offensive line, and its special teams. The age of players, especially on the defensive line, should be addressed. While the secondary needs to find players long term, the offensive line must be completely overhauled, hopefully with some of the young guys on the roster now. In short, this franchise has many problems to solve on defense and offense before becoming a power in the NFC.

FRANCHISE BUSINESS

Besides performing as teams in regular season and postseason games, NFL franchises are also commercial enterprises. To that end, their economic objective is to earn maximum revenue and obtain the greatest amount of profit on a fiscal basis from their operations. Although they share revenue with each other from such sources as national television contracts and other deals, it is important for them to efficiently allocate resources, determine, and distribute payrolls, set non-premium and premium ticket prices, and schedule investments in short- and long-term assets. To reveal and manage these activities, this section focuses on different parts of four NFC franchises' business and how these organizations rank and succeed or not succeed from a financial perspective.

Dallas Cowboys

Born in Los Angeles, California, Jerald "Jerry" Jones spent his childhood in North Little Rock, Arkansas, where his father owned an insurance company. While at North Little Rock High School, Jerry was a running back on the football team. After graduating from there, he accepted a football scholarship to the University of Arkansas and was co-captain and a starting guard on the team. With such teammates as Glen Ray Hines and Jimmy Johnson, Arkansas won a national championship in 1964 under the college Hall of Fame coach Frank Broyles.[15]

In 1970, Jones earned a master's degree in business and tried many business ventures but success eluded him until he started an oil and gas exploration company in Oklahoma, which became hugely successful. Over the next two decades, his business expanded rapidly. As a result, he established offices throughout western America and in provinces of Canada.

Jerry purchased the Dallas Cowboys and their stadium for approximately $140 million in 1989 from the previous owner H. R. "Bum" Bright. Prior to the purchase, the team underperformed with a 3–13 record. Immediately after the acquisition he fired existing coach Tom Landry, much to the chagrin of fans and replaced him with his friend and former teammate, Jimmy Johnson. Also, general manager Tex Schramm lasted only a few months but was then replaced by Jones. During the next few years, with Jones personally involved in every aspect of the team's operations, the Cowboys improved and appeared in consecutive playoffs from 1991 to 1996 including victories in three Super Bowls. In 2014, he won the Professional Football Writers Association executive of the year award.

Team Financials

According to data and other financial information published in *Forbes* for sixteen franchises in the NFC as of their 2015–2016 season, the Cowboys ranked first in market value at $4 billion, total revenue at $620 million, gate receipts at $94 million, and operating income at $270 million. In addition, the team was fifteenth in player expenses at $148 million and also tied for thirteenth with the Saints each with a debt-to-value ratio of 5 percent. Among the conference's ED team, Dallas's amounts were first except for its player expenses and debt ratio. From a financial perspective, the Cowboys are the most valuable NFC team because of their location, market size and wealth, income from home games including television broadcasts, city's expanding economy, and the club's large and enthusiastic fan base (Table A.7).

Based on data of the other thirty-one NFL clubs as of their 2015 season, the Cowboys had the highest market value, total revenue and operating income, and also ranked second in gate receipts following the Patriots, twenty-eighth in player expenses, and tied for twenty-seventh with the Saints and Chiefs in their debt-to-value percentage. From a financial perspective, this Dallas-based football organization is very profitable and the league's richest franchise with a relatively low payroll for its players and small debt compared to its large but estimated net worth as a business enterprise (Table A.8).

For several years a company in Chicago named Team Marketing Report (TMR) has prepared and published a Fan Cost Index (FCI) for the home games of teams in professional sports leagues. To attend a game for a typical family with two kids, an FCI includes the costs of four average-priced tickets, two cheapest-priced draft beers, four each cheapest-priced soft drinks and hot dogs, parking for one vehicle, and two each game programs and least-expensive, adult-size adjustable caps. Costs are determined by telephone calls with team representatives, venues, and concessionaires, and from asking questions during interviews.[16]

For the 2015 season, the Cowboys' FCI was approximately $634 or second highest in the league with no change in percent from 2014. Listed from most to least in amount by item for one person, the club's nonpremium tickets averaged about $110, space for parking a vehicle $75, a cap $20 and program $10, one beer almost $9, and a hot dog and soft drink each $5 to $6. Among FCIs of three other ED teams, the Giants ranked third $629, Redskins sixth at $597, and Eagles ninth at $530. While the 49ers' index of $640 placed first in the league, the average of all teams equaled $480.

Given these amounts, Cowboys' home games are expensive for fans who attend them at 85,000-seat AT&T Stadium in Arlington, Texas. Because of the team's success especially during the 1990s and competing in five playoffs since 2000, and other social and economic factors, the franchise sets relatively high nonpremium and premium (average $346) ticket prices for seats and other items sold to spectators at games in order to increase revenue and, in part, to maximize the franchise's operating income or profit.

Business Highlights

Using fifteen years of data on such things as NFL team performances, home-game ticket prices, and market populations and their median incomes, Emory University researchers created an equity index to determine which clubs had the most avid, engaged, passionate, and/or supportive fans before the NFL's 2015 season. Among the NFC's ED teams, the Cowboys ranked first and ahead of the Giants at third, Eagles at eleventh and Redskins at fifteenth.[17]

For various reasons, including owner Jerry Jones' decision to provide the team with a plush stadium, the index suggests that Cowboys fans are, on average, very engaged or passionate about their football team partly because of the sport's popularity in Texas and the team's potential to perform above expectations in its division and conference. Meanwhile, in another index titled Social Media Equity, the Cowboys had the league's second best fan base followed by the ED's Eagles at seventh, Giants at nineteenth, and Redskins at thirtieth. Although this index reflects whether teams over- or under-perform with respect to their Twitter following, Dallas fans are more involved with their hometown team on social media than those of other NFC clubs although the AFC Steelers ranked first and Patriots third.

The recent sale of the NFL Buffalo Bills was 1.497 times bigger—and National Basketball Association's Los Angeles Clippers 3.48 greater—than their respective valuations in *Forbes*. Based on an average of these multiples, the Cowboys' estimated worth could be approximately $8 billion. Since Terry Pegula paid $1.4 billion for the Bills in tiny Buffalo and Stephen Ballmer $2 billion for the Clippers in large-market Los Angeles, someone might buy the most popular sports team in America for at least $6–$8 billion. In other words, Jerry Jones's purchase of the Cowboys for just $140 million in 1989 was a very lucrative investment.

To further review this Texas franchise, the Cowboys are the NFL's most valuable team for the tenth straight year thanks to record league revenue of $620 million or $126 million more than any other football team. The Cowboys generate $90 million annually from its stadium's 350 luxury suites and more than $100 million from sponsors. In addition the club won a playoff game in 2014 for only the second time in eighteen years with a thrilling come-from-behind win against the Lions. Meanwhile AT&T Stadium is an attractive site for big sporting events with the venue hosting the first college football national championship game in January 2015.[18]

New York Giants

Born in 1954, John Mara graduated from Iona Prep High School in New Rochelle, New York. He attended Boston College and received an undergraduate degree in marketing. Mara earned his law degree from Fordham University in 1979 and then began his career as an attorney with a New York law firm specializing in labor and employment law and litigation.[19]

After spending two years with another law firm, John joined the Giants organization in 1991 as its general counsel and later added the title of executive vice president and chief operating officer. When his father Wellington Mara died in 2005, John became the franchise's president and chief executive officer and also its co-owner.

The team's other co-owner, Steve Tisch, has been involved with the Giants since his father, Preston Robert Tisch, purchased 50 percent of the franchise in 1991. Steve joined the front office as executive vice president in July 2005, and following his father's death, assumed the additional title of chairman. Steve worked closely with John Mara on the planning and construction of MetLife Stadium. In 2011, they were named "Best Owners" in the NFL by *Forbes* magazine for their success both on and off the field.

Team Financials

According to data and other financial information published in *Forbes* for sixteen franchises in the NFC as of their 2015–2016 season, the Giants ranked third in market value at $2.8 billion and also fourth in both total revenue at $400 million and operating income at $105 million, second in gate receipts at $92 million, ninth in player expenses at $165 million, and fifth with a debt-to-value ratio of 18 percent. Among only ED teams, the franchise's amounts placed third except for its gate receipts and debt ratio. From a financial perspective, the ninety-one-year-old Giants are a rich and powerful organization with plenty of liquidity primarily because of their location in a very large market, history of success, and playing home games before large crowds primarily against rivals in their division and others in the conference (Table A.7).

Based on data of the other thirty-one NFL clubs as of their 2015 season, the Giants had the fourth highest market value and also fifth most revenue, third largest gate receipts and seventh greatest operating income and debt ratio, but only the fourteenth highest player expenses in the league. In short, this is a popular, profitable, and wealthy franchise in the nation's most populated city despite the team's mediocre performances in 2009–2010 and 2012–2015 (Table A.8).

Because of differences in their competitiveness and number of seasons, results in postseasons, and other factors, the Giants are 8 percent more valuable than the crosstown rival New York Jets. As of 2014, the former team's revenue, gate receipts, and players expenses—but not their operating income or debt ratio—were significantly greater when compared to those of the Jets. In short, the Giants have become a more successful business organization and team in New York area's sports market than its nearby competitor in the AFC.

For the NFL's 2015 season, the Giants' FCI was approximately $629 or third highest in the league and 8 percent more than in 2014. Listed from most to least in amount by item for one person, the club's nonpremium tickets averaged about $123, space for parking a vehicle $30, a cap $25 and hot dog $6, one beer and a program each $5, and a soft drink $3. Among FCIs of three other ED teams, the Cowboys ranked second at $634, Redskins sixth at $597, and Eagles ninth at $530. While the 49ers' index of $640 was first overall, the league averaged $480.[20]

The Giants, on average, had the NFL's second most expensive price for premium tickets at $509 with the division's Redskins' at $375, Cowboys' at $346, and Eagles' at $217. Consequently, New York football fans including any businessmen, politicians, and professionals, are willing to pay $386 or 413 percent more for at least one additional amenity in their premium versus nonpremium seat at games in MetLife Stadium.

Business Highlights

Using fifteen years of data on such things as NFL team performances, home-game ticket prices, and market populations and their median incomes, Emory University researchers created an equity index to determine which clubs had the most avid, engaged, passionate, and/or supportive fans before the NFL's 2015 season. Among the NFC's ED teams, the Giants ranked third and higher than the Eagles at eleventh and Redskins at fifteenth but lower than the top-rated Cowboys.[21]

In another Emory University index titled Social Media Equity, the Giants had the league's nineteenth best fan base followed by the Redskins at thirtieth but below the Cowboys at second and Eagles at seventh. Although this index reflects whether teams over- or underperform with respect to their Twitter following, Giants fans are less involved or not as passionate about their hometown team on social media as those of eighteen other NFL clubs and also the Jets at ninth. Interestingly, the Steelers had the most dedicated and fervent fan base while the Cardinals ranked thirty-second.

Believed to be a first among NFL clubs, one of the league's most venerable teams has extended its brand into health care and fitness. The first Hackensack UMC Fitness & Wellness Center powered by the Giants opened during December 2013 in Maywood, New Jersey, about five miles from the team's home field. The 112,000-square-foot health, rehabilitation, wellness, and education facility features everything from occupational therapy and kids' swim lessons to instruction in Zumba and healthy cooking. The Center, which has sponsored the team for several years, projects membership from eight to ten thousand people.[22]

Although primarily a pro football team, the Giants franchise also operates a store that offers accessories, hats, polos, shorts and pants, sweatshirts and fleece, T-shirts, jerseys, and swimwear for men; accessories, dresses and skirts, hats, jackets, shorts and pants, sleepwear, sweats, T-shirts, and jewelry for women; and accessories, jerseys, shorts and pants, T-shirts, sweatshirts and fleece, newborn and infant products, preschool and toddler products, and toys and games for kids.

Philadelphia Eagles

Born to wealthy parents in 1951, Jeffrey Lurie earned an undergraduate degree from Clark University, master's degree in psychology from Boston University, and a doctorate in social policy from Brandeis University where he wrote his thesis on the depiction of women in Hollywood movies. Prior to entering business, Lurie served as an adjunct assistant professor of social policy at Boston University.[23]

In 1983, Lurie left academia to join General Cinema Corporation (GCC), a major film company founded by his grandfather, Philip Smith. He worked as an executive in the company and served as a liaison between it and the production community in Hollywood and also as an advisor in the General Cinema national film purchasing office.

A fan of Boston sports teams, Lurie had been a season-ticket holder of the AFL's New England Patriots since the franchise's birth in 1960. He tried to buy the team in the early 1990s but dropped out of the bidding at $150 million because his uncle Richard Smith nixed the deal based on the financials. Five months later, Smith agreed to let his nephew Jeffrey acquire the Philadelphia Eagles.

After contacting Eagles owner Norman Braman, Lurie bought the team from him for $195 million during May 1994. Lurie and his mother Nancy Lurie Marks—Philip Smith's only daughter—borrowed an estimated $190 million from the Bank of Boston to make the acquisition. To finance a loan, Lurie put up millions of dollars' worth of personal stock in Harcourt General and GCC, as equity capital. Furthermore, he and his mother pledged their stock in the family trust as collateral so that Lurie could borrow the remaining amount.

Team Financials

According to data and other financial information published in *Forbes* for sixteen franchises in the NFC as of their 2015–2016 season, the Eagles ranked sixth in market value at $2.4 billion and also fifth in total revenue at $370 million, gate receipts at $69 million, and operating income at $88 million. Additionally the team tied for sixth with the Rams in player expenses at $167 million and tied for eighth with the Redskins and Rams in their debt-to-value ratio of 8 percent. Among only ED clubs in the conference, Philadelphia's pro football team had the lowest amounts except for player expenses and its debt ratio. From a financial perspective, the Eagles are below-average within their division but above-average in value and earnings with respect to all NFC teams (Table A.7).

Based on the data of thirty-one other NFL clubs as of their 2015 season, Philadelphia was ninth in both market value and operating income, eighth in total revenue and gate receipts, tied for tenth with the Rams and Browns in player expenses, and tied for sixteenth with the Redskins and Rams in their debt percentages. Regarding these rankings, the Eagles are in the upper half of the league financially and also they prosper as a business organization but less than operations of such clubs as the Cowboys, Giants, Bears, 49ers, and Patriots. One or two more championship seasons would certainly improve the team's gate receipts and revenue and likely the franchise's market value (Table A.8).

For the league's 2015 season, the Eagles' FCI was approximately $530 or ninth highest in the league but with zero percent increase from 2014. Listed from most to least in amount by item for one person, the club's nonpremium tickets averaged about $98, space for parking a vehicle $35, a cap $18 and beer almost $9, hot dog and program each $5, and a soft drink between $4 and $5. Among FCIs of other ED teams, the Cowboys ranked second in the league at $634, Giants third at $629, and Redskins sixth at $597. While the 49ers' index of $640 placed first among all teams, $480 was the average amount.[24]

The Eagles had relatively low premium tickets at $217 in 2015 compared to the Giants' $509, Redskins' $375, and Cowboys' $346. Because Philadelphia is a blue-collar community and professional baseball, basketball, and hockey teams are popular that play there, these differences in ticket prices suggest that football fans, including businessmen, politicians, and professionals are simply unable or not willing to pay an excessive price for another amenity in a premium seat at Lincoln Financial Field.

Business Highlights

Using fifteen years of data on such things as NFL team performances, home-game ticket prices, and market populations and their median incomes, Emory University researchers created an equity index to determine which clubs had the most avid, engaged, passionate, and/or supportive fans before the NFL's 2015 season. Among the NFC's ED teams, the Eagles ranked eleventh and higher than the Redskins at fifteenth but below the first-place Cowboys and also the Giants in third. Thus Philadelphia has more enthusiastic football fans than twelve other NFC teams and a majority of those in the AFC.

In another Emory University index titled Social Media Equity, the Eagles had the league's seventh best fan base followed by the ED's Giants at nineteenth and Redskins at thirtieth but below the Cowboys at second. Although this index reflects whether teams over- or underperform with respect to their Twitter following, Eagles fans are more involved or passionate about their hometown team on social media than those of twenty-five other NFL clubs. Interestingly, the Steelers had the most dedicated and fervent fan base while the Cardinals ranked thirty-second.

Regarding the franchise's other business news, the Eagles and Apple Vacations recently signed a multiyear corporate partnership agreement. The deal's centerpiece is an opportunity for fans to take a four- or seven-night luxury vacation with players and alumni to Mexico initially during April 2016. The trip includes round-trip airfare, hotel accommodations at the Now Sapphire Riviera Cancun resort, a private welcome party, an autograph and photo session with a group of not-yet-named players and alumni, and a commemorative gift. It costs individuals $1,389 for four-nights and $1,699 for three additional nights. Besides that agreement, the team also renewed or entered into new multiple-year sponsorship deals with Aramark, Wawa, and America Airlines.[25]

During 2014, the Eagles refinanced about $120 million of existing stadium debt and $70 million of other debt related to renovations of Lincoln Financial Field. The team borrowed $180 million in 2001 for construction of its stadium and the interest rate on the refinancing was less than 5 percent. The Eagles refinancing was arranged by Bank of America, which acted as the placement agent, but not the lender.

Washington Redskins

Born in 1964, Daniel Snyder attended Hillandale Elementary School in Silver Spring, Maryland . After graduating from high school, his first job was at B. Dalton bookstore in the White Flint Mall in Rockville, Maryland. By age twenty, he dropped out of college and operated his own business, leasing jets to fly college students to spring break in Fort Lauderdale, Florida, and the Caribbean. Supposedly, Snyder cleared $1 million by running the business from his parents' bedroom with a friend and several telephone lines.[26]

During the 1980s to early 1990s, he and his sister Michelle started a wallboard advertising company—Snyder Communications (SNC)—whose revenue exceeded $9 million in 1993. In an initial public offering in 1996, he became the youngest chief executive officer ever of a company on the New York Stock Exchange. Three years later SNC was sold to a French services group in an all-stock transaction valued in excess of $2 billion, the largest transaction in the history of the advertising market industry.

Following the death of former Redskins franchise owner Jack Kent Cooke, Snyder purchased the team and its two-year-old stadium for $800 million in 1999. The deal was financed largely through borrowed money and $155 million debt assumed on the stadium. While interested in the appearance of the team and surrounding area, he renamed the stadium FedEx Field.

Team Financials

According to data and other financial information published in *Forbes* for sixteen franchises in the NFC as of their 2015–2016 season, the Redskins ranked second in market value at $2.85 billion, total revenue at $439 million, and operating income at $124 million. In addition the club was third in both gate receipts at $85 million and player expenses at $170 million, and tied for eighth with the Eagles and Rams in their debt-to-value ratio of 8 percent. Among only ED teams in the conference, Washington was first in player expenses and second highest in market value, total revenue, and operating income, and also third in gate receipts and tied for second in its debt-to-value percentage. Based on these results, this is a rich, profitable, and successful franchise compared to others in the conference's three divisions (Table A.7).

Regarding thirty-one other teams as of the league's 2015–2016 season, the Redskins were third in market value, total revenue, and operating income, fourth in gate receipts, tied for fourth with the Steelers and Broncos in player expenses, and tied for sixteenth with the Eagles and Rams in their debt ratio. Besides the NFC's Cowboys and Giants and AFC's Patriots, this NFL franchise is a wealthy business enterprise that generates millions from its home games at FedEx Field and also its partnerships and sponsorship, television broadcasts, and other revenue sources (Table A.8).

During the NFL's 2015 season, the Redskins' FCI was approximately $597 or sixth highest in the league but with no change in percent from 2014. Listed from most to least in amount by item for one person, the team's non-premium tickets averaged $102, parking for one vehicle about $58, a cap $30 and beer $9, hot dog $6, and a program and soft drink each $5. For FCIs of other ED clubs, the Cowboys ranked second in the league at $634, Giants third at $629, and Eagles ninth at $530. In other words, it is expensive for a family of four to attend an NFL game at FedEx Field in Washington even though the hometown team had appeared in only four playoffs from 1993 to 2014.[27]

At $375 each the Redskins had the third highest average premium ticket prices in the league following the Patriots' $566 and Giants' $509, and also $120 or approximately 47 percent more than amounts of the typical NFL team. Therefore, Washington is an expensive, important, and lucrative market for professional football while also being a home site for the MLB Nationals, NBA Wizards, and NHL Capitals.

Business Highlights

Using fifteen years of data on such things as NFL team performances, home-game ticket prices, and market populations and their median incomes, Emory University researchers created an equity index to determine which clubs had the most avid, engaged, passionate, and/or supportive fans before the NFL's 2015 season. Among the NFC's ED teams, the Redskins ranked fifteenth and below the Cowboys in first, Giants in third, and Eagles in eleventh. Overall this Washington, D.C.–based franchise has more enthusiastic football fans than eight other NFC teams and a majority of those in the AFC.

In another Emory University index titled Social Media Equity, the Redskins had the league's thirtieth best fan base following the ED Cowboys in second, Eagles in seventh, and Giants in nineteenth. Although this index reflects whether teams over- or underperform with respect to their Twitter following, Redskins fans are less involved or passionate about their hometown team on social media than those of twenty-nine other NFL clubs. Interestingly, the Steelers had the league's most dedicated and fervent fan base while the Cardinals ranked thirty-second.

For other important business news, the club's media ventures include Redskins Nation—produced by the Redskins Broadcast Network—which is the league's only year-round, daily thirty-minute television show. The team also produces television and radio broadcasts via Redskins.com, has a robust editorial and social media staff, and features a fan forum named Extremeskins.com. There is a variety of other television programs, which are broadcast independently as well as in partnerships with local television outlets.

During mid-2015, the franchise lost some protection for its controversial name after a federal judge ruled it may be disparaging to Native Americans. Although the decision does not bar the team's commercial use of the trademarked name, it opens the door to copycats seeking to profit from it. The Redskins cannot add the name to a federal registry, which provides additional protection from such infringement. Meanwhile, Redskins president Bruce Allen said the team will appeal the ruling.[28]

The Redskins recently removed thousands of seats from FedEx Field for the third time in five seasons as demand has waned for tickets. According to owner Dan Snyder, the team had a waiting list for season tickets of 200,000 names and wants to build a new stadium in Washington, D.C., although its lease at FedEx Field, which is in Landover, Maryland, exists through the 2026 NFL season.

The Obama administration would likely block Washington authorities from building a new stadium there because of objections to the team's name. The National Park Service owns the land underneath the fifty-four-year-old Robert F. Kennedy Memorial Stadium, a venue two miles east of the Capitol that hosted the Redskins from 1961 to 1996. Some city leaders want to demolish the current stadium and build a new one to lure the football team back from suburban Maryland. Snyder, who vowed to never change the name of his team, may have to if he wants political support and taxpayer funding for a new, billion-dollar stadium.

NOTES

1. Two prominent books on the NFL and its seasons and teams are Frank P. Jozsa Jr., *Football Fortunes: The Business, Organization and Strategy of the NFL* (Jefferson, NC: McFarland, 2010), and James Quirk and Rodney D. Fort, *Pay Dirt: The Business of Professional Team Sports* (Princeton, NJ: Princeton University Press, 1992).
2. Season performances of the Cowboys and their players and also other ED teams are in the *NFL Record & Fact Book 2014* (New York: NFL, 2014) and reported in more detail on such websites as nfl.com, pro-football-reference.com, and sportsencyclopedia.com.
3. Besides pages 488 to 494 in the Data Supplement of *Pay Dirt*, NFL teams' attendances are available in "Rod Fort's Sports Business Data," http://www.sites.google.com, cited September 1, 2015.
4. The best article to read is "Ranking All 31 NFL Stadiums," http://www.sportingnews.com, cited August 31, 2015.
5. This information is in "2015 NFL Future Power Rankings," http://www.insider.espn.go.com, cited October 10, 2015.
6. Two references for the Giants' history are "Teams," http://www.profootballhof.com, cited September 1, 2015 and "Teams," http://www.pro-football-reference.com, cited August 25, 2015.
7. See note 3 for historical attendances of the New York Giants.
8. A brief evaluation of MetLife Stadium and its amenities is in "Ranking All 31 NFL Stadiums," http://www.sportingnews.com, cited August 31, 2015.
9. Besides note 6, another reading is "Power Rankings: Rating the Likeability of Every NFL Franchise," http://www.foxsports.com, cited August 31, 2015.
10. See various sources and references including websites in notes 1 and 2.

11. This quote appears in "Ranking All 31 NFL Stadiums," http://www.sportingnews.com, cited August 31, 2015.

12. The article in note 5 contains the power rankings of the Eagles and other clubs in the NFC's ED.

13. As mentioned in other notes of the chapter, this book's bibliography contains articles and Internet sources that provide details about Redskins' team performances.

14. Another study of current football venues, besides *Sporting News*, is "Ranking the Best and Worst NFL Stadiums," http://www.athlonsports.com, cited August 31, 2015.

15. The history of Jerry Jones and other WD franchise owners in the NFC is available on their team's website and also in articles, reports, and studies published online in various journals, magazines, and newspapers. For more about these leaders and their personal and business careers, see "NFL Team Owners," http://www.biography.yourdictionary.com, cited December 24, 2015.

16. Read "2015 NFL Fan Cost Index," http://www.teammarketing.com, cited November 20, 2015 and Jon Greenberg, "2014 NFL Fan Cost Index," http://www.teammarketing.com, cited August 26, 2015.

17. For both indexes from Emory University, see Manish Tripathi, "2015 NFL Fan Equity Rankings," https://scholarblogs.emory.edu, cited September 4, 2015, and Michael Lewis, "2015 NFL Social Media Equity Rankings," https://scholarblogs.emory.edu, cited September 4, 2015.

18. Two articles with business news about the franchise are Terry Lefton, "AT&T Naming Deal Years in the Making," *SportsBusiness Journal* (October 28, 2013): 28, and Don Muret, "Cowboys Plug Feedback Tool Into App," *SportsBusiness* Journal (October 7, 2013): 10.

19. There is more information about John Mara in the article, "NFL Team Owners" and on his team's website at http://www.nfl.com.

20. Read about these costs in "2015 NFL Fan Cost Index," https://www.teammarketing.com, cited November 20, 2015.

21. See note 13 in this chapter.

22. Terry Lefton, "N.Y. Giants Make Rare Move, Extend Brand to Health Center." *SportsBusiness Journal* (April 1, 2013): 4.

23. "NFL Team Owners" also has facts about Jeffrey Lurie's business and personal careers.

24. The same readings as in notes 12, 13, and 14 of this chapter were used to discuss the FCI and indexes for the Eagles.

25. One reference is John George, "Here's How You Can Take a Vacation with Some Eagles," http://www.bizjournals.com, cited October 20, 2015. For another revenue source of the team, see Terry Lefton, "Eagles Making Sponsorship Connections," *SportsBusiness Journal* (September 7, 2015): 11.

26. Research the club's website on http://www.nfl.com and "NFL Team Owners" for information about Daniel Snyder's personal and business careers.

27. For the Washington Redskins' FCI and the club's rankings in the fan and social equity indexes, see notes 13 and 14 in this chapter.

28. To read more details about this topic, see Ian Shapira, "Federal Judge Orders Cancellation of Redskins' Trademark Registrations," http://www.washingtonpost.com, cited October 21, 2015, and Joe Palazzalo, "U.S. Justice Department Intervenes in Football Redskins' Trademark Case." *Wall Street Journal* (January 9, 2015): 1.

Chapter Six

North Division

When the postseason of the National Football League (NFL) concluded in early 2016 with the Denver Broncos defeating the Carolina Panthers in Super Bowl 50, which team or teams in the North Division (ND) of the National Football Conference (NFC) had the least number of all-time wins, smallest winning percentage, most titles and championships, and appeared in the fewest playoffs? Did the Chicago Bears have a higher market value as a franchise than the Green Bay Packers, and were the Detroit Lions' revenue and gate receipts larger or smaller than those of the Minnesota Vikings?

To answer these and other questions, next are some interesting but important, realistic, and relevant facts that highlight the historical performances of four teams in the NFC's North Division as of the league's 2015–2016, or simply 2015, season. Besides their winning percentage and number of wins, titles, and championships, this information includes special coaches, players, and events regarding each of them while competing in the NFL's regular seasons and any playoffs. In the chapter's final section—labelled Franchise Business—is an analysis of these franchises' success or failure as business enterprises both individually and in comparison to each other from a financial perspective.

TEAM PERFORMANCES

Chicago Bears

In 1920, the Decatur Staleys finished second to the champion Akron Pros in the fourteen-team American Professional Football Association (APFA). Despite the team's success and growing popularity of the sport in the Midwest, franchise owner A. E. Staley's problem was the limited population of Decatur, Illinois, as a viable, long-term sports market as opposed to moving his club to a larger city with a bigger stadium. In fact, Staley Field had only 1,500 seats for spectators with space for another 1,000 for those not seated.[1]

Based on his team's dilemma, Staley had to make a crucial decision. Was he in the corn-processing industry or the emerging business of professional sports? After meeting with Coach George Halas, Staley made Halas a proposition because big-time football needed more fans. As a result, they agreed that Halas would take control of the team and then in October 1921 move it from Decatur to Chicago and play its home games at Wrigley Field but retain "Staleys" as a nickname for the league's 1921 season.

The nineteen players on the club's roster remained on the payroll one year and Staley agreed to pay the team $5,000 to help with its move to Chicago. Although he had no legal or moral obligation to promote the continuation of the football club, Staley realized the potential impact of it in the sport. Later, he attended games at Wrigley Field and referred to the Chicago team as "transplants." In 1922 the team—co-owned by Halas and player Dutch Sternaman—changed its name to Chicago Bears.

Historical Results

A member of the NFL during 1921–1932 and within its Western Division from 1933 to 1949, in the National Conference during 1950–1952 and Western Conference from 1953 to 1966 and the conference's Central Division (CD) to 1969, and then in the NFC's CD to 2001 and finally the conference's ND to its 2014–2015 season, the Bears played 1,325 games and won approximately 55 percent of them. Among other teams in the conference as of the league's 2015–2016 season, Chicago ranked first in number of wins, third in winning percentage, fourth in division titles, tied for sixth with the Lions and Vikings in conference titles, second in total number of championships including one Super Bowl victory, and fifth with twenty-six playoff appearances (Table A.5).

Compared to the conference's ND teams, the Bears had the most wins, a smaller winning percentage and fewer titles, championships, and total playoffs than the Packers but more than the Lions. In addition, the club ranked third in qualifying for playoffs behind the Packers and Vikings. Based on these results, Chicago has been a competitive team in the NFC and especially competent at winning division and conference titles and championships. Since 1995, however, the team has played in only four postseasons.

Regarding the performances of thirty-one other NFL teams as of their 2015–2016 season, the ninety-five-year-old Bears ranked first in number of wins and sixth in winning percentage, and also fifth in division titles, tied for tenth with the Lions, Vikings, and Bills in winning their conference, second in championships including one Super Bowl, and sixth in qualifying for the playoffs. These and other results prove that, except for such periods as the 1920s, early-1950s to 1960s, mid-1960s to 1970s, late 1990s, and several seasons between 2002 and 2015, Chicago's NFL team has been above average competitively while playing clubs in the NFC and against teams in the league's other conference (Table A.6).

To be successful in regular seasons and the playoffs, the Bears had some dedicated, popular, and smart coaches since 1921. In number of wins, these included George Halas with 248 victories, Mike Ditka 112, and Lovie Smith 84. For their leadership, the team's Associated Press (AP) coaches of the year were Halas in 1963 and 1965, Ditka in 1985 and 1988, Dick Jauron in 2001, and Smith in 2005. Meanwhile, such men as Ralph Jones, Luke Johnson, John (Paddy) Driscoll, Jim Dooley, Jack Pardee, and Abe Gibron each had fewer than 25 wins and several losing seasons.

Because of their skill and talent, several Bears players set career, single season, and single game records at their position for the franchise. For examples of career records, Walter Payton rushed for 16,726 yards, caught 492 passes, and scored 125 touchdowns; Gary Fencik intercepted 38 passes; Gale Sayers averaged 30.6 yards on his kickoff returns; and Richard Dent sacked quarterbacks 124.5 times. During a single season, Erik Kramer passed for 3,838 yards and 29 touchdowns in 1995; Bobby Joe Green averaged 465.5 yards on punts in 1963; Robbie Gould kicked 32 field goals in 2006; and Kevin Butler scored 144 points in 1985.

In a single game, Johnny Lujack passed for 468 yards and Sid Luckman 7 touchdowns; Jim Keane received 14 passes; Alston Jeffrey had 249 receiving yards; and Gale Sayers scored 6 touchdowns and 36 points. As a group, these players' remarkable career, single season, and single game records resulted in many wins for Chicago during various NFL seasons.

Each year the Associated Press (AP) rewards players for their exceptional performances in games at their respective positions on the field. Running back Walter Payton, for example, was the league's Most Valuable Player (MVP) and offensive player of the year in 1977 for his 1,828 yards while running the football and 16 total touchdowns. Besides him, other winners included offensive rookie of the year Mike Ditka in 1961, Ron Bull in 1962, Gale Sayers in 1965, and Anthony Thomas in 2001; defensive player of the year Mike Singletary in 1985 and 1988 and Brian Urlacher in 2005; and defensive rookie of the year Wally Chambers in 1973, Mark Carrier in 1990, and Urlacher in 2000. Moreover Payton, Sayers (twice), and defensive Doug Atkins were each pro bowl MVPs.

As of the league's 2015–2016 season, there were twenty-seven Bears in the pro football Hall of Fame. Unmentioned before and not record holders, three all-time great players were quarterback George Blanda, linebacker Dick Butkus, and the great running back Red Grange. Inducted in 1982, for example, Doug Atkins won all-NFL honors three times, all-Western Conference acclaim seven years, and defensive end in the pro bowl eight of his twelve seasons as a Bears player. For sure, these were special athletes who deserved recognition for their accomplishments.

Performance Highlights

Among its years in the league, Chicago's most successful periods consecutively were 1932–1934, 1940–1943, 1984–1988, 1990–1991, and 2005–2006. In large part, these seasons of playoffs and winning titles occurred because of such quarterbacks as Keith Molesworth, Jim McMahon, and Jim Harbaugh, rushers Bronko Nagurski, Walter Payton, and Neal Anderson, and receivers Ken Kavanaugh, Willie Gault, and Mushin Muhammad. Alternatively, the team's worst back-to-back performances happened during 1923–1931, 1951–1955, 1957–1962, 1964–1976, and 1995–2000. Poor coaching decisions, inferior player performances, and other problems caused losses during these seasons

At its games in 61,500-seat Soldier Field, which opened in 1924 and home of the Bears since 1971, the club's attendances have been among the smallest in the league. While the NFL's average per season was in the mid-500,000s, the number of spectators at the team's games from 2004 to 2015 have been in the high 400,000s and ranked near the bottom of the NFC. Simply put, thousands of Chicago football fans are not passionate about their hometown team's games, in part, because of its failure to consistently defeat the Lions, Packers, and Vikings in the ND and appearing in only five playoffs since 1992 but losing in a divisional or the conference's title game.[2]

Among other NFL venues, Soldier Field was twenty-fourth in a recent study. According to an article about it in an edition of *Sporting News*, the author stated:

> A dozen years after venerable Soldier Field went through a $606 million renovation, the Bears and their landlord, the Chicago Park District, are renovating concession spaces and developing The Den, a new upscale sports bar. In addition, Bears fans will enjoy new video boards this season [2014], and the venue remains a heckler's paradise. The 2003 reconstruction reduced the number of stadium parking spaces and tailgate sports. Fans parking remotely can enjoy a bite to eat at restaurants along Michigan Avenue and bars in the South Loop neighborhood.[3]

In the Entertainment Sports Programming Network's (ESPN) future power rankings, the network assigned three experts to rate each NFL team for three seasons (2015–2017) on a scale of 0 to 100 percent in five categories including roster (excluding quarterback), quarterback, draft, front office, and coaching. In their analysis, the Bears ranked twenty-fifth in the NFL and last among ND teams. After a 5–11 season in 2014, the club's average was 63.1.

More specifically, the roster scored 61, quarterback 47, draft 65.3, front office 71, and coaching 75.[4]

In 2013, quarterback Jay Cutler and his teammates had received a 78.3. However, after arguably his worst season as a pro, that number considerably declined in 2014. Although the Bears do not expect Cutler to become a great player, they hope he returns to his middle-tier status. If Cutler has another year like 2014, the Bears will look elsewhere for his replacement and that might set the franchise back again.

Although the Bears fell fourteen spots in the overall rankings from 2014, they moved up from tenth to thirteenth in coaching after hiring John Fox. In every other category, however, the club suffered a double-digit dip as the experts reassessed where Chicago stood after a disappointing season. Nevertheless, few believe the team's appreciably worse off in the front office or in its drafting. Plus, nobody knows if Ryan Pace will be a better general manager than Phil Emery. From the 2015 to 2017 NFL seasons, the Bears will win or lose games and thus determine their actual scores as a power in the NFC's ND.

Detroit Lions

An expansion team in the NFL, the Portsmouth Spartans had a 28–16–7 record and from 1930 to 1933 they finished eighth, second, and third in the league and then second in the Western Division. Owned by the Portsmouth NFL Corporation, which issued 250 shares at $100 each, the team had a $16,000 loss in 1931 and two years later went bankrupt.[5]

In 1934, radio executive George A. Richards led a group of investors who purchased the franchise for the staggering price of $7.9 million. Because of financial problems and also small attendances at its home games at 8,200-seat Universal Stadium in Portsmouth, Ohio, Richards moved his club in 1934 to a much larger sports market in southeast Michigan. Renamed Detroit Lions, the club played its home games at the 25,000-seat University of Detroit Stadium. Interestingly, the Lions became the fourth APFA/NFL team in Detroit following those with such nicknames as Heralds (1920), Panthers (1921), and Wolverines (1925).

Historical Results

While a member of the league's Western Division from 1934 to 1949, National Conference during 1950–1952, Western Conference from 1953 to 1966 and in the conference's Western Division during 1967–1969, and finally in the NFC's CD to 2001 and then the ND since 2002, the Lions played 1,150 games and won approximately 44 percent of them. Among fifteen other teams in its conference as of the NFL's 2015–2016 season, Detroit ranked seventh in number of wins, twelfth in winning percentage, tenth in division titles and also tied for sixth with the Bears and Vikings in conference titles, seventh with four championships but zero Super Bowls, and ninth in playoff appearances (Table A.5).

Compared to the conference's ND clubs, the Lions had the third most number of victories and worst winning percentage, fewest division titles and playoff appearances, and also less number of championships than the Bears and Packers but more than the Vikings. Based on these results, Detroit has been a mediocre performing team while playing against rivals in the NFC and especially against those in its division.

Regarding the all-time performances of thirty-one other NFL teams as of their 2015–2016 season, the eighty-two-year-old Lions ranked eighth in number of wins, twenty-fifth in winning percentage, eighteenth in division titles and also tied for tenth with the Bears, Vikings, and Bills in winning their conference, tied for eighth with the Patriots in number of championships including any NFL and Super Bowl victories, and fourteenth in qualifying for postseasons. These and other results prove that, except for such periods as the mid-1930s to early 1950s, late 1950s to 1960s, early 1970s to 1980s, and early 2000s, Detroit's NFL team has been primarily average—but sometimes above-average—in its performances in games while playing clubs in the NFC and also against others in the league's AFC (Table A.6).

To be competitive in a number of regular seasons and the playoffs since 1934, the Lions had some superior coaches but also several with few victories. In number of wins, the former group includes Wayne Fontes with 67, George Wilson 55, Raymond (Buddy) Parker 50, and George (Potsy) Clark 49. Wilson was AP coach of the year in 1957 and Fontes in 1991. Alternatively, the club had several coaches with fewer than ten wins each such as Elmer (Gus) Henderson, George (Potsy) Clark, Bill Edwards, and John Karcis in the 1940s, Don McCafferty in the 1970s, and Gary Moeller, Marty Mornhinweg, and Dick Jauron in the 2000s.

Because of their determination, talent, and training, several Lions players set career, single season, and single game records at their position for the franchise. For examples of career records, Barry Sanders rushed for 15,269 yards and scored 109 touchdowns; Jason Hanson kicked 495 field goals while scoring 2,150 points; Calvin Johnson had 9,328 yards as a receiver; and Bobby Lane passed for 118 touchdowns.

During a single season, Matthew Stafford passed for 5,038 yards and 41 touchdowns in 2011; Herman Moore caught 123 passes in 1995; Calvin Johnson rushed for 1,964 yards in 2012; Yale Lary punted 48.9 yards each time in 1963; and Robert Porcher had 15 sacks in 1999. For a single game, Don Doll intercepted 4 passes; Garo Yepremian and Jason Hanson each kicked 6 field goals; and Bill Gay had 5.5 sacks. Sanders, Stafford, Moore, and Johnson also set records in a game for their team.

Each year, the AP awards players for outstanding performances at their respective positions. In 1997, the Lions' Barry Sanders was the league's co-MVP because he rushed for an all-time but second-best record of 2,053 yards including fourteen consecutive 100-yard games. Other awards winners were offensive player of the year Sanders in 1994 and 1997, and Billy Sims in 1980; offensive rookie of the year Nick Pietrosante in 1959, Gail Cogdill in 1960, Mel Farr in 1967, Earl McCullouch in 1968, and Sanders in 1989; defensive rookie of the year Lem Barney in 1967, Al Baker in 1978, and Ndamukong Suh in 2010; and comeback player of the year Matthew Stafford in 2011. For sure, these athletes had unforgettable years for Detroit.

As of 2015, there were several Lions in the pro football Hall of Fame. Besides Barry Sanders, Lem Barney, and Bobby Lane, five others were Dick (Night Train) Lane, Charley Culp, Alex Wojciechowicz, Dick LaBeau, Doak Walker, and Dick Stanfel. In short, these were all-time great NFL players at various positions and deserve recognition for their contribution to Lions teams.

Performance Highlights

Among its years in the league, the Lions' most successful periods consecutively were 1952–1954, 1982–1983, and 1993–1995. In large part, these seasons of playoffs and winning titles occurred because of such quarterbacks as Bobby Layne, Gary Danielson, and Calvin Peete; rushers Bob Hoernschemeyer, Billy Sims, and Barry Sanders; and receivers Dorne Dibble, Leonard Thompson, and Herman Moore. Alternatively, the team's worst back-to-back performances took place during 1936–1951, 1958–1969, 1971–1981, 1984–1990, and 2000–2010. Mostly, competition from strong and talented Bears, Packers, and Vikings teams in the ND and ineffective Lions coaches and their inferior players caused losses in these seasons.

At its home games in 64,500-seat Ford Field, which opened in 2002, the club's attendances have been below average in the league. While the NFL's average per season was in the mid-500,000s, the numbers of spectators at the team's games from 2004 to 2015 were in the high 400,000s to low 500,000s and thus ranked near the bottom of the NFC. Simply put, thousands of Detroit football fans have not been thrilled about their home team's games, in part, because of the club's failure to consistently defeat the ND's Bears, Packers, and Vikings and appearing in only four playoffs since 1996 but then losing in a wild card game each of these postseasons.[6]

Among other NFL venues, Ford Field ranked tenth in a recent study. According to an article about it in an edition of Sporting News:

> Another underrated stadium—its hard-nosed industrial look speaks to the city's automotive industry and the incorporation of a historic department store into the building design is a unique feature. For this season [2015], the Lions

> are upgrading a field level club sponsored by the MGM Grand Detroit. Several bars are within walking distance of the stadium, including the Hockeytown Café, owned by Red Wings owner Mike Illitch. The Eastern Market, another game-day food destination, is about one mile from Ford Field.[7]

In ESPNs future power rankings, the network told three experts to rate each NFL team for three seasons (2015–2017) on a scale of 0 to 100 percent in five categories including roster (excluding quarterback), quarterback, draft, front office, and coaching. In their analysis, the Lions ranked twelfth in the NFL, seventh in the NFC, and third in their division following the Packers, who were first, and Vikings seventh. With an overall score of 71.9, the Lions' roster scored 71.3, quarterback 74, draft 69.3t, front office 71.3, and coaching 73.[8]

With respect to their rating, the Lions placed higher in the front office at seventeenth and coaching at eighteenth. The front office did not change much, but the coaching changes—bringing in Jim Caldwell to replace Jim Schwartz—went over well enough to improve the perception of those responsible for doing the hiring. The Lions deserve credit for putting into place a winning formula built around a strong defense. The question moving forward is whether that formula remains viable without all-pro defensive tackle Ndamukong Suh, whose departure affected a rank of fifteenth in the roster.

Other than winning NFL championships in 1935 and again in 1952–1953 and 1957, the Lions have not played in a Super Bowl. For that to happen, the club needs to unify its front office and hire better coaches and more talented players especially at such key positions as quarterback and offensive guard and tackle. Otherwise the Packers, Bears, and/or Vikings will continue to dominate the ND and win more titles and championships

Green Bay Packers

During August 1919, a group of young athletes, headed by Earl "Curly" Lambeau and George Calhoun, gathered in the dingy editorial room of the old *Green Bay Press-Gazette* building and organized a football team. Later they spoke to and convinced Curly's employer, the Indian Packing Company (IPC), to buy their team equipment. Because IPC permitted the use of its athletic field for practices and also provided jerseys, the club was identified publicly as a project. Although the team adopted "Packers" as a nickname, IPC decided to reduce its support of them about midway into the club's first year of operation.[9]

In their first season as an independent team, the Packers won ten games and lost only once while competing against others from Wisconsin and Michigan. These were played in a field with no fences or bleachers, and interested fans "passed the hat" to collect money as payments for players and other expenses. During the Packers' second season, a small bleacher with a capacity of a few hundred seats was built on one side of the field, and a fee charged to spectators who sat there.

Since the Packers were successful in games after two years, IPC officials helped Lambeau obtain an expansion franchise in the new APFA, which had formed in 1920. After finishing seventh at 3–2–1 in the APFA's 1921 season, the league—renamed National Football League—revoked the Packers' franchise because it used college players during the season. As a result, Lambeau purchased a new franchise for $250 in order to compete in the NFL's 1922 season.

Historical Results

As member of the APFA/NFL during 1921/1922–1932, Western Division from 1933 to 1949, National Conference during 1950–1952, Western Conference from 1953 to 1966 and in the conference's Central Division during 1967–1969, and finally in the NFC's CD to 2001 and then the ND since 2002, the Packers played 1,304 games and won approximately 55 percent of them. Among other conference teams as of the NFL's 2015–2016 season, Green Bay ranked second in wins and also winning percentage and division and conference titles, first in number of championships including four Super Bowls, and tied for first with the Cowboys and Giants in total playoff appearances (Table A.5).

Compared to only ND clubs in the NFC as of their 2015 season, the Packers were second in victories to the Bears but first in winning percentage, total titles and championships, and qualifying for postseasons. Based on these results, this Wisconsin-based franchise has a culture, tradition, and record of being an elite team among others in its division and also the league's conference. From a historical perspective, the club's closest rivals in all-time performances are the NFC's Cowboys and Giants and AFC's Steelers.

Regarding the performances of thirty-one other NFL teams as of their 2015–2016 season, the Packers ranked second in number of wins and also division and conference titles, fifth in winning percentage, first in number of total championships including four Super Bowl victories, and tied for first in qualifying for thirty-one postseasons. These and other results prove that, except for such periods as the 1920s, mid-1940s to late 1950s, mid-1970s to early 1980s, and mid-1980s to early 1990s, Green Bay's NFL teams have been superior in their performances while playing clubs in the NFC and also against those in the league's other conference (Table A.6).

To win titles and championships and succeed in their seasons and postseasons, the Packers had several former coaches who provided leadership to their teams since 1921. In number of wins Lambeau had 212, Vince Lombardi 98, and Mike Holmgren 84. Lombardi was AP coach of the year in 1959 and Lindy Infante in 1989. Besides Infante, several others won fewer than 50 games and had losing records including such coaches as Gene Ronzani, Lisle Blackbourn, Phil Bengston, Dan Devine, Bart Starr, and Forest Gregg. As of 2014, head coach Mike McCarthy was 100–54–1 and in seven playoffs since 2006.

While playing for the Packers, some players were outstanding and set career, single season, and single game records for the franchise. For example, Ahman Green rushed for 8,322 yards; Brett Favre passed for 61,655 total yards and 442 touchdowns (both NFL records); Donald Driver caught 743 passes for 10,137 yards; Bobby Dillon intercepted 52 passes; and Ryan Longwell kicked 226 field goals and scored 1,054 points.

In a single season, Aaron Rodgers passed for 4,643 yards and 45 touchdowns in 2011; Irv Comp had 10 interceptions in 1943; Tim Masthay averaged 45.6 yards per punt in 2011; and Paul Hornung scored 176 points in 1960. During a single game, Rodgers and Matt Flynn passed for 480 yards; Don Hutson caught 14 passes; Hornung scored 5 touchdowns and also 33 points; and Vonnie Holiday had 5 sacks. In short, these athletes set remarkable career, single season, and single game records that resulted in winning games and titles for Green Bay.

Besides coaches Lombardi and Infante, some Packers players won AP awards at their positions. Running backs Hornung and Jim Taylor (each once), wide receiver Hutson (twice), and quarterbacks Starr (once), Favre (four times), and Rodgers (twice) became MVPs for their great performances in various NFL seasons. In addition to them, John Brockington was offensive rookie of the year in 1971 and Eddie Lacy in 2013; Reggie White defensive player of the year in 1998 and Charles Woodson in 2009; and Willie Buchanon defensive rookie of the year in 1972. Other award winners for Green Bay were pro bowl MVPs Henry Jordon, Dave Robinson, and John Jefferson.

The Packers have twenty-four individuals in the pro football Hall of Fame including 2015 inductee Ron Wolf. Their total is second only to the Bears with 27 but more than the Steelers' 21, Giants' 20, Redskins' 19, and Browns' 16. Four Packers inductees were charter members in 1963 while five others who played briefly for the team—defensive end Len Ford, linebacker Ted Hendricks, guard/coach Walt Kiesling, kicker Jan Stenerud, and safety Emlen Tunnell—also have their busts displayed in the Hall of Fame. Former quarterback Brett Favre joined them in 2016.

Performance Highlights

Among its years in the league, Green Bays' most successful periods consecutively were 1929–1931, 1960–1962, 1965–1967, 1993–1998, 2001–2004, and 2009–2015. In large part, these seasons of playoffs and winning titles and perhaps championships occurred because of such quarterbacks as Starr,

Favre, and Rodgers; running backs Taylor, Edgar Bennett, and Eddie Lacy; and receivers Max McGee, Sterling Sharpe, and Jordy Nelson. Alternatively, the team's worst back-to-back performances took place during 1921–1928, 1945–1955, 1973–1981, and 1983–1992. For the most part, too much rigorous competition from teams in their division and conference and also ineffective Packers coaches and unproductive players were reasons for the latter group of disappointing seasons.

At its home games in 80,750-seat Lambeau Field, which opened in 1957, the club's attendances have been above the league's average number. While the NFL's average each season was in the mid-500,000s, the number of spectators at the team's games from 2004 to 2015 ranged from the mid to high 500,000s into occasionally the low 600,000s. Simply put, Green Bay football fans are dedicated and passionate about attending their hometown team's games, in part, because of the club's success defeating the Bears, Lions, and Vikings in the ND and from appearing in twelve playoffs since 2000 and winning a Super Bowl in 2010.[10]

Among thirty-one other venues, Lambeau Field ranked first in a recent study. According to an article about it in an edition of the Sporting News:

> Simply put, it's the NFL's best fan experience. Tailgating is second to none and the tight seating bowl reflects a college game-day atmosphere. The brats and beer just go down better on a crisp fall Sunday. Plus, the Pack, through its unique publicly held status, has invested about $500 million over the past 12 years to pay for facility upgrades, including a south end zone expansion. This year, Delaware North Sportservice, the Packers concessionaire, updated the old Curly's pub into the 1919 Kitchen & Tap.[11]

In ESPN's future power rankings, the network asked three experts to rate each NFL team for three seasons (2015–2017) on a scale of 0 to 100 percent in five categories including roster (excluding quarterback), quarterback, draft, front office, and coaching. In their analysis, the Packers ranked first in their division and ahead of the Vikings (seventh), Lions (twelfth), and Bears (twenty-sixth). With an overall 91.3, the roster scored 88.3, quarterback 98.3, draft 91.7, front office 93, and coaching 87.3.[12]

According to these results, Green Bay overtook the Seattle Seahawks in rank since 2014. While the Packers' draft improved its score, the team earned top spots in the quarterback and front office categories. More specifically, the 2014 draft class helped the club when such players as receiver Davante Adams, center Corey Linsley, and tight end Richard Rodgers each made key rookie contributions to reach the NFC championship game. That had a tremendous impact for a team already a contender.

The Packers are incredibly well-positioned in terms of having most of their core players under contract on both offense and defense. The lone exception is along the offensive line, where Josh Sitton and a few other players will become unrestricted free agents following the team's 2016 season. How will the offense—which finished fifth, eighth, and first in scoring from 2012 to 2014, respectively—respond to a new offensive coordinator for the first time since Mike McCarthy became head coach in 2006? This is an important question going forward, as it was situational play calling that arguably cost the Packers a berth in Super Bowl XLIX.

For sure, the Packers' top overall ranking occurred primarily because of quarterback Aaron Rodgers, and a roster built almost exclusively with players who started their careers in Green Bay. General manager Ted Thompson has been successful at getting three or four starters out of every draft, signing most of them to second contracts, and drafting an excellent offensive line. For these reasons, the club will compete for more titles and championships in the future.

Minnesota Vikings

Professional football began in the Twin Cities with the Minneapolis Marines, who played in the APFA in 1921 and then in the NFL for another three years before the franchise folded during its 1924 season. Then in 1929–1930, the Minneapolis Red Jackets played as an NFL team but cancelled operations after the league's 1930 season.

A new professional football team in the area formed in August 1959 when three Minneapolis businessmen—Bill Boyer, H. P. Skoglund, and Max Winter—were awarded a franchise in the new AFL. However, five months later, the ownership group along with newspaper publisher Bernie Ridder forfeited its AFL membership and for a $600,000 expansion fee, became the NFL's fourteenth franchise and began to play in the league's 1961 season.

In 1960, sports executive Ole Haugsrud was added as an owner because of an agreement he had with the NFL since the late 1920s when he sold his NFL Duluth Eskimos team back to the league. The agreement allowed him 10 percent of any future Minnesota team. Nicknamed Vikings, it partly reflected Minnesota's place as a center of Scandinavian American culture. Interestingly the Vikings embraced a marketing program that produced first-year season ticket sales of nearly 26,000 and an average home attendance of about 85 percent of 40,800-seat Metropolitan Stadium.

Historical Results

A member of the league's Western Conference from 1961 to 1966 and the conference's Central Division until 1969, then the NFC's CD during 1970–2001 and finally the ND since 2002, the Vikings played 838 games and won approximately 53 percent of them. Among NFC teams as of their 2015–2016 season, Minnesota ranked ninth in number of wins, tied for fourth with the 49ers in winning percentage, tied for fifth with the 49ers in division titles and also tied for sixth with the Bears and Lions in winning their conference, tied for thirteenth with the Falcons, Panthers, and Cardinals in total championships, and fourth in qualifying for twenty-eight playoffs (Table A.5).

Compared to only ND clubs as of their 2015 season, the Vikings had the fewest wins and championships, tied for second in conference titles, but achieved a higher winning percentage and more division titles and playoff appearances than the Lions. Based on these results, this Minnesota-based NFL team has been mediocre in performances within the NFC but also below average against the Bears and Packers in its division.

Regarding the performances of thirty-one other NFL teams as of their 2015 season, the fifty-five-year-old Vikings ranked tenth both in wins, tied for eighth in winning percentage, tied for sixth in division titles, tied for tenth with the Bears, Lions, and Bills in conference titles and also tied for twentieth with twelve other teams in total number of championships each with zero of them, and fifth in qualifying for twenty-eight postseasons. These and other results prove that, except for such periods as the early to mid-1960s, mid-1980s, and early 2000s, Minnesota's NFL team has been competitive and primarily above average in performances while playing clubs in the NFC and against teams in the league's other conference (Table A.6).

While competing in the league's seasons and postseasons since 1961, the Vikings were led by both superior and inferior coaches. In number of wins, Bud Grant had 161, Dennis Green 101, and Jerry Burns 55. For their leadership, Grant was AP coach of the year in 1969 and twenty-three years later, Green won it in the NFC. In contrast to them, coaches Norm Van Brocklin, Les Steckel, Mike Tice, and Brad Childress each won fewer than 45 games.

Some of Minnesota's players were successful and established career, single season, and single game records for the franchise in various games and seasons. For example, career record holder Fran Tarkenton passed for 33,098 yards and 239 touchdowns; Chris Carter caught 1,004 passes for 12,383 yards; Fred Cox kicked 282 field goals; and John Randle had 114 sacks.

During a single season, Adrian Peterson rushed for 2,097 yards in 2012; Daunte Culpepper passed for 4,717 yards and 39 touchdowns in 2004; Paul Krause intercepted 10 passes in 1975; and Gary Anderson scored 164 points in 1998. In one game, Joe Kapp passed for 7 touchdowns (NFL record); Rickey Young caught 15 passes; Chuck Foreman and Ahmad Rashad each scored 24 points; and Randy Holloway had 5 sacks. Individually, these men were outstanding athletes while performing on various Vikings teams.

Beside coaches Grant and Green, some Vikings players won AP awards for playing at their position on the field. Defensive tackle Alan Page, quarterback Fran Tarkenton, and running back Adrian Peterson were each MVPs in the league. Other winners included offensive player of the year Tarkenton in 1975 and Peterson in 2012; offensive rookie of the year Paul Flatley in 1963,

Chuck Foreman in 1973, Sammy White in 1976, Randy Moss in 1998, and Percy Harvin in 2009; and defensive player of the year Page in 1971 and Keith Millard in 1989. In addition to Tarkenton, Rashad, Moss, and Peterson, tight end Kyle Rudolph was the pro bowl MVP in 2013.

Several of Minnesota's former players have been inducted into the pro football Hall of Fame. Michael Tingelhoff is the latest to be honored in Canton, Ohio. From 1962 to 1978, he played his entire career at center and never missed a start in 240 consecutive games. Tingelhoff made six pro bowls and was named first-team all-pro five times despite not being drafted. Besides appearing in three Super Bowls, he was a part of the team that won the Western Conference title game in 1969. Forty-six years later, Tingelhoff joined such athletes as Chris Doleman, Gary Zimmerman, and Carl Eller in the Hall of Fame.

Performance Highlights

Among its years in the league, Minnesota's most successful periods consecutively were 1968–1971, 1973–1978, 1987–1989, 1992–1994, and 1996–2000. In large part, these seasons of playoffs and winning titles occurred because of such quarterbacks as Joe Kapp, Fran Tarkenton, and Brad Johnson; rushers as Dave Osborn, Chuck Foreman, and Robert Smith; and receivers Gene Washington, Sammy White, and Randy Moss. Alternatively, the team's worst back-to-back performances took place during 1961–1967, 1983–1986, 2001–2003, and 2005–2007. For the most part, intense competition from teams in their division and conference and also ineffective Vikings players and inferior players were three reasons for these groups of dismal seasons.

At its home games in 52,000-seat TCF Bank Stadium, which opened in 2009, the club's attendances have been among the smallest in the league. While the NFL's average each season was in the mid-500,000s, the number of spectators at the team's games from 2009 to 2015 ranged from the low 400,000s to the 500,000s. Simply put, Minnesota football fans are not dedicated or very passionate about attending their hometown team's games, in part, because of the club's performances against the Bears, Lions, and Packers in the ND and from appearing in only five playoffs since 2001.

Among other NFL venues, TCF Bank Stadium ranked twenty-fifth in a recent study. According to an article published about it in an edition of *Sporting News*, the author wrote:

> Until that time [2016], the NFL club plays in one of the nicer facilities in college football [University of Minnesota's football venue]. The video board is one of the nicest screens in the FBS [Football Bowl Subdivision] and in a 50,000-seat stadium; the views are still decent at the top of the building. For

> fans walking around the campus, the student hangouts along the Dinkytown drag provide options to eat and drink outside of traditional tailgating.[13]

Minnesota's bid for Super Bowl LII was successful when selected on May 20, 2014 as the host community for the world-renowned event. The game itself will be played at the new Minnesota Stadium but the entire greater Twin Cities metro area will accommodate the week-long festivities. Announced on November 14, 2014, the iconic new Minnesota Stadium was awarded 2019 NCAA Men's Final Four to be held April 6–8, 2019. Minnesota was awarded the high profile event after a multi-year bid process.[14]

FRANCHISE BUSINESS

Besides performing as teams in regular season and postseason games, NFL franchises are also commercial enterprises. To that end, their economic objective is to earn maximum revenue and obtain the greatest amount of profit on a fiscal basis from their operations. Although they share revenue with each other from such sources as national television contracts and other deals, it is important for them to efficiently allocate resources, determine and distribute payrolls, set nonpremium and premium ticket prices, and schedule investments in short and long-term assets. To reveal and manage these activities, this section focuses on different parts of four NFC franchises' business and how these organizations rank and succeed or not succeed from a financial perspective.

Chicago Bears

Born in 1923, Virginia Halas McCaskey is the principal owner of the franchise. She is the eldest child of legendary Bears coach and former owner George Halas, who left the team to his daughter upon his death in 1983. Along with her children and grandchildren, she controls the majority of the club's operations.[15]

Virginia's son Michael was team president from 1983 to 1999 and chairman of the board until May 2011, when his brother George assumed the position. During early 2011, former team vice president Tim McCaskey died from cancer. The second oldest of Ed and Virginia McCaskey's eleven children, he had held that position since 1993.

Team Financials

According to data and other financial information published in *Forbes* for sixteen franchises in the NFC as of their 2015–2016 season, the Bears ranked fifth in market value at $2.45 billion and also sixth in revenue at $352 million, gate receipts at $67 million, and operating income at $85 million. In addition, the club tied for fourth with the 49ers in player's expenses at $168 million, and tied for fifteenth with the Panthers' debt-to-value ratio of 4 percent. Within the conference's ND, Chicago had the highest amounts but the lowest debt ratio among the group (Table A.7).

Regarding thirty-one other NFL teams in 2015, Chicago ranked eighth in market value, ninth in revenue, tenth in both gate receipts and operating income, tied for eighth with the 49ers in player expenses, and tied for fifteenth in its percent of debt-to-value. Based on these results, the Bears are an above-average team from a financial perspective and also a valuable franchise and prosperous business enterprise (Table A.8).

For several years a Chicago-based company named Team Marketing Report (TMR) has prepared and published a Fan Cost Index (FCI) for the home games of teams in professional sports leagues. To attend a game for a typical family with two kids, an FCI includes the costs of four average-priced tickets, two cheapest-priced draft beers, four each cheapest-priced soft drinks and hot dogs, parking for one car, and two each game programs and least-expensive, adult-size adjustable caps. Costs are determined by telephone calls with team representatives, venues, and concessionaires, and from asking questions during interviews.[16]

For their 2015 season, the Bears' FCI was approximately $601 or fifth highest in the league and almost 1 percent more than in 2014. Listed from most to least in amount by item for one person, the team's nonpremium tickets averaged about $108, parking for one vehicle $49, cap $25 and a beer more than $9, and a soft drink, hot dog, and program each $5. For FCIs of other ND clubs in the NFC, the Packers were eleventh at $495, Vikings sixteenth at $474, and Lions twentieth at $437. Based on the league's FCI of $480, it is relatively expensive for spectators to buy any nonpremium tickets and attend a Bears game at Soldier Field.

At $322 each, the Bears had the sixth highest average premium ticket price in the league or approximately 26 percent more than the typical team's. Thus, Chicago, Illinois, is a large, lucrative, and popular market for professional football while also being the home site of the Major League Baseball (MLB) Cubs and White Sox, National Basketball Association (NBA) Bulls, National Hockey League (NHL) Blackhawks, and Major League Soccer (MLS) Fire.

Business Highlights

Using fifteen years of data on such things as NFL team performances, home-game ticket prices, and market populations and their median incomes, Emory University researchers created an equity index to determine which clubs had the most avid, engaged, passionate, and/or supportive fans before the NFL's

2015 season. Among the NFC's ND teams, the Bears ranked sixth and above the Packers at seventh, Vikings eighteenth, and Lions twenty-fifth. As such, Chicago has more enthusiastic football fans than thirteen other NFC teams and a majority of those in the AFC.[17]

In another Emory University index titled Social Media Equity, the Bears had the league's eleventh best fan base following the division's Packers in fourth but ahead of the Lions in fourteenth and Vikings in twentieth. Although this index reflects whether teams over- or underperform with respect to their Twitter following, Bears fans are more involved or passionate about their hometown team on social media than those of twenty-one other NFL clubs. Interestingly, the Steelers had the leagues most dedicated and fervent fan base while the Cardinals ranked thirty-second.

For other important business news regarding the Bears franchise, Cook County will make it harder for ticket brokers to do business in Chicago. Its plan is to apply a 3 percent amusement tax to event tickets that are resold for more than face value. The county currently collects the tax from the city's professional sports teams when they sell their tickets, but does not get it from people who profit from reselling tickets to high-demand games for more than they originally paid. The county's goal is to recapture revenue from the secondary market for important events, when tickets change hands for much more than people paid when they bought them from the team.[18]

In addition to that news event, daily fantasy website FanDuel was among the new brands on display at Soldier Field at the opening game in September 2015. The Bears signed a new sponsorship deal with the New York-based site, which has been on an advertising spending spree to get as many people as possible into daily fantasy sports. FanDuel, which offers fantasy sports games that last only one day or week instead of an entire season, added the Bears to a list of fifteen other NFL teams that signed marketing partnerships with the site this year [2015].[19]

According to one source, the club's advertising campaign is not drastically different from the new billboards it debuted in 2014. However, it's trying to be more precise in reaching specific groups of fans. That means using more of its ads to call fans to action for specific events such as the team's Family Fest and second-annual 5,000-meter run, as well as target specific demographic populations. Some billboards, aimed specifically at Chicago's growing Latino population, will rove around summer festivals in various largely Hispanic neighborhoods.[20]

The newly built, 15,000-square-foot-plus club space behind sections 136 and 138 on Soldier Field's west side changed names before it opened. Originally dubbed by the team and its corporate partner Comcast as "The Den," the area's new official name is "The Midway" with Xfinity as the space's presenting sponsor. The club section, which includes an upscale sports bar that fans are able to pay to use during games, made its debut during late July

2015 at the International Champions Cup soccer match between Manchester United and Paris St. Germain. The Bears and Soldier Field Management Company used funding from stadium concessionaire Aramark to build out the space during the offseason. Aramark, meanwhile, committed $10 million toward stadium infrastructure upgrades when it signed a ten-year concessions contract with the Chicago Park District–owned venue in 2013.[21]

In sum, the Bears are one of only six NFL teams to play in a venue without a corporate name attached to it. However, in April 2015, the team inked a naming rights deal with PNC Financial Services Group for Halas Hall and luxury seats at Soldier Field. The deal is expected to net as much as $35 million as PNC replaces Chase as the club's official bank. Nonetheless, the Bears' sponsorship revenue still lags behind other big-market NFL teams.

Detroit Lions

When her husband William Clay Ford Sr. as the last surviving grandson of Henry died of pneumonia, eighty-nine-year-old Martha Firestone Ford became owner of the franchise in the spring of 2014. Their son, William Clay Ford Jr., is a vice chairman and his sisters—Martha Ford Morse, Sheila Ford Hamp, and Elizabeth Ford Kontulis—are vice chairwomen.[22]

According to various sources, Martha attends all the team's games and frequently speaks to president Tom Lewand, general manager Martin Mayhew, and head coach Jim Caldwell about the club's performances and strategies in games and seasons. Apparently she reads about, studies, and really understands football, and asks questions regarding specific players and the coaching staff. Besides that information, Mrs. Ford has been in the team's war room during a recent NFL draft. She has also represented the franchise at league meetings.

Martha Ford is among a small group of female team owners. The others are Virginia Halas McCaskey, ninety-two, owner of the Chicago Bears since 1983, when her father, George, died. Also Carol Davis, along with her son Mark, own the largest stake in the league's Oakland Raiders since her husband, Al Davis, died in 2011.

Team Financials

According to data and other financial information published in *Forbes* for sixteen franchises in the NFC as of their 2015 season, the Lions ranked sixteenth in market value at $1.44 billion and fourteenth in both revenue at $298 million and player expenses at $156 million, thirteenth in both gate receipts at $52 million and operating income at $36 million, and fourth in its debt-to-value ratio of 19 percent. Among only ND clubs in the conference, Detroit had the smallest value and player expenses, second lowest revenue, gate receipts and operating income, but also second highest debt ratio. Based on these results the Lions are a low-valued team from a financial perspective and also a marginally profitable franchise with too much debt and not enough revenue from its operations with respect to fifteen different clubs in the conference (Table A.7).

Compared to thirty-one other NFL teams as of their 2015 season, the Lions were thirty-first in market value, twenty-seventh in revenue, tied for twenty-fourth with the Titans in gate receipts, twenty-eighth in operating income, twenty-fifth in player expenses, and tied for fifth with the Dolphins in their debt ratio. Overall, this team is an inferior organization financially because of these below-average amounts and their current and future impact on operations. Owner Martha Ford and her executive staffs need to demand realistic but accurate and current budgets and pro forma statements that reflect the team's financial shortcomings including its cash, income, and profit (Table A.8).

For their 2015 season, the Lions' FCI was approximately $437 or twentieth highest in the league and 6.2 percent more than in 2014. Listed from most to least in amount by item for one person, the team's nonpremium tickets averaged approximately $79, a cap $25 and parking for one vehicle $11, a beer between $7 and $8, hot dog $6, and a soft drink $5. For FCIs of other ND clubs in the conference, the Bears ranked fifth at $601, Packers eleventh at $495, and Vikings sixteenth at $474. In other words, it is relatively inexpensive for a family of four to attend an NFL game at Ford Field in Detroit partly because the hometown team has appeared in only two playoffs since 2000 and also seeks more attendance and spending from fans while there.[23]

At $159 each, the Lions had the second lowest average premium ticket price in the league and significantly below the Bears' $322, Packers' $255, and Vikings' $203, and also $96 or approximately 60 percent less than the typical team's. Consequently Detroit is not a lucrative or popular market for professional football and Lions games, in part, because of its weak economy and being a home site for the NBA Pistons, MLB Tigers, and NHL Red Wings.

Business Highlights

Using fifteen years of data on such things as NFL team performances, home-game ticket prices, and market populations and their median incomes, Emory University researchers created an equity index to determine which clubs had the most avid, engaged, passionate, and/or supportive fans before the NFL's 2015 season. Among the NFC's ND teams, the Lions ranked twenty-fifth and inferior to the Bears at sixth, Packers at seventh, and Vikings at eighteenth. Apparently, Detroit has less enthusiastic football fans than the other NFC teams and a majority of those in the AFC.

In another Emory University index titled Social Media Equity, the Lions had the league's fourteenth best fan base following the division's Packers in fourth and Bears in eleventh but ahead of the Vikings in twentieth. Although this index reflects whether teams over- or underperform with respect to their Twitter following, Lions fans are more involved or passionate about their hometown team on social media than those of eighteen other NFL clubs. Interestingly, the Steelers had the league's most dedicated and fervent fan base while the Cardinals ranked thirty-second.

Eight months after the 2014 season, one of the Lions' top executives left the team on the eve of the regular season. Luis Perez, who had joined the franchise as chief executive officer in 2011 and later became its senior vice president of business development and strategy, resigned from his position with the club. It was not clear why Perez left or whether he accepted another job in the sport. Perez was replaced by chief financial officer Allison Maki. He was a former managing director of Maryland-based Modell Ventures Limited Liability Corporation (LLC) and before that, the chief financial officer of the Baltimore Ravens from 1998 to 2004.

During May 2015, the Lions and a nonprofit organization named the Detroit Sports Commission submitted a bid to host the 2019 college football national championship game. The game's executives toured and evaluated the team's stadium and also the downtown area to determine if the city and its facilities fit the game's requirements. Detroit opted for 2019 because it was the only one of three years that did not conflict with the media preview days for the annual North American International Auto Show at the Cobo Center. The city estimates a cost of $13 million to stage the championship event. That cost, which would likely increase, includes travel, housing, and renting different venues for the various activities planned around the game such as concerts and fan fests.[24]

Although the Lions lost to the Cowboys in the conference's 2014 wild card playoffs, they still might cash in on their winning season because of making the playoffs for the second time in four years. In Ford Field's variable-pricing system for seats in regular seasons, games are designated as "touchdown" or "field goal" levels. In the 2015 season, for example, there are three premier "touchdown" games while the other five at Ford Field each cost spectators less money.[25]

Green Bay Packers

After owner Curly Lambeau and the Packers went broke following the 1923 NFL season, a group of Green Bay, Wisconsin–based businessmen made a loan to the team and also established a non-profit, publicly-owned corporation to operate it. The corporation, which has more than 350,000 stockholders who collectively own in excess of five million shares of stock, is governed by a seven-member executive committee, elected from among the board of directors. The committee directs corporate management, approves major capital expenditures, establishes board policy, and monitors management's performance in conducting the business and affairs of the corporation.

For official shareholder rules as outlined in the official Green Bay Packers Inc. shareholder and financial history, stock shares include voting rights but the redemption price is minimal. There are no dividends or season-ticket privileges associated with stock ownership. No shareholder is allowed to own more than 200,000 shares, a safeguard to ensure that an individual is unable to assume financial control of the club.

Team Financials

According to data and other financial information published in *Forbes* for sixteen franchises in the NFC as of their 2015–2016 season, the Packers ranked seventh in both market value at $1.95 billion and revenue at $347 million, tied for seventh with the Panthers in gate receipts at $65 million, ninth in operating income at $63 million, twelfth in player expenses at $159 million, and tied for eleventh with the Seahawks in their debt-to-value ratio of 6 percent. Among only the conference's ND teams, Green Bay was second in market value, revenue, gate receipts, operating income and player expenses, and also had the third highest debt ratio (Table A.7).

Compared to thirty-one other NFL teams as of their 2015 season, the Packers were tenth in both market value and revenue, tied for eleventh in gate receipts, sixteenth in operating income, tied for twentieth in player expenses, and tied for twenty-fourth in their debt ratio. Because of its enthusiastic fan base, culture, tradition, and all-time performances, this club is average to above average financially among others in both the NFC and league despite being located in a remote urban area with a relatively small and slow-growing population (Table A.8).

For their 2015 season, the Packers' FCI was approximately $495 or eleventh highest in the league and 1.9 percent more than in 2014. Listed from most to least in amount by item for one person, the team's nonpremium tickets averaged about $89, parking for one vehicle $40, a cap almost $15, one beer $8, program $6, and a hot dog and soft drink each between $4 and $6. Other ND teams' FCIs were the Bears' $601 at fifth, Vikings' $474 at sixteenth and Lions' $437 at twentieth. In other words, Green Bay charged spectators $4 more for its regular-season games at Lambeau Field than the league's average non-premium ticket price or an additional $15 in total costs.

In addition to these amounts, the Packers' premium ticket price averaged $255 in 2015 and the same as a typical team in the league. While the ND's Bears' was $322, Vikings' $203, and Lions' $159; Green Bay's was less than those charged by five NFC teams. Based on several factors including home attendances, stadium amenities, and costs for families to attend other entertainment events in the area, the Packers set prices for premium seats and food, beverage, merchandise, and other items at Lambeau Field to maximize revenue and increase their gate receipts and operating income.

Business Highlights

Using fifteen years of data, Emory University researchers created an equity index to determine which clubs had the most avid, engaged, passionate, and/or supportive fans before the NFL's 2015 season. Among the NFC's ND teams, the Packers ranked seventh and below the Bears at sixth but above the Vikings at eighteenth and Lions at twenty-fifth. Thus, Green Bay has more enthusiastic and engaged football fans than a dozen other NFC teams and also a majority of those in the AFC.

In another Emory University index titled Social Media Equity, the Packers had the league's fourth best fan base and superior to the Bears in eleventh, Lions in fourteenth, and Vikings in twentieth. Although this index reflects whether teams over- or underperform with respect to their Twitter following, Packers fans are more involved or passionate about their hometown team on social media than those of twenty-eight other NFL clubs.

For other news about the Packers' organization, its officials unveiled plans for the development of a commercial district near Lambeau Field that could cost up to $130 million in private money. Named "Titletown District," the development may include a luxury hotel, sports medicine center, a public square complete with ice-skating rink, a brewery, and perhaps more attractions. Constructed on thirty acres of land, it will also contain some residential units. The Packers expect to invest roughly $65 million into the project, while at least three local companies will contribute a combined $65 million.[26]

In contrast to for-profit professional sports franchises, the Packers will never leave Wisconsin even though they exist in the NFL's least-populated market. When the team needed money to upgrade their stadium in 2011, they did not hold local taxpayers hostage and force the city to choose between keeping them and cutting public services. Rather, they simply sold 185,000 shares at $250 each. Even though Green Bay competes with some teams located in markets ten times its size, the club's shareholders are committed and do a responsible job of managing them. In fact, they are favorites to win consecutive titles while still being one of about fifteen franchises that pay into the NFL's reserve fund, rather than withdraw money from it.

In some ways, the Packers and local taxpayers are ahead of others when it comes to stadium debt payments even though the Brown County sales tax used to renovate Lambeau Field in 2003 expired in 2015. The Green Bay/Brown County Professional Football Stadium District, which receives money from a 0.5 percent county sales tax, paid off bonds used for the stadium's $295 million renovation in 2011 and needs $91 million to cover its maintenance responsibilities through the end of the Packers' lease in 2031. Even so, they will meet their financing goals.[27]

Minnesota Vikings

Born in Germany, Zygmunt "Zigi" Wilf—whose father Joseph was a well-known real estate developer in the country and escaped the Holocaust in Nazi-occupied Poland with his wife Elizabeth—migrated to America with his family during the early 1950s to live and become citizens. An excellent student with a keen aptitude for business, Zigi completed his bachelor's degree in economics from Fairleigh Dickinson University in 1971 and later graduated from Manhattan's New York Law School.[28]

After working awhile as an attorney, Wilf joined the family business and later headed the Garden Commercial Properties. From four shopping centers, the company expanded into more than a hundred real estate properties which included two large malls. An avid fan of the New York Giants in the 1960s, billionaire Zigi and five partners acquired the Minnesota Vikings for $600 million in 2005 after which he became majority owner of the franchise.

Team Financials

According to data and other financial information published in *Forbes* for sixteen franchises in the NFC as of their 2015–2016 season, the Vikings ranked tenth in market value at $1.59 billion, sixteenth in revenue at $281 million, fifteenth in gate receipts at $47 million, tied for fourteenth with the Rams in operating income at $34 million, thirteenth in player expenses at $157 million, and second in their debt-to-value ratio of 31 percent. Among the conferences' ND teams, Minnesota had the third highest market value and player expenses, the smallest revenue, gate receipts and operating income, but the most debt-to-value percentage-wise (Table A.7).

Compared to thirty other NFL teams as of their 2015 season, the Vikings were eighteenth in market value, thirty-second or last in revenue, thirtieth in gate receipts, tied for twenty-ninth in operating income, twenty-fourth in player expenses, and second in their debt ratio. Although the team appeared in ten playoffs from 1996 to 2015, it struggles fiscally to generate enough money from its gate receipts and other operations at games in TCF Bank Stadium. From a financial perspective, it is one of the least profitable and most indebted franchises in the league (Table A.8).

For its 2015 season, the Vikings' FCI was approximately $474 or sixteenth highest in the league although 3.2 percent less than in 2014. Listed from most to least in amount by item for one person, the team's nonpremium tickets averaged $84, a cap $25 and parking one vehicle $15, a beer $7, program $5, and a hot dog and soft drink each $3. Among other ND teams, the Bears FCI ranked fifth at $601, Packers eleventh at $495, and Lions twentieth at $437.[29]

In addition to these amounts, the Vikings' premium ticket price averaged $203 in 2015 but below the league's by $53 or 26 percent. While the Bears' was $322, Packers' $255, and Lions' $159, Minnesota's was less than those charged by most NFL teams. Based on several factors including home attendances, stadium amenities, and costs for families to attend the games of the MLB Twins and NBA Timberwolves, the Vikings set prices for tickets, food, beverage, merchandise, and other items at TCF Bank Stadium to maximize revenue and increase their operating income.

Business Highlights

Using fifteen years of data, Emory University researchers created an equity index to determine which clubs had the most avid, engaged, passionate, and/or supportive fans before the NFL's 2015 season. Among the NFC's ND teams, the Vikings ranked eighteenth and below the Bears at sixth and Packers at seventh but above the Lions at twenty-fifth. Thus, Minnesota has fewer enthusiastic football fans than eight NFC teams and several of those in the AFC.

In another Emory University index titled Social Media Equity, the Vikings had the league's twentieth best fan base and inferior to the Packers in fourth, Bears in eleventh and Lions in fourteenth. Although this index reflects whether teams over- or underperform with respect to their Twitter following, Vikings fans are less involved or passionate about their hometown team on social media than those of nineteen other NFL clubs.

For other news about the organization, the Vikings have a redevelopment plan that would dramatically reshape the former Northwest Airlines headquarters in Eagan, Minnesota, by making the area a high school football hub and adding housing, shops, and offices to the city's landscape. The team has agreements to purchase 194 acres at the former airline's campus near the intersection of Interstate 494 and Dodd Road.[30]

More specifically the project will include a thirty-acre practice facility to anchor the development with three outdoor grass fields, a roughly 150,000-square-foot indoor training facility, and a 7,000 to 10,000-seat outdoor stadium to host high school football games. The Northwest Airlines office building, totaling about 275,000 square feet, will be demolished and replaced by shops. While a new office building is constructed on the east side of the property, the west side of the property will contain a hotel with 120 to 150 rooms and a 100,000 to 200,000 square-foot conference center. In the northwest corner of the site, plans are to build 500 to 800 housing units of an undetermined type.

To highlight them as a business enterprise, the Vikings will move into a new $1 billion stadium for the 2016 NFL season. The stadium received a corporate name when U.S. Bancorp, fifth largest in America by assets, inked a twenty-year deal worth more than $200 million. The team's share of stadium costs is expected to be $550 million, but $125 million of it will be covered by "stadium-builder" licenses that season ticket holders must obtain for the right to purchase regular-season tickets. The franchise also accepted $200 million from the NFL as part of its G-4 stadium financing program. Those proceeds will be repaid from club seat revenue normally shared with the NFL's other thirty-one teams. As of mid-June 2015, the Vikings had leased 70 percent of the stadium's 131 suites.[31]

In sum, the Bears are the most prosperous and valuable team in the conference's ND. They have the highest market value, total revenue, gate receipts and operating income, and the most player expenses. Ranked next in the group, from a financial perspective, are the Packers and then the Vikings or Lions. While they compete in home and away games during NFL seasons and perhaps in postseasons, these clubs are unique and thus different in other ways especially regarding their business models, financial accounts and amounts, and levels of commercial success.

NOTES

1. Historical team performances and their coaches and players, by season, are in the *NFL Record & Fact Book 2014* (New York: NFL, 2014) and online at "Teams," http://www.pro-football-reference.com, cited August 25, 2015.
2. Besides the Data Supplement on pages 409–34 of *Pay Dirt*, other information including NFL team attendances and financial amounts are contained at the website of "Rod Fort's Sports Business Data," http://www.sites.google.com, cited September 1, 2015.
3. The reference is "Ranking All 31 NFL Stadiums," http://www.sportingnews.com, cited August 31, 2015.
4. The article to read is "2015 NFL Future Power Rankings," http://www.insider.espn.go.com, cited October 10, 2015.
5. Along with those in note 2, another research source for information about teams is "NFL Links," http://www.sportsecyclopdia.com, cited August 25, 2015.
6. For attendance data of all clubs in various seasons and postseasons of the league, see nfl.com, pro-reference.com, and the sources in note 3 above.
7. Besides note 3, another reference is Michael Potts, "Ranking All NFL Stadiums for 2015—From Worst to Best," http://www.whatculture.com, cited September 2, 2015.
8. The Lions' performance expectations for three seasons are in "2015 NFL Future Power Rankings," http://www.insider.espn.go.com cited October 10, 2015.
9. The historical performances of Packers teams are reported in the same readings as the Bears, Lions, and Vikings.
10. For attendances of NFL teams, there is a data base at "Rod Fort's Sports Business Data," http://www.sites.google.com, cited September 1, 2015, and http://www.espn.go.com.
11. "Ranking All 31 NFL Stadiums," http://www.sportingnews.com, cited August 31, 2015.
12. See note 8 for the future power ranking of the Green Bay Packers in 2015–2017.
13. This quote about the Vikings venue appeared in *Sporting News* article "Ranking All 31 NFL Stadiums."

14. "Minnesota Vikings History Timeline," http://www.vikings.com, cited December 16, 2015.

15. One source is: "NFL Team Owners," http://www.biography.yourdictionary.com cited December 24, 2015.

16. For two recent years of FCIs for the Bears, Lions, Packers, and Vikings, see "2014 NFL Fan Cost Index," https://www.teammarketing.com, cited August 26, 2015, and "2015 NFL Fan Cost Index," https://www.teammarketing.com, cited November 20, 2015.

17. To review indexes for teams in the conference's ND, the articles are Manish Tripathi, "2015 NFL Fan Equity Rankings," https://scholarblogs.emory.edu cited September 4, 2015, and Michael Lewis, "2015 NFL Social Media Equity Rankings," https://scholarblogs.emory.edu, cited September 4, 2015.

18. See Danny Ecker, "The Game Is Getting Harder for Chicago Ticket Brokers," http://www.chicagobusiness.com, cited October 22, 2015.

19. The reading for this information is Danny Ecker, "FanDuel among New Bears Corporate Partners," http://www.chicagobusiness.com, cited October 22, 2015.

20. The reference is Danny Ecker, "Here's the Bears' 2015 Ad Campaign," http://www.chicagobusiness.com, cited December 8, 2015.

21. Steve Seiferheld, "Total Recall: Which On-Site Factors Make Fans Remember Brands?" *SportsBusiness Journal* (April 22, 2013): 15.

22. For Lions owners, see John Bacon, "William Clay Ford: The Detroit Lions' Company Man," *Wall Street Journal* (March 12, 2014): 1.

23. The FCI and fan equity and social equity media indexes for the Lions appear in the same articles as the Bears, Packers, and Vikings.

24. Bill Shea, "Detroit Bids to Host 2019 College Football Championship Game at Ford Field," http://www.crainsdetroit.com, cited October 21, 2015.

25. Daniel Kaplan, "Lions' Variable Pricing Will be the First for NFL," *SportsBusiness Journal* (January 27, 2014): 5. Another reading about the team's business is Sharon Terlep, "A Mystery in the Lions' Den," *Wall Street Journal* (December 23, 2015): D6.

26. "Packers Unveil 'Titletown' Development Plans for Area Near Lambeau Field," http://www.espn.go.com, cited October 22, 2015.

27. Daniel Kaplan, "Future Bodes Well for Packers' Income," *SportsBusiness Journal* (July 14, 2014): 3.

28. "Minnesota Vikings History Timeline" and "NFL Team Owners" have facts about Zigi Wilf's personal and business careers.

29. "2015 NFL Fan Cost Index" contains amounts for the Vikings.

30. See Nick Halter, "Vikings Redevelopment Plan Adds to Ongoing Eagan Retail Boom," http://www.bizjournals.com, cited October 21, 2015.

31. Rochelle Olson, "New Vikings Stadium Will Be Named for U.S. Bank," http://www.startribune.com, cited October 29, 2015, and Don Muret, "Finance Still Bullish on Naming Rights," *SportsBusiness Journal* (June 22, 2015): 3.

Chapter Seven

South Division

Which National Football League (NFL) team or teams in the South Division (SD) of the National Football Conference (NFC) won the most games all-time as of early 2016 and also had the lowest winning percentage, largest number of division and conference titles, least Super Bowl championships, and appeared in the fewest playoffs? Are the Atlanta Falcons a more valuable franchise than the New Orleans Saints and approximately what do the Carolina Panthers and Tampa Bay Buccaneers each earn in revenue, gate receipts, and operating income?

In response to these and other questions, next are some interesting but important, realistic, and relevant facts that highlight the historical performances of four teams in the NFC's SD as of the league's 2015–2016, or simply 2015, season. Besides their winning percentage and number of seasons, wins, titles, championships, and playoffs, this information includes special coaches, players, and events regarding each of them while competing in the NFL's regular seasons and any playoffs. In the chapter's final section—labelled Franchise Business—are these franchises' success or failure as business enterprises both individually and in comparison to each other from a financial perspective.[1]

TEAM PERFORMANCES

Atlanta Falcons

To keep his team from joining the rival AFL, NFL Commissioner Pete Rozelle granted an expansion franchise for $8.5 million in June 1965 to forty-one-year-old Rankin M. Smith Sr., an executive vice president of Life Insurance Company of Georgia. Falcons—which a high school teacher from

Griffin, Georgia, had suggested in a contest—became the team's nickname. Before late December, Georgia fans purchased 45,000 season tickets, an NFL record for a new team.[2]

As his first pick in the 1966 NFL Draft, Smith chose University of Texas linebacker Tommy Nobis, making him the first ever Falcons' player. Early speculation on the team's first head coach focused on a host of men including former University of Oklahoma's Bud Wilkerson, University of Arkansas's Frank Broyles, Cleveland Browns' Paul Brown, and Green Bay Packers' Vince Lombardi. In the end Smith selected Lombardi's six-year assistant, Norb Hecker. Although Lombardi did not recommend Hecker, Smith hired him anyway thinking Lombardi was not being totally straightforward about his assistant.

Historical Results

A member of the Eastern Conference in 1966, Western Conference's Coastal Division from 1967 to 1969, NFC's Western Division during 1970–2001 and then the conference's South Division (SD) since 2002, the Falcons played 768 games and won approximately 43 percent of them. Among clubs in the NFC as of their 2015 season, Atlanta ranked eleventh in number of wins, fourteenth in winning percentage, tied for thirteenth with the Saints in division titles and also with three different teams in conference titles, tied for thirteenth with three teams in number of championships, and eleventh in qualifying for twelve playoffs (Table A.5).

Compared to only SD teams in the conference as of the league's 2015–2016 season, Atlanta had fewer total wins than the Saints, third highest winning percentage, and most playoff appearances of the group, and tied for first or second with one or more clubs in division and conference titles and also in their number of championships. According to these results, the Falcons have performed below average in the SD and NFC during their fifty-year history because of coaching problems, inferior and/or inexperienced players, strong competition from their rivals, and such other things as failing to draft competent college athletes and trying to solve franchise ownership issues.

With respect to the performances of thirty-one other NFL teams as of their 2015 season, the Georgia-based Falcons ranked eighteenth in number of wins, twenty-eighth in winning percentage, tied for twenty-third with the Saints in division titles, tied for twenty-second in winning their conference, and tied for twentieth in number of championships and also with the Jets in qualifying for twelve playoffs. These and other results prove that, except for nine years during 1978–2008 and from 2010 to 2012, Atlanta's NFL team has been below average competitively while playing clubs in the NFC and against those in divisions of the AFC (Table A.6).

In regular season and postseason games since 1966, Atlanta had some successful and unsuccessful coaches as leaders of its teams. Based on number of wins as of 2014, coach Mike Smith had 67, Dan Reeves 52, and Leeman Bennett 47. For their excellent leadership, Reeves was Associated Press (AP) coach of the year in 1998 and Smith in 2008. Since each of them won fewer than 5 games, the least successful coaches besides Norb Heckler include Pat Peppler, Jim Hanifan, Wade Phillips, Bobby Petrino, and Emmitt Thomas.

Some Falcons players established career, single season, and single game records for the franchise. For example, a few career record holders are Steve Bartkowski passing for 23,470 yards and 154 touchdowns; Roddy White receiving 685 passes for 9,436 yards; and Morten Andersen kicking 184 field goals and scoring 806 points. In a single season, Jamal Anderson rushed for 1,846 yards in 1998; Scott Case intercepted 10 passes in 1988; and John Abraham sacked opposing quarterbacks 16.5 times in 2008.

During a single game, Chris Chandler passed for 431 yards and Wade Wilson 5 touchdowns; William Andrews caught 15 passes; and T. J. Duckett and Michael Turner each scored 4 touchdowns and 24 points. Individually and as a group, these were outstanding performances by Atlanta's players in seasons and specific games for the team.

Besides coaches, the AP gives awards to NFL players each year for performances at their respective positions on the field. While no Falcons became NFL Most Valuable Player (MVP) and/or offensive or defensive player of the year, quarterback Matt Ryan was offensive rookie of the year in 2008 and end Claude Humphrey defensive rookie of the year in 1968 and linebackers Buddy Curry and Al Richardson in 1980. In addition to them, Andre Rison won the pro bowl MVP award in 1994 for his performance as wide receiver of the NFC team.

Five former Falcons players are in the pro football Hall of Fame. Inducted in 2014, Claude Humphrey was a first-round pick in the league's 1968 draft and completed his career as the all-time sack leader in franchise history with 94.5 of them. He also ranks third in Atlanta annals with 15.6 sacks in a single season and tied for the franchise lead with six pro bowl selections including five straight from 1970 to 1974. Besides him, other Hall of Famers includes cornerback Deion Sanders in the 2011 class; running backs Tommy McDonald in 1998 and Eric Dickerson in 1999; and defensive end Chris Doleman in 2012. These were all-time great players and well respected by their opponents in Falcons games.[3]

Performance Highlights

While in the league since 1966, Atlanta's most successful periods consecutively were 2010–2012 and then previously during one year in the 1970s, two in the 1980s, three in the 1990s, and another three within 2002 to 2008. In large part, these seasons of playoffs and winning titles occurred because of such quarterbacks as Steve Bartkowski, Mike Vick, and Matt Ryan; rushers William Andrews, Warrick Dunn, and Michael Turner; and receivers Alfred Jenkins, Bert Emanuel, and Roddy White. Alternatively, the team's worst back-to-back performances happened during 1966–1977, 1983–1990, 1992–1994, 1999–2001, 2005–2007, and 2013–2015. For the most part, Falcons' coaching problems and poor player performances in games contributed to losses during these regular seasons of the NFL.

At its home games in the 71,281-seat Georgia Dome, which opened in 1992, the club's attendances have been neither the lowest nor highest in the league. While the NFL's average each season was in the mid-500,000s, the number of spectators at Falcons games between 2004 and 2015, for example, ranged from 515,000 to 575,000 and ranked in the middle part of the NFC. Simply put, thousands of Atlanta football fans are not extremely passionate about their hometown team because of its failure to consistently defeat the Panthers and Saints in the SD and also for appearing in only six playoffs and one conference final since 2000. Another year like 1998, when they played in a Super Bowl game, would boost fan attendances at least temporarily for the Falcons.[4]

Among thirty-one NFL venues, the Georgia Dome ranked twenty-ninth in a recent study. According to an article published about it in an edition of *Sporting News*, the author wrote:

> The dirty birds will play out their string at the Georgia Dome before moving to a new stadium next door in 2017. The new venue features a radical retractable roof design influenced by a popular children's toy. The 23-year-old dome has served its purpose, though. It's played host to the National Collegiate Athletic Association [NCAA] and also the Final Four, Super Bowl, and SEC [Southeast Conference Conference] football championship. Many fans take public transportation to Falcons games and those driving must pick their spots to find parking. One lot south of the dome, dubbed 'The Gulch,' is named for the original street level of Atlanta in the 1880s.[5]

In the Entertainment Sports Programming Network's (ESPN) future power rankings, the network asked three experts to rate each NFL team for three seasons (2015–2017) on a scale of 0 to 100 percent in five categories including roster (excluding quarterback), quarterback, draft, front office, and coaching. In their analysis, the Falcons ranked nineteenth in the NFL and third among SD teams following the Panthers in tenth and Saints in eighteenth but ahead of the Buccaneers in the bottom third of the league.[6]

For a few seasons in the future, there is no question about the Falcons' talent offensively. With a passing game that features quarterback Matt Ryan and wide receivers Julio Jones and Roddy White, Atlanta will be difficult to slow down from scoring for most teams. If the club develops a consistent rushing attack, they should be one of the league's top offenses. To further improve, they hired former Seattle Seahawks defensive coordinator Dan Quinn to be the team's new head coach and also spent their first round pick on Vic Beasley, an explosive outside linebacker with game-changing ability. Yet, they still have weaknesses with defensive linemen, linebackers, and cornerbacks. Whether the Falcons win their division depends, for the most part, on their ability to keep opponents out of the end zones.

After the departure of Coach Mike Smith, who led his team to four playoffs from 2008 to 2014, Atlanta will need to regroup under new head coach Dan Quinn. General manager Thomas Dimitroff and his staff are expected to operate the franchise and continue its improvement in 2015 and years thereafter by drafting college players with potential at their positions, signing free agents to fill positions particularly on defense, and provide fans with an exciting and successful club in the conference's SD.

Carolina Panthers

During 1992 the NFL released the name of five cities including Charlotte, North Carolina, as potential sites for expansion. After team owners delayed their vote to late 1993, an investment group named Richardson Sports to promote its bid by announcing the sale of permanent seat licenses (PSLs) to primarily finance the construction of a new 72,300-seat stadium in uptown Charlotte and complete it before the league's 1996 season.[7]

Within twenty-four hours 41,632 PSLs were ordered, all of the proposed stadium's 8,314 club seats had been sold, and 104 luxury boxes reserved and ultimately leased to buyers of them. Impressed by these efforts, the NFL awarded its twenty-ninth franchise to Charlotte and more specifically, to majority owner Jerry Richardson and his syndicate. Nicknamed Panthers, the team played its home games for one season at Memorial Stadium on the campus of Clemson University in South Carolina. During August 1996, Ericsson Stadium in Charlotte officially opened to initially host Panthers preseason home games and later those in the regular season.

Historical Results

A member of the league's NFC Western Division from 1996 to 2001 and then the conference's SD since 2002, the twenty-one-year-old Panthers played 336 games and won approximately 49 percent of them. Among teams in the conference as of their 2015–2016 season, Carolina ranked fifteenth in number of wins, ninth in winning percentage, tied for eleventh with the Buccaneers in division titles and with the Rams in conference titles, tied for thirteenth with the Vikings, Falcons, and Cardinals each with zero championships, and fourteenth in qualifying for seven playoffs (Table A.5).

Compared to other clubs in the SD as of their 2015–2016 season, the Panthers had the fewest wins and playoff appearances, highest winning percentage, more division plus conference titles than the Falcons, Saints, and Buccaneers, and tied for second with the Falcons with each winning zero championships. Based on these results, Carolina has been an average but improving team in its division but below average in the NFC because of the club's relatively short history, mediocre coaches, motivated but inferior players, and better performances by several teams and occasionally the Falcons, Saints, and Buccaneers in regular seasons.

In evaluating the performances of thirty-one other NFL teams as of their 2015–2016 season, the Panthers ranked twenty-seventh in total wins, sixteenth in winning percentage, tied for twentieth with the Buccaneers in division titles, tied for seventeenth in winning their conference, tied for twentieth with several teams in number of championships, and twenty-sixth in qualifying for their conference's playoffs. These and other results prove that, except for seven of its seasons, Carolina's NFL team has been below average competitively while playing clubs in the NFC and also against those within divisions of the AFC (Table A.6).

During its regular season and postseason games, Carolina had coaches with different success while leading their teams. Based on number of wins as of the league's 2014–2015 season, John Fox had 78 victories, Ron Rivera 47, and Dom Capers 31. For their leadership, Capers was AP coach of the year in 1996 and Rivera in 2013 and 2015. The team's other multiyear coach, George Seifert, was 16–32–0 in three seasons and replaced by Fox in 2002.

Some Panthers players have established career, single season, and single game records for the franchise as of the league's 2015–2016 season. For example, a few career record holders include quarterback Jake Delhomme with 19,258 yards and 120 touchdowns; receiver Steve Smith with 836 catches and 12,197 yards; and kicker John Kasay with 351 field goals and 1,482 points. During a single season, quarterback Steve Beuerlein passed for 4,436 yards and 36 touchdowns in 1999; running back DeAngelo Williams rushed for 1,515 yards and scored 20 touchdowns in 2008; and defensive ends Kevin Greene in 1998 and Greg Hardy in 2013 each had 15 sacks.

In one of their games, quarterback Cam Newton passed for 432 yards; cornerback Deon Grant intercepted 3 passes; and players Williams, Beuerlein, Smith, Kasay, and Hardy each set records respectively in rushing, passing, receiving and kicking, and sacking the opposing quarterback. These were significant performances by various players in setting records for Panthers teams in games between 1995 and 2015.

For having an outstanding NFL season at their position in games, players receive one or more awards from the AP. Quarterback Newton was offensive rookie of the year in 2011 and offensive player of the year and the league's MVP in 2015; Luke Kuechly defensive player of the year in 2013; Julius

Peppers defensive rookie of the year in 2002; and Steve Smith co-comeback player of the year in 2005. In addition, veteran Thomas Davis was Walter Payton man of the year in 2014 for his community service activities and excellence on the field as a linebacker.

Reggie White is the only former Panthers player in the pro football Hall of Fame as of 2014. Inducted in 2000 as a defensive end, he had 198 sacks in 132 career games, 2 fumble recoveries for touchdowns, and 3 interceptions. White was a three-time defensive player of the year, elected to thirteen consecutive pro bowls, and named all-pro thirteen of his fifteen seasons including ten as a first-team selection. Unfortunately, he died in December 2004 at forty-three-years-old.

Performance Highlights

While competing in its division of the league's NFC since 1995, Carolina's most successful period consecutively was 2013–2015 and then during one year in the 1990s and three within 2002 to 2009. In large part, these seasons of playoffs occurred because of such quarterbacks as Jake Delhomme and Cam Newton, running backs DeShaun Foster and DeAngelo Williams, and receivers Mushin Muhammad and Steve Smith. Alternatively, the club's worst performances consecutively happened during 1997–2002 and from 2009 to 2012. Wrong coaching decisions, lack of talent and too many injured players, and the team's poor draft choices were a few reasons for the Panthers' losing records.

At its home games in the 73,778-seat Bank of America Stadium, which opened in 1996, the club's attendances have been neither the smallest nor largest in the league. While the NFL's average each season was in the mid-500,000s, the number of spectators at Panthers games between 2004 and 2015, for example, ranged from 570,000 to 595,000 while ranked in the upper half of the NFC. Consequently, thousands of sports fans from Charlotte and the surrounding areas are really enthusiastic about their pro football team because of its ability to consistently compete against the Falcons, Saints, and Buccaneers in the SD although qualifying for only two championship games and playing in two conference finals in twenty-one years. Another postseason like 2003 and 2015, when they competed in Super Bowls, would generate more fan attendances in Charlotte at least temporarily for the Panthers.[8]

Among thirty-one NFL venues, Bank of America Stadium ranked eighteenth in a recent study. According to an article published about it in an edition of *Sporting News*, the author stated:

> The 19-year-old building [as of 2015] celebrates its "stadium-in-the-park setting," which is heavy on landscaping outside the facility. Inside, the Panthers have upgraded with new video boards in both end zones, open-air bars in the

> upper deck and escalators for aging PSL [Permanent Seat License] owners to more easily access the upper levels. For this season [2015], the Panthers refreshed 158 suites and opened two new premium clubs. Parking is scattered and there are plenty of tailgates, but the stadium is a short walk from uptown Charlotte's bar scene, a piece of the city that's grown tremendously in the past decade.[9]

The CBS Sports writer Brad Gagnon predicted the Panthers to be the twentieth best NFL team in 2017. While the franchise broke the bank signing Cam Newton, Greg Olsen, Luke Kuechly, and Thomas Davis to multiyear contracts, it still lacks consistency and usually does not contend for a championship. Carolina needs money to keep impending unrestricted free agents Charles Johnson, Star Lotulelei, and Ryan Kalil, which might not be possible. Although its defense is very good, the team has problems passing and running effectively. With Newton, however, the Panthers have a chance to win a title and championship in 2016 to 2017.[10]

Carolina's general manager Dave Gettleman believes that successful professional sports franchises have a winning culture that withstands change. The Panthers, according to Gettleman, are taking steps to becoming more successful. For the first time in its history in the league, the club qualified for the postseason in consecutive seasons [2013–2015].

The Panthers also became the first franchise to win consecutive NFC SD titles. The challenge for them, however, is to sustain that success and make more frequent postseason appearances and to win their playoff games. For better performances in regular-season home and away games, the club needs to improve its special teams and overall roster besides keeping their coaching coordinators and adding replacements for starting defensive and offensive linemen and cornerbacks.

New Orleans Saints

Before the mid-1960s, New Orleans was primarily a boxing, baseball, and college football town with the annual Sugar Bowl headlining the local sports calendar. High school rivalries in the city's Catholic League earned front-page news. The 1892 world heavyweight title fight between heavyweight boxers Jim Corbett and John L. Sullivan was the city's biggest sports event in its history.[11]

During the summer of 1966 the NFL announced plans to merge with the AFL, which would consolidate interest in the sport, eliminate bidding wars for players, and create a true world championship game. However, the chairman of the House Judiciary Committee and congressional subcommittee on antitrust, Representative Emanuel Celler of New York, opposed the merger and any legislation to approve it.

In a deal involving NFL Commissioner Pete Rozelle, New Orleans civic leader Dave Dixon's political advisor David Kleck, and powerful politicians in Washington, D.C., Representative Hale Boggs of Louisiana attached the NFL-AFL congressional antitrust exemption as a rider to an anti-inflation tax bill supported by President Lyndon Johnson. This moved the bill from Celler's committee to the Senate Finance Committee, led by Louisiana Senator Russell Long.

After a quid pro quo agreement between Rozelle, Kleck, and Boggs, Long's committee passed the bill and indirectly approved the merger. In November 1966, Rozelle appeared in New Orleans's Pontchartrain Hotel and awarded the sixteenth NFL franchise to the state of Louisiana and more specifically to the city. Besides Rozelle, other headliners in attendance were Boggs, Long, Governor John McKeithen, Tulane University President Herbert Longenecker, City Councilman Moon Landrieu and Jefferson Parish President Thomas Donelon. Dixon said he specifically asked to be seated in the rear of the Patio Room that day so that the attention could shine on Boggs, Long, and McKeithen. The franchise's majority owner, John Mecom Jr., paid an expansion fee of $8 million for the new team nicknamed "Saints."

Historical Results

While playing in the Eastern Conference's Capitol Division in 1967 and the conference's Century Division in 1968, Capitol Division again in 1969, and the NFC's Western Division from 1970 to 2001 and then in the conference's SD since 2002, New Orleans played 754 games and won approximately 44 percent of them. Among other teams in the conference as of their 2015 season, the Saints ranked tenth in total wins, thirteenth in winning percentage, tied for thirteenth with the Falcons in division titles and also with three different teams in number of conference titles, tied for ninth with three others in winning championships, and tied for twelfth with the Buccaneers in qualifying for the conference's playoffs (Table A.5).

Compared to performances of three other SD teams in the NFC as of their 2015 season, the Saints had the most wins, second highest winning percentage, tied for first in championships but not playoff appearances, and tied for second in total division and conference titles. Based on these results, New Orleans has been a competitive and occasionally successful team within its division but otherwise below average while performing against several of those in the NFC's East, North, and West Division.

With respect to the performances of thirty-one other NFL teams as of the league's 2015 season, the Saints were seventeenth in total wins and ranked twenty-sixth in winning percentage, tied for twenty-third with the Falcons in division titles, tied for twenty-first with five different teams in winning their conference, tied for fifteenth in number of championships including Super

Bowls, and tied for twenty-third with the Buccaneers and Ravens each qualifying for ten playoffs. These and other results prove that, except for its seasons in the playoffs, New Orleans' NFL team has been below average competitively while playing most clubs in the conference and league but average against those only in its division (Table A.6).

In its regular season and postseason games, the Saints had a number of successful and unsuccessful head coaches to lead their teams. According to their number of wins as of the league's 2015 season, Jim Mora and Sean Payton each had 93 and Jim Haslett 46. Mora was the AP coach of the year in 1987, Haslett in 2000, and Payton in 2006. Because they resigned, were released, or served during an interim period, some head coaches each won fewer than 10 games including J. D. Roberts, Ernie Hefferle, Hank Stram, Dick Stanfel, Wade Phillips, Rick Venturi, Aaron Kromer, and Joe Vitt.

A group of Saints players established career, single season, and single game records for the franchise as of 2014. During their seasons with the club, for example, Drew Brees passed for 38,733 yards and 283 touchdowns; Marques Colston received 607 passes for 8,337 yards and 63 touchdowns; and Morten Andersen kicked 302 field goals and scored 1,318 points.

In a single season, George Rogers rushed for 1,674 yards in 1981; Dave Whitsell intercepted 10 passes in 1967; Mel Gray returned punts 14.7 yards, on average, in 1987; and Dalton Hilliard scored 18 touchdowns in 1989. During one game, Tony Galbreath caught 14 passes, and Wes Chandler had 205 receiving yards; Joe Horn and Reggie Bush each scored 4 touchdowns and 24 points; and Wayne Martin and several other players each had 4 sacks of opposing quarterbacks. In short, these were exceptional performances by New Orleans players who set career, single season, and single game records.

Annually the AP gives awards to NFL players for being excellent performers at their positions during games on defense or offense. Although none have been the league's MVP or defensive rookie of the year as of 2014, Saints honored include offensive player of year Drew Brees in 2008 and 2011; offensive rookie of the year George Rogers in 1981 and Ruben Mayes in 1986; defensive player of the year Pat Swilling in 1991; and comeback player of the year Joe Johnson in 2000. Indeed these athletes had one or more great seasons for the franchise and earned their awards from the AP.

Six former New Orleans players and coach Hank Stram have been inducted into the pro football Hall of Fame. Among the group, Rickey Jackson and Willie Rolf had the most years with the club. Linebacker Jackson recorded double-digit sacks in six seasons, named all-pro four times, and appeared in six pro bowls. Tackle Rolf was voted to eleven pro bowls and named first-team all-pro seven times, and also a member of both the NFL's all-decade teams of the 1990s and 2000s. Besides them, other Hall of Fame players from Saints teams are Doug Atkins, Earl Campbell, Jim Finks, and Jim Taylor.

Performance Highlights

While competing in a division of its conference since the NFL's 1967 season, New Orleans' most successful periods consecutively were from 1990 to 1992 and 2009 to 2011. These occurred because of such quarterbacks as Bobby Herbert and Drew Brees, running backs Fred McAfee and Pierre Thomas, and receivers Eric Martin and Jimmy Graham. Alternatively, the club's worst seasons consecutively were from 1967 to 1986, 1993 to 1999, and 2001 to 2005. This happened because of coaching issues, lack of enough talented players at their positions, and mistakes by both groups in games of regular seasons.

At its home games in the 73,000-seat Mercedes-Benz Superdome, which opened in 1975, the club's attendances have been average to slightly above average in the league. While the NFL's average each season was in the mid-500,000s, the number of spectators at Saints games between 2004 and 2015, for example, ranged from a low of 490,000 to a high of 585,000, while ranked in the upper half of the NFC.

Simply put, thousands of sports fans from New Orleans and surrounding areas are enthusiastic about their pro football team because of the sport's popularity among residents and tourists in Louisiana and also for consistently competing against the Falcons, Panthers, and Buccaneers in the SD despite appearing in only one championship game since the late 1960s. Another postseason like 2009, when they won a Super Bowl, would boost fan attendance at least for a few years at Saints home games

Among thirty-one NFL venues, the Mercedes-Benz Superdome ranked eighth in a recent study. According to an article published about it in an edition of the *Sporting News*, the author wrote:

> There's a soft spot among many locals for this stadium. Ten years ago, the dome served as a shelter after Hurricane Katrina crushed the city. It underwent a post-storm restoration and renovation to the tune of about $350 million. The dome may not have the noisy reputation of a Century Link Field, but try standing at field level for the opening kickoff. It can be deafening. Champions Square, the Saints' official tailgate space outside the dome, clicks [entertains fans] with live bands cranking up the energy. In NOLA, it's not difficult to find a party somewhere, anywhere, on game day.[12]

In ESPN's future power rankings, the network asked three experts to rate each NFL team for three seasons (2015–2017) on a scale of 0 to 100 percent in five categories including roster (excluding quarterback), quarterback, draft, front office, and coaching. In their analysis the Saints ranked eighteenth, for the most part, because both Coach Sean Payton and quarterback Drew Brees proved fallible during the club's 7–9 collapse in the 2014 season.

Furthermore, Brees's contract expires after 2016, which leaves some uncertainty at that critical position.

For changes in ratings from the league's 2014 to 2015 season, the Saints fell from fourth to eleventh in coaching and third to twelfth in quarterback. They need a roster overhaul after losing key players such as tight end Jimmy Graham, receiver Kenny Stills, and middle linebacker Curtis Lofton, while adding athletes like running back C. J. Spiller, center Max Unger, and cornerback Brandon Browner. Regarding young talent on the roster, the Saints loaded up with nine draft picks to build for the future. It was a key draft for New Orleans since the team has just seven starters left from the previous four classes. If all goes according to plan, the Saints could have a bright future.

The team's failure in their 2014–2015 season should help everyone from both a motivational and strategy standpoint, most importantly on defense. Players who admitted to getting caught up in the preseason hype then are more grounded now. The Saints have simplified defensive coordinator Rob Ryan's scheme to cut down on assignment errors and missed tackles that plagued them.

Tampa Bay Buccaneers

According to the football leagues' merger during the late 1960s and end of the AFL, the NFL agreed to expand from sixteen teams in 1969 to twenty-eight. After the actual merger in 1970, however, twenty-six teams played in the league with each of them in a division of the AFC or NFC. But following the league's 1973 season, Commissioner Pete Rozelle announced that Tampa Bay, Florida, would be the first city to get an expansion franchise for a fee of $16 million.[13]

One reason for delaying expansion a few years was because of uncertainties about some newly integrated stadiums such as those of the Buffalo Bills and Boston—renamed New England—Patriots. Meanwhile, business syndicates and other groups from Tampa Bay had tried but failed to encourage both teams to move to their area. However, when Rich Stadium in Buffalo and Schaefer Stadium in Boston were built respectively for the Bills and Patriots, the league was stable enough to expand in size.

The proposed Tampa Bay expansion franchise was originally awarded to Tom McCloskey, a construction company owner from Philadelphia, Pennsylvania. Shortly thereafter, McCloskey became dissatisfied with the NFL about financial matters and then backed out of the deal a month later. Hugh Culverhouse, a wealthy tax attorney from Jacksonville, Florida, who failed in his bid to buy the NFL's Los Angeles Rams after an unannounced sale of the team to Robert Irsay, instead received the Tampa Bay franchise. In a reference to pirates along Florida's Gulf Coast during the seventeenth century, "Buccaneers" became the team's nickname.

Historical Results

As a member of the AFC's Western Division in 1976, NFC's Central Division from 1977 to 2001 and then the conference's SD since 2002, the Buccaneers or simply "Bucs" played 628 games and won approximately 38 percent of them. Among teams in the conference as of the league's 2015–2016 season, Tampa Bay ranked thirteenth in total wins, sixteenth in winning percentage, tied for eleventh with the Panthers in division titles, tied for thirteenth with three other clubs in conference titles, tied for ninth in championships, and tied for twelfth with the Saints in qualifying for ten playoffs (Table A.6).

Compared to three other clubs in the SD as of their 2015–2016 season, the Bucs had more wins than the Panthers but the lowest winning percentage of the group, and also ahead of the Falcons and Saints in division titles, and tied for second in conference titles and first in number of championships including a Super Bowl victory in 2002. Except for its dismal winning percentage, forty-year-old Tampa Bay has been average within the SD but below average in performances especially after playing teams in the East, North, and West divisions of the conference.

When contrasted to the performances of thirty-one other NFL teams as of their 2015 season, the Bucs ranked twenty-fourth in total wins, thirty-first in winning percentage, tied for twentieth with the Panthers and Chiefs in division titles, tied for twenty-second with several other clubs in winning their conference, tied for fifteenth in number of championships including Super Bowls, and tied for twenty-third in qualifying for the playoffs. These and other results prove that, except for its ten playoffs, Tampa Bays' NFL team has been below average competitively while playing clubs in regular seasons of the league for four decades (Table A.7).

During games in seasons and postseasons since 1976, the Bucs were led by both superior and inferior coaches. In number of wins, head coach Jon Gruden had 60 of them, Tony Dungy 56, and John McKay 45. Although Gruden and Dungy had winning records and had their team in conference playoffs, the AP did not select them as coaches of the year. Alternatively, Tampa Bay's least successful coaches were Leeman Bennett and Richard Williamson each with 4 wins and then Raheem Morris with 17, Ray Perkins 19, and Sam Wyche 23. The latter group simply failed to inspire their players and win enough games in their division to appear in a playoff.[14]

Some Buccaneers were outstanding players who set career, single season, and single game records for the franchise as of 2015. For example, during their careers with the club, James Wilder rushed for 5,957 yards and caught 430 passes; Josh Freeman passed for 80 touchdowns and Vinny Testaverde for 14,820 yards; and Martin Gramatica kicked 137 field goals and scored 592 points.

During a single season, Keyshawn Johnson caught 106 passes in 2001 and Mark Carrier 1,422 yards as a receiver in 1989; Ronde Barber intercepted 10 passes in 2001; Josh Bidwell's punts averaged 45.6 yards in 2005; and Warren Sapp had 16.5 sacks of the opposing quarterback in 2000. For individual records in a game, Doug Martin rushed for 251 yards, and Doug Williams passed for 486; Vincent Jackson received passes for 216 yards; and Jimmy Giles scored 4 touchdowns and 24 points. As a group, these athletes played great while at their positions on the field and established records for Bucs teams.

Annually the AP gives awards to NFL players for their outstanding performances on defense or offense in games of a regular season. Tampa Bay winners included offensive rookie of the year Warren Dunn in 1997 and Carnell Williams in 2005, and defensive player of the year Lee Roy Selmon in 1979, Warren Sapp in 1999, and Derrick Brooks in 2002. In addition, Selmon was the pro bowl MVP in 1982 and Brooks in 2006. For sure, Dunn and the others were standouts during specific games and also seasons of the league.

Three former Bucs players, who played at least nine years for the franchise, are in the pro football Hall of Fame. Besides Selmon in 1995 and Sapp in 2013, Derrick Brooks was inducted in 2014. He never missed a game, won a defensive player of the year award in 2002, and named to the league's all-decade team of 2000s. Besides them, former head coach Tony Dungy joined the group in 2016.

Performance Highlights

While competing in divisions of its conference since 1976, Tampa Bays' most successful periods consecutively were during 1981–1982 and from 1999 to 2002. These occurred because of such quarterbacks as Doug Williams and Trent Dilfer, running backs James Wilder and Mike Alstott, and receivers Kevin House and Keshawn Johnson. Alternatively, because of coaching mistakes and player problems, the club's worst seasons were during 1983–1996 and from 2008 to 2015.

At its home games in the 65,908-seat Raymond James Stadium, which opened in 1998, the club's attendances have been below average in the league. While the NFL's average per season was in the mid-500,000s, the number of spectators at Bucs games between 2004 and 2015, for example, ranged from the high 400,000s to low 500,000s and ranked in the lower half of the NFC. Thus, thousands of sports fans in Tampa Bay and surrounding areas are not enthusiastic or passionate about their NFL team.[15]

Among thirty-one NFL venues, Raymond James Stadium ranked twenty-second in a recent study. According to an article published about it in an edition of *Sporting News*:

> It wasn't that long ago that Raymond James hosted the 2009 Super Bowl. But since that time, newer stadiums have opened and the Bucs face a challenge in upgrading a 14-year-old facility to get the Big Game back in town. The big question, as always, is how much will it cost for improvements and who will pay for it? Regardless, the pirate ship, the stadium's signature feature, remains intact. Bars and restaurants a short drive away include Lee Roy Selmon's, named after the team's first Pro Football Hall of Famer.[16]

For various reasons the Bucs are set up for long-term success on offense and similar to their defense a few years ago. The club invested in a lot of talented players during the past few years, using all but one of their draft picks on that side of the football. As a result they have a core of young, quality players who can learn a system together, and hopefully thrive in the long run. If everything goes right, the Bucs could have one of the best offenses in the NFL in a couple of years to complement their defensive players.

FRANCHISE BUSINESS

Besides performing as teams in regular season and postseason games, NFL franchises are also commercial enterprises. To that end, their economic objective is to earn maximum revenue and obtain the greatest amount of profit on a fiscal basis from their operations. Although they share revenue with each other from such sources as national television contracts and other deals, it is important for them to efficiently allocate resources, determine and distribute payrolls, set nonpremium and premium ticket prices, and schedule investments in short- and long-term assets. To reveal and manage these activities, this section focuses on different parts of four NFC franchises as businesses and how these organizations rank and succeed or not succeed from a financial perspective.

Atlanta Falcons

A native of Flushing, New York, Arthur Blank attended Stuyvesant High School in Manhattan where he competed on the football, baseball, and track teams. He received a Bachelor of Science degree in business administration with distinction from Babson College, where he was active in a variety of extracurricular activities. He cofounded Home Depot in 1978 and retired from the company as cochairman in 2001. During Blank's last year as chief executive officer of the company, Home Depot ranked first in social responsibility in an annual survey conducted by Harris Interactive, Inc.[17]

In February 2002, Blank bought the Atlanta Falcons for $545 million. The team had endured an up-and-down existence for thirty-six years under the ownership of the Rankin Smith family. The highlight of the Smith's family ownership came in 1999 when Atlanta played in Super Bowl XXXIII but lost the game to the Denver Broncos at Pro Player Stadium in Miami, Florida.

When Blank acquired the Falcons, his twin missions were to upgrade the team's roster and also bring fans back to its home stadium, the Georgia Dome. He made the unprecedented move of lowering ticket prices on nearly 25,000 seats in the Dome, which gave the Falcons their first sold-out season in more than two decades. Besides purchasing land to ensure that Falcons fans had parking spots in downtown Atlanta, he helped turn home games into exciting and entertaining events with pregame and halftime concerts. In other words, Blank injected some of the customer service principles—that worked for Home Depot—into the Falcons organization and quickly won him acclaim as an NFL maverick.

Team Financials

According to data and other financial information published in *Forbes* for sixteen franchises in the NFC as of their 2015–2016 season, the Falcons ranked ninth in market value at $1.67 billion, thirteenth in total revenue at $303 million, eleventh in gate receipts at $57 million, sixteenth in operating income at $25 million, and first in player expenses at $187 million and also in its debt-to-value ratio of 57 percent. Among SD teams in the conference, Atlanta was first in market value, player expenses, and the debt ratio, but fourth in revenue, gate receipts and operating income. Based on these results the Falcons have been below average while operating as a business enterprise within its division and conference, and moreover, from a financial perspective (Table A.7).

Compared to thirty-one other NFL teams as of its 2015 season, Atlanta was seventeenth in estimated market value, twenty-sixth in revenue, tied for eighteenth with the Dolphins in gate receipts, thirty-second or last in operating income, and first both in its player expenses and the debt ratio. These rankings indicate, in part, that the Falcons are commercially inferior to most teams in the league. Therefore, this franchise is a mediocre sports business with too much debt and players expenses but not enough revenue and operating income to be financially successful (Table A.8).

For several years a Chicago-based company named Team Marketing Report (TMR) prepares and publishes a Fan Cost Index (FCI) for the home games of teams in professional sports leagues. To attend a game for a typical family with two kids, an FCI includes the costs of four average-priced tickets, two cheapest-priced draft beers, four each cheapest-priced soft drinks and hot dogs, parking for one car, and two each game programs and least-expensive, adult-size adjustable caps. Costs are determined by telephone calls with team representatives, venues, and concessionaires, and from asking questions during interviews.[18]

For the 2015 season, the Falcons' FCI was approximately $438 or nineteenth highest in the league and 0.2 percent higher than in 2014. Listed from most to least in amount by item for one person, the team's nonpremium tickets averaged about $78, parking for one vehicle and a cap each $20, a beer almost $8 and soft drink $7, and a hot dog $6. For FCIs of other SD clubs, the Saints ranked tenth at $507, Panthers twenty-fourth at $415, and Buccaneers thirty-first at $373. While the Buccaneers had the lowest FCI in the conference, the 49ers had the highest at $640.

At $280 each, the Falcons' premium ticket prices exceeded the league's average by $25 or approximately 10 percent and also those of the Saints and Bucs but not the Panthers. Thus, Atlanta is a mid-sized sports market where fans at the team's home games in the Georgia Dome will pay more for premium seats but $7 less than the NFL average for nonpremium seats. This suggests that Falcons' ticket prices are set by the club to maximize gate receipts but also to collect more revenue from operations during games of their season.

Business Highlights

Using fifteen years of data on such things as NFL team performances, home-game ticket prices, and market populations and their median incomes, Emory University researchers created an equity index to determine which clubs had the most avid, engaged, passionate, and/or supportive fans before the NFL's 2015 season. Among the NFC's SD teams, the Falcons ranked twentieth and above the Bucs at twenty-first and Panthers twenty-second but below the Saints at eighth. According to this index, Atlanta has more enthusiastic football fans than five NFC teams and seven in the AFC.[19]

In another Emory University index titled Social Media Equity, the Falcons had the league's twenty-seventh best fan base following the SD's Saints at fifth, Bucs at seventeenth, and Panthers at twenty-first. Although this index reflects whether teams over- or underperform with respect to their Twitter following, Falcons fans are less involved or passionate about their hometown team on social media than those of twenty-six other NFL clubs. Interestingly, the AFC Steelers had the league's most dedicated and fervent fan base while the NFC Cardinals ranked thirty-second.

For other important business news about Atlanta's NFL franchise, the Falcons signed a new sponsorship deal in 2015 with a liquor company from Dripping Springs, Texas, named Deep Eddy Vodka. The multiyear agreement, whose terms were not disclosed, provides for vodka being sold before and during the team's home games at concession bars, mobile bars, and for order in luxury suites throughout the stadium.[20]

The cost of the Falcons new stadium doubled to $1.5 billion since originally proposed several years ago. Taxpayers will pay $200 million of the cost while the NFL committed $200 million. Team owner Arthur Blank is on the hook for the remainder including any cost overruns. Operated by the Falcons, the new stadium is also the future home of Atlanta United FC, the expansion Major League Soccer team owned by Blank that begins to play in 2017, the same year the stadium opens. An $850 million loan put together by Bank of America is being used by Blank to build it. Automobile manufacturer Mercedes-Benz, meanwhile, signed a twenty-seven-year deal in August 2015 for naming rights to the new venue.[21]

Carolina Panthers

Born in Spring Hope, North Carolina, Jerry Richardson completed high school and then graduated from Wofford College where he played football and became an AP Little All-America selection in 1957 and 1958. Drafted in the thirteenth round by the defending champion Baltimore Colts, Richardson played two seasons in the NFL and earned Colts rookie of the year honors in 1959.[22]

Following his years as an athlete, Richardson embarked on a successful business career. Supposedly he used his 1959 NFL championship bonus, with the help of Charles Bradshaw, to open the first Hardee's franchise in Spartanburg, South Carolina. As a result, the business expanded rapidly under Richardson's hands-on management style.

From his headquarters in Spartanburg, he cofounded Spartan Foods, which was the first franchisee of Hardee's. Later he became chief executive officer of Flagstar, the sixth largest food service company in the nation controlling 2,500 restaurants and 100,000 employees, but retired from there in 1995. Two years before retirement, Richardson became the first former NFL player—since the Chicago Bears' George Halas—to become a team owner when his syndicate was unanimously awarded the NFL's twenty-ninth franchise and nicknamed "Panthers,"

Team Financials

According to data and other financial information published in *Forbes* for sixteen franchises in the NFC as of their 2015–2016 season, the Panthers ranked eleventh in market value at $1.56 billion, ninth in total revenue at $325 million, tied for seventh with the Packers in gate receipts at $65 million, seventh in operating income at $77 million, sixteenth or last in player expenses at $137 million, and tied for fifteenth with the Bears' 4 percent debt-to-value ratio. Among only SD teams in the conference, Carolina had the second highest market value and also the most revenue, gate receipts, and operating income, but the least player expenses and smallest debt ratio (Table A.7).

Compared to the operations of thirty-one other NFL teams as of their 2015 season, the Panthers' value was nineteenth, revenue fifteenth, gate receipts tied for eleventh, operating income eleventh, and player expenses thirty-second and last in the league, and debt-to-value tied for thirtieth. According to these amounts and rankings, Carolina is above average in the SD from a financial perspective but only average among teams in its conference and also across the NFL. In fact, the franchise is profitable, successful, and well-managed as a business enterprise within the professional sports industry (Table A.8).

For the 2015 NFL season, the Panthers' FCI was approximately $415 and twenty-fourth highest in the league or 2.6 percent more than in 2014. Listed from most to least in amount for one person to attend a home game in Bank of America Stadium, the club's average nonpremium ticket cost $78, parking for one vehicle $20 and a cap $15, and a beer, hot dog, and soft drink each $5. For other SD teams in the NFC, their FCIs and rankings were respectively the Saints' $507 at tenth in the league, Falcons' $438 at nineteenth, and Buccaneers' $373 at thirty-first. Among all teams in the league, the NFC 49ers had the highest FCI at $640 and AFC Jaguars lowest at $347.[23]

The Panthers' average-priced premium tickets at $295 each cost $40 or 16 percent more than those of a typical team and greater than prices paid by fans at home games of the Falcons, Saints, and Buccaneers. While Carolina underpriced spectators for its nonpremium tickets, it overpriced them for premium seats. Because of the sport, team's popularity in its market, and location and size of the stadium in Charlotte, local executives, corporations, and other organizations purchase tickets to hometown games for their employees, clients, and similar groups.

Business Highlights

Prepared by researchers at Emory University, their equity index indicated which clubs had the most avid, engaged, passionate, and/or supportive fans before the NFL's 2015 season. According to results from the study, the Panthers placed twenty-second in the league and inferior to the Saints at eighth, Falcons at twentieth, and Buccaneers at twenty-first. Simply put, Carolina fans are less engaged or passionate about their hometown team than those of twelve other NFC clubs and the majority of them in the AFC.[24]

In another Emory University index titled Social Media Equity, the Panthers had the league's twenty-first best or most impressive fan base following the SD Saints at fifth and Bucs at seventeenth, but ahead of the Falcons at twenty-seventh. Although this index reflects whether teams over- or underperform with respect to their Twitter following, Panthers fans are less concerned or involved with their favorite team on social media than those of twenty other NFL clubs. Interestingly, the AFC Steelers had the league's most dedicated and fervent fan base while the NFC Cardinals ranked thirty-second.

For other business news about the franchise, Charlotte-based PSL Source pairs buyers and sellers and handles the title transfers for permanent seat licenses (PSLs), which are one-time fees charged by teams for fans to have the rights to purchase specific tickets in perpetuity, but only if they buy their season tickets every year. According to the company's managing partner, owners should consider selling their PSLs because of the team's popularity and recent success, scarcity of licenses, growth in the population of fans, and other factors.[25]

The Panthers, for example, have sold 62,000 seats as PSLs, totaling about 25,000 accounts. According to the team, there are only 1,200 of them available at the 74,000-seat stadium. Most of them cost $2,000 to $7,500 each, with a limited number selling for less—$1,000 in the upper corners of the stadium and more—$15,000 to $20,000—for the best locations.

Carolina made the playoffs in their 2013–2015 seasons, which meant consecutive boosts in ticket prices for home games. The latest bump was $2 to $5 for most tickets, although 2,200 seats in the lower level of the stadium increased $30 for the 2015 season. Ticket prices were flat between 2010 and 2013 when Carolina was shut out of the playoffs. Furthermore, the Panthers added two new private clubs in 2015 at Bank of America Stadium. One-time membership fees for them generate about $1.4 million for the Panthers. In addition, there is a per-game price of $650 as well and that includes food, beer, soft drinks, and parking. The number of luxury suites in the stadium was reduced from 158 to 153 to provide room for the new private clubs.[26]

New Orleans Saints

Born in New Orleans, Louisiana, in 1927, Tom Benson served in the U.S. Navy and after being discharged, obtained an accounting degree in 1948 at Loyola University of New Orleans. Following college, he worked as a car salesman in the city but then in 1956 moved to San Antonio to revive a failing car dealership. For his efforts, the eager young businessman was given a 25 percent interest in the dealership. In 1962 he opened Tom Benson Chevrolet, the first of several dealerships he would eventually own in New Orleans and San Antonio.[27]

Benson showed his financial wisdom by investing profits from his car dealerships in local commercial banks. This led him to acquire a group of small Southern banks to form Benson Financial. Tom sold Benson Financial to Norwest in 1996 for a huge amount.

In 1985 Benson learned that the Saints were on the verge of being sold to a group that wanted to move them from New Orleans to Jacksonville, Florida. Being a successful businessman, he could not let that happen to his beloved city. Indeed Benson recognized the negative economic implications of the team moving to Florida on not just New Orleans, but also Louisiana.

The state was in a deep economic recession in the mid-1980s due to the severe drop in crude oil prices. In 1984, team owner John W. Mecom Jr. offered the Saints for sale but demanded a nonnegotiable $75 million. A year later, however, Benson negotiated Mecom's price for the franchise down to $70.2 million. As a result, Mecom sold his club to Benson.

Team Financials

According to data and other financial information published in *Forbes* for sixteen franchises in the NFC as of 2015, the Saints ranked thirteenth in market value at $1.515 billion, tenth in revenue at $322 million, ninth in gate receipts at $63 million, eighth in operating income at $70 million, eleventh in player expenses at $162 million, and tied for thirteenth with the Cowboys' 5 percent debt-to-value ratio. Among the conference's SD clubs, New Orleans had the third highest market value and players expenses and also second highest revenue, gate receipts, and operating income, and second smallest debt ratio (Table A.7).

Compared to the operations of thirty-one other NFL teams as of their 2014–2015 season, the Saints' market value was twenty-third, revenue tied for sixteenth with the Dolphins, gate receipts fourteenth, operating income twelfth, player expenses eighteenth, and their debt-to-value ratios tied for twenty-seventh. According to these different financials, New Orleans is an average franchise in its division and conference but also average to below average among all teams in the league. In other words, the club is a profitable business organization but for various reasons, a relatively low-valued sports enterprise (Table A.8).

For the 2015 NFL season, the Saints' FCI was approximately $507 and tenth highest in the league with zero percent change from 2014. Listed from most to least in amount for one person at a home game in the Mercedes-Benz Superdome, the club's average nonpremium ticket cost $84, parking for one vehicle $35, a cap $32 and beer $9, and a hot dog, soft drink, and program each between $4 and $6. Regarding FCIs of other SD teams in the conference, the Falcons ranked nineteenth at $438, Panthers twenty-fourth at $415, and Bucs thirty-first at $373. Because of tourists and football fans in the New Orleans metropolitan area, the Saints charged more for food and other items at their games than did the typical NFL team.[28]

At Saints games, the average price for a premium ticket was about $187 or 36 percent less than the league's $255. Because of competitive ticket prices for nonpremium and premium seats, New Orleans gets greater attendances at—and more revenue from—their home games than by charging higher amounts for admission to them.

Business Highlights

Prepared by researchers at Emory University, their equity index indicated which clubs had the most avid, engaged, passionate, and/or supportive fans before the NFL's 2015 season. According to results from the study, the Saints placed eighth in the league and superior to the Falcons at twentieth, Buccaneers at twenty-first, and Panthers at twenty-second. Simply put, New Orleans fans are more engaged or passionate about their team than those of twelve other NFC clubs and a majority of them playing in the AFC.

In another Emory University index titled Social Media Equity, the Saints had the league's fifth best or most impressive fan base while such SD rivals as the Bucs were seventeenth, Panthers twenty-first, and Falcons twenty-seventh. Although this index reflects whether teams over- or underperform with respect to their Twitter following, New Orleans fans are more concerned or involved about their favorite team on social media than those of twenty-seven other NFL clubs. Interestingly, the AFC Steelers had the league's most dedicated and fervent fan base while the NFC Cardinals ranked thirty-second.

In contrast to these indexes, the magazine *Business Insider* found New Orleans to be the most supportive city of its NFL team. On average, 45 percent of all households in the local television market tuned into Saints games the first two weeks of the 2014 season. However, having the highest participation rate among the local population does not mean the Saints had the largest audiences in raw numbers. While the New York Giants attracted only 14 percent of the television market, that amounted to about 2.6 million households. In contrast, New Orleans' percentage meant 666,564 households watched them play games.[29]

Early in 2015, team owner Tom Benson made some changes regarding who will control his empire upon his death. The eighty-seven-year-old's initial plans were to grant ownership of his NFL Saints and National Basketball Association (NBA) New Orleans Pelicans franchises to his granddaughter, Rita Benson LeBlanc. But after Benson announced that he would transfer command to his third wife, Gayle, his daughter Renee and her children Rita and Ryan became petitioners in a lawsuit filed against Benson that stated, in part, he was mentally incompetent to make correct decisions. During the summer Benson won a trial against his heirs that officially ruled him competent and fit to continue running the two pro sports organizations.

Tampa Bay Buccaneers

During May 2014, Buccaneers' former owner/president Malcolm Glazer died at the age of eighty-five. Since being purchased by Glazer in 1995, his NFL franchise qualified for seven playoff berths and had five wins, and also captured its first and only Super Bowl championship in 2002. Known among his league peers as a pioneering thinker, Glazer infused his team and employees with the determination and dedication to be the best in the league. His commitment to building a championship organization provided the foundation for continued success both on and off the field.[30]

A longtime member of the Forbes 400, Malcolm became a billionaire in 2003. He made a fortune in real estate and his First Allied Corporation owned 6.7 million square feet of shopping center space across the country. During the years, Glazer invested his money into a handful of businesses including Harley Davidson, Tonka, and the Zapata Corporation.

Glazer's long-established estate succession plan assures everyone that the Buccaneers will remain with the Glazer family for generations. His wife Linda, along with their five sons and daughter, will continue to operate the team as they have throughout the family's ownership of it.

Team Financials

According to data and other financial information published in *Forbes* for sixteen franchises in the NFC as of their 2015–2016 season, the Bucs ranked fourteenth in both market value at $1.51 billion and gate receipts at $48 million, eleventh in both total revenue at $313 million and operating income at $55 million, tenth in player expenses at $163 million, and sixth in its debt-to-value ratio at 12 percent. Within the conference's SD, Tampa Bay was least valuable in market value of the group and third in both total revenue and operating income, fourth in gate receipts, and second in player expenses and also its percent of debt-to-value ratio (Table A.7).

Compared to thirty-one other NFL teams as of their 2015–2016 season, the Bucs were twenty-fourth in market value, tied for twenty-first with the Browns in total revenue, twenty-ninth in gate receipts, tied for nineteenth with the Bengals in operating income, tied for sixteenth with the Bills in player expenses, and twelfth in its debt-to-value percent. From a financial perspective, Tampa Bay's NFL team is not an elite or very wealthy and prosperous enterprise because of several factors including its small to mid-sized fan base, strong competition from others in the conference's SD, history of losing seasons and mediocre performances, and location. In other words, the club is below average as a business operation compared to the Cowboys, Giants, and most other franchises in the NFC and league (Table A.8).

For the 2015 NFL season, the Bucs' FCI was approximately $373 and thirty-first highest in the league or 3.8 percent less than in 2014. Listed from most to least in amount for one person to attend a home game at Raymond James Stadium, the average nonpremium ticket cost $63, parking for one vehicle $25, a cap $20, single beer about $8, and a hot dog and soft drink each between $4 and $6. For the FCIs of other SD clubs, the Saints ranked tenth at $507, Falcons nineteenth at $438, and Panthers twenty-fourth at $415. Thus it cost a four-person family $107 or 28 percent less to attend Tampa Bay's home games in Florida than those of thirty other NFL teams, especially the NFC's 49ers, Cowboys, and Giants, and AFC's Patriots, Jets, and Ravens.

While their average nonpremium ticket price was $22 or 35 percent below the typical teams' in 2015, the Bucs' average premium ticket cost $222 compared to the league's $255. Based on these amounts, Tampa Bay keeps its prices competitive in order to boost attendance at its home games and maximize revenue from gate receipts. In turn, this means additional profit or less financial loss from the club's operations.

Business Highlights

Prepared by researchers at Emory University, their equity index indicated which clubs had the most avid, engaged, passionate, and/or supportive fans before the NFL's 2015 season. According to results from the study, the Bucs placed twenty-first in the league and inferior to the Saints at eighth and Falcons at twentieth, but superior to the Panthers at twenty-second. Simply put, Tampa Bay fans are less engaged or passionate about their team than those of eleven other NFC clubs and also a majority of any playing in the AFC.[31]

In another Emory University index titled Social Media Equity, the Bucs had the league's seventeenth best or most impressive fan base while such division rivals as the Saints were fifth, Panthers twenty-first, and Falcons twenty-seventh. Although this index reflects whether teams over- or underperform with respect to their Twitter following, Tampa Bay's fans are more concerned or involved about their local team on social media than those of fifteen other NFL clubs. Interestingly, the AFC Steelers had the league's most dedicated and fervent fan base, but unfortunately the NFC Cardinals ranked thirty-second.

During late 2015, the Bucs applied for a piece of a Florida incentive program that could get the team as much as $1 million a year while it plays games at Raymond James Stadium. The application puts the Bucs in competition with the Jaguars, Dolphins, and Daytona International Speedway for money to upgrade their facility. The annual amount is for the duration of the stadium agreement between the Tampa Bay Sports Authority and Buccaneers

Stadium Limited Partnership dated August 28, 1996. Legislators decide which upgrades, if any, get funded. Although the Bucs did not apply in 2014, state lawmakers refused all four proposals for stadium renovations under the same program.[32]

The Buccaneers turned over the keys to the franchise in the league's 2015 season to quarterback Jameis Winston, who won the 2013 Heisman Trophy while playing at Florida State University and was then selected first in the 2015 NFL draft. The Bucs won only six games combined in 2013–2014 and hope Winston can stem the tide. The losing has kept fans away from Raymond James stadium with the team ranked in the NFL's bottom four in attendance each of the past five seasons. After Malcolm Glazer—who bought the franchise for $192 million in 1995—died in 2014, his wife Linda and their six children continued family ownership under a long-established estate succession plan.[33]

NOTES

1. Two books about the NFL's regular seasons and postseasons and the league's teams and their success are Frank P. Jozsa Jr., *Football Fortunes: The Business, Organization and Strategy of the NFL* (Jefferson, NC: McFarland, 2010), and James Quirk and Rodney D. Fort, *Pay Dirt: The Business of Professional Team Sports* (Princeton, NJ: Princeton University Press, 1992).
2. For the Atlanta Falcons' performances including their seasons and postseasons, see the *NFL Record & Fact Book 2014* (New York: NFL, 2014) and "Teams," http://www.pro-football-reference.com, cited August 25, 2015.
3. The most important and reputable online source to verify the careers of Hall of Fame owners, administrators, coaches, and players is "Teams," http://www.profootballhof.com, cited September 1, 2015.
4. Attendances of NFL teams are reported on pages 488–94 of *Pay Dirt* and online at "Rod Fort's Sports Business Data," http://www.sites.google.com, cited September 1, 2015.
5. "Ranking All 31 NFL Stadiums," http://www.sportingnews.com, cited August 31, 2015 contains these results.
6. To learn about this topic in greater detail, read "2015 NFL Future Power Rankings," http://www.insider.espn.go.com, cited October 10, 2015.
7. Notes 1–4 above were used to research performances of the Carolina Panthers including their coaches' and players' records, attendances, future power ranking, and other information.
8. Sources include "Rod Fort's Sports Business Data" and home-site attendances of NFL teams at http://www.espn.go.com.
9. See note 5 for the ranking of the Panthers' Bank of America Stadium.
10. The reference is Brad Gagnon, "The NFL All-Time Power Rankings of the Super Bowl Era," http://www.cbssports.com, cited August 26, 2015.
11. Most of the historical information for the Saints' performances was taken from the literature cited in notes 1–4 and also "Teams," http://www.pro-football-reference.com, cited August 25, 2015.
12. Readings include "Ranking All 31 NFL Stadiums" and Michael Potts, "Ranking All NFL Stadiums for 2015—From Worst to Best," http://www.whatculture.com, cited September 2, 2015.
13. Decisions by the NFL to expand and to which sites and when are discussed in Frank P. Jozsa Jr., *National Football League Strategies: Business Expansions, Relocations, and Mergers* (New York: Springer, 2014).

14. Sources for the Falcons, Panthers, and Saints were also used to determine performances of the Buccaneers.

15. "Rod Fort's Sports Business Data" and NFL attendances at http://www.espn.go.com are references.

16. See note 12 for the Mercedes-Benz Superdome's rank among NFL venues.

17. The source is "NFL Team Owners," http://www.biography.yourdictionary.com, cited December 24, 2015.

18. The articles to research and study online about the franchises are the "2015 NFL Fan Cost Index," http://www.teammarketing.com, cited November 20, 2015, and the "2014 NFL Fan Cost Index," http://www.teammarketing.com, cited August 26, 2015.

19. For both the fan equity and social media equity indexes, see Manish Tripathi, "2015 NFL Fan Equity Rankings," https://scholarblogs.emory.edu, cited September 4, 2015, and Michael Lewis, "2015 NFL Social Media Equity Rankings," https://scholarblogs.emory.edu, cited September 4, 2015.

20. To read more about this team's current business, see Phil W. Hudson, "Atlanta Falcons Ink Sponsorship Deal with Texas Vodka Distiller," http://www.bizjournals.com, cited November 5, 2015.

21. Regarding this facility, one reading is Belinda Lanks, "Atlanta Falcons New Stadium Makes a Spectacle of Its Retractable Roof," *Business Week* (September 1, 2014): 1.

22. "NFL Team Owners" has information about Jerry Richardson's career.

23. Jon Greenberg, "2014 NFL Fan Cost Index," https://www.teammarketing.com, cited August 26, 2015.

24. These indexes for the Panthers are in readings of note 19.

25. For more information and data, see "Carolina Panthers PSL," http://www.pslsource.com, cited November 5, 2015.

26. This topic is discussed in Eric Spanberg, "Panthers Double Up on New Private Clubs," *SportsBusiness Journal* (May 11, 2015): 8.

27. "NFL Team Owners" highlights Tom Benson's personal and business careers including his ownership of the Saints.

28. The FCI and other costs are discussed in the article contained in note 18.

29. Mark Waller, "Business Insider Finds the New Orleans Saints Enjoy Highest Level of Devotion from Local Fans," http://www.nola.com, cited November 5, 2015. Also see David Broughton, "Saints Dominate Local Preseason Ratings," *SportsBusiness Journal* (July 28, 2014): 8.

30. For Glazer's career, see the team's website and also the article, "NFL Team Owners."

31. See note 18 for fan equity and social media indexes of the Buccaneers and their rankings among NFC and AFC teams.

32. The primary reference is Chris Wilkerson, "Bucs Asking State to Chip In for Stadium Upgrades," http://www.bizjournals.com, cited November 5, 2015.

33. For recent news about the franchise, see "Bucs Set Sail with Fresh Approach to Business," *SportsBusiness Journal* (September 2, 2013): 1.

Chapter Eight

West Division

While being a member of the National Football League (NFL), which team or teams in the West Division (WD) of the National Football Conference (NFC) won the least number of games all-time and also had the highest winning percentage, most division titles and championships but qualified for the fewest playoffs? Are the Arizona Cardinals a more valuable franchise than the Seattle Seahawks and do the San Francisco 49ers earn more revenue, gate receipts, and operating income than the St. Louis Rams?

To answer these and other questions, this chapter contains some interesting but important, practical, and relevant facts that highlight the historical performances of four teams in the NFC's WD as of the league's 2015–2016, or simply 2015, season. Besides their winning percentage and also number of wins, titles, championships, and postseasons, this information also includes special coaches, players, and events regarding each of them while competing in the NFL's regular seasons and any playoffs. In the chapter's final section—labeled Franchise Business—are these franchises' success or failure as business enterprises both individually and in comparison to each other from a financial perspective.

TEAM PERFORMANCES

Arizona Cardinals

After playing home games in Chicago from 1921 to 1959 and winning two NFL championships, the Cardinals moved to St. Louis, Missouri. While there, they appeared in only three playoffs during twenty-eight seasons. In addition to being a mediocre club, the Cardinals also played their games before sparse crowds at 54,392-seat Busch Stadium. Moreover, most sports fans in the St. Louis metropolitan area rooted more for the Major League Baseball (MLB) Cardinals than their local NFL team.[1]

Upon failing to establish a sizable fan base in St. Louis and get a new publicly financed stadium for his NFL franchise while financially operating it at a deficit, Cardinals owner Bill Bidwill—who purchased his brother Charles's share of the team in 1972—received offers from officials in such cities as Baltimore, Jacksonville, and Memphis, to move his team to their area after the league's 1987 regular season.

With an opportunity for the Cardinals to play in 70,491-seat Sun Devil Stadium in the Phoenix suburb of Tempe, the league overwhelmingly approved Bidwill's request to relocate them from eastern Missouri to Arizona before their 1988 season. Renamed Phoenix Cardinals, the club was assigned to the NFC's Eastern Division and join the Dallas Cowboys, New York Giants, Philadelphia Eagles, and Washington Redskins.

Historical Results

While in the conference's Eastern Division from 1988 to 2001 and then in the West Division (WD) during 2002–2015, the team—renamed Arizona Cardinals in 1994—played 448 games and won approximately 41 percent of them. Among other teams in the NFC as of their 2015–2016 season, the club ranked fourteenth in total wins, fifteenth in winning percentage, tied for fifteenth with the Rams in number of division titles, tied for thirteenth with three other teams in conference titles, tied for thirteenth with three other teams each with zero championships, and tied for fifteenth with the Rams in number of playoffs (Table A.5).

Compared to only WD clubs as of their 2015–2016 season, the Cardinals had the lowest winning percentage and fewer titles and championships than those of the 49ers, Seahawks, and Rams, and the same number of playoff appearances but more victories than the Rams. Based on these results and other data, Phoenix, or simply Arizona, has been an inferior performing team against its division and conference rivals despite playing in a Super Bowl in 2008. This record occurred, in part, because of their coaching problems, inexperienced and also unmotivated and injured players, competition from rivals, and such other things as failing to draft competent college football athletes and struggling with franchise ownership issues.

In contrast to the performances of thirty-one other NFL teams as of their 2015–2016 season, the Cardinals ranked twenty-fifth in total wins, thirtieth in winning percentage, tied for twenty-sixth with the Rams, Texans, and Titans each with three division titles, tied for twenty-second with several teams in winning their conference, tied for twentieth in number of championships each with zero, and tied for twenty-ninth in qualifying for the conference's playoffs. These and other results prove that, except for nine years during 1998, 2008–2009 and 2014–2015, Arizona's NFL team has underperformed and been a below-average competitor while playing clubs in the league but especially against those in its division (Table A.6).

In its regular season and postseason games, Arizona had a few successful but mostly unsuccessful coaches since 1988. Based on number of wins as of the league's 2015–2016 season, Ken Whisenhunt had 49, Vince Tobin 29, and Bruce Arians 22. For leading his team to the conference playoffs with eleven victories, Arians was the Associated Press (AP) coach of the year in 2014. Alternatively, several head coaches including Hank Kuhlmann, Joe Bugel, Buddy Ryan, Dave McGinnis, and Dennis Green each had more losses than wins while with the club.

Since 1988 some Cardinals players have established career, single season, and single game records for the franchise. For example, two career record holders were Larry Fitzgerald, who caught 846 passes for 11,367 yards and 87 touchdowns, and Dave Zastudil with 45.9 yards per punt. During a single season, Kurt Warner passed for 30 touchdowns in 2008; Ben Graham averaged 47 yards per punt in 2009; Neil Rackers kicked 40 field goals and scored 140 points in 2005; and David Boston received passes from quarterbacks for 1,598 yards in 2001. In a single game, Beanie Wells rushed for 228 yards; Boomer Esiason passed for 522 yards; and Kwamie Lassiter intercepted 4 passes. Individually, these players had significant performances, and as of 2014, their records continued to exist for the club.

Each year, the AP honors players for being outstanding at their position during games of a season. Between 1988 and 2015, those winning awards for Cardinals teams were offensive rookie of the year Anquan Boldin in 2003 and defensive rookie of the year Simeon Rice in 1996. In addition to them and their awards, quarterback Kurt Warner was Walter Payton NFL Man of the Year in 2008; Larry Fitzgerald the pro bowl Most Valuable Player (MVP) in 2009; and safety Pat Tillman's number retired by the organization after his career ended in 2001.

Cornerback/safety Aeneas Williams, who played for the Cardinals from 1991 to 2004, was inducted into the pro football Hall of Fame in 2014. He participated in 8 pro bowl games, had 55 interceptions for 807 yards and 9 touchdowns, and was named to the NFL's all-decade team of the 2000s. Williams started 159 of 160 games, and his interceptions rank second in franchise history. Because of these performances, Williams was inducted into the Cardinals' Ring of Honor in 2008.[2]

Performance Highlights

While located in Arizona since 1988, the club's most successful period was 2008–2009 and also in NFL seasons' 1998 and 2014–2015. In large part, these playoffs and winning titles occurred because of quarterbacks Jake

Plummer, Kurt Warner, and Drew Stanton; rushers Adrian Murrell, Edgerrin James, and Andre Ellington; and receivers Michael Sanders, Larry Fitzgerald, and Michael Floyd. Alternatively, the team's worst back-to-back performances happened during 1988–1997, 1999–2007, and 2010–2013. For sure, coaching problems and poor player performances contributed to losses in games during these seasons.

At its home games in the 65,000-seat University of Phoenix Stadium, which opened in 2006, the club's attendances have been among the smallest in the league. While the NFL's average each season was in the mid-500,000s, the number of spectators at Cardinals games between 2006 and 2014, for example, ranged from the high 400,000s to low 500,000s. Simply put, thousands of Arizona sports fans are not really passionate about their hometown pro football team because of its failure to consistently defeat the 49ers, Seahawks, and Rams in the WD while appearing in only four playoffs and one Super Bowl.[3]

Among thirty-one NFL venues, University of Phoenix Stadium ranked ninth in a recent study. According to an article published about it in an edition of *Sporting News*, the author wrote:

> People tend to forget about the cool technology tied to the facility's removable field, making the venue a true multi-purpose building. Whether there's any connection to the natural grass surface ranked as the league's best by NFL players is another question. But the sightlines are spectacular and last year, it became the first NFL stadium to upgrade to LED sports lighting. The loft-style seats provide a funky look to premium seating. The Green Lawn, an eight-acre, shaded green space, gives kids a chance to throw the football on grass. Next door to the stadium, the Westgate entertainment district's bars and restaurants provide hangouts for fans before and after Cardinals games.[4]

In the Entertainment Sports Programming Network's (ESPN) future power rankings, the network asked three experts to rate each NFL team for three seasons (2015–2017) on a scale of 0 to 100 percent in five categories including roster (excluding quarterback), quarterback, draft, front office, and coaching. In their analysis, the Cardinals had a 72.4 and ranked eleventh in the NFL following the WD's Seahawks at second but above the Rams at seventeenth and 49ers at twenty-second. The team received its highest score in coaching at 84.3 and then the front office 82.3, draft 76.7, roster 73.3, and quarterback 48.3.[5]

More specifically the Cardinals have improved in rank because general manager Steve Keim and coach Arians succeeded to lead them in the conference's 2013 and 2014 seasons. As a result the organization signed both of them to contract extensions, which is a foundation for the future. Even though quarterback Carson Palmer returned after major knee surgery, Arizona's offensive-minded head coach seems capable of building a winning club with or without him.

San Francisco 49ers

After five years petitioning the NFL for a franchise, trucking executive Anthony Morabito and his brother Victor and Louis Spadia spent a total of $25,000 to finance and organize the San Francisco 49ers that, in turn, became a charter member of the All America Football Conference (AAFC) in 1946. During its four years in the league's Western Division, the team had a 38–14–2 regular-season record, and in 1949, the Cleveland Browns defeated the 49ers in the championship game. Thus, San Francisco was a competitive club and premier organization in the AAFC.[6]

Because the Browns dominated the league by winning four consecutive titles, attendances dwindled at some teams' games causing financial problems for them including their owners, coaches, and players. As a result, two days before the AAFC's championship game in early December, 1949, the AAFC and NFL merged their operations. Along with the Browns and Baltimore Colts, the 49ers joined the NFL in 1950 because San Francisco was a natural fit as a geographic rival to the Los Angeles Rams. For several years, the Morabito brothers continued to own the 49ers until Anthony died of a heart attack in 1957.

Historical Results

A member of the league's National Conference from 1950 to 1952, Western Conference during 1953–1966 and the conference's Coastal Division to 1969, and then in the NFC's Western Division from 1970 to 2001 and finally the WD to their 2015–2016 season, the 49ers played 970 games and won approximately 54 percent of them. Among fifteen other teams in the conference as of their 2015 season, San Francisco ranked sixth in total wins, tied for fourth with the Vikings in winning percentage, tied for fifth with the Vikings in number of division titles, fourth in conference titles, tied for fourth with the Cowboys and Redskins in winning championships, and also sixth in qualifying for twenty-five playoffs (Table A.5).

Compared to only clubs in the conference's WD as of their 2015 season, the 49ers had the most victories and highest winning percentage, and also the largest number of titles, championships, and playoff appearances. Based on these results, San Francisco's NFL team has been above average to superior while performing against other teams in its division and the NFC. For sure, the 49ers are a popular and successful sports organization that vigorously competes against its rivals during most regular seasons and frequently wins a title and occasionally a league championship.

In contrast to the performances of thirty-one other NFL teams as of 2015, the 49ers ranked seventh in total wins and conference titles, eighth in winning percentage, tied for sixth in number of division titles, tied for fourth with the Cowboys and Redskins each winning five championships including Super Bowls, and seventh in qualifying for twenty-five playoffs. These and other results prove that, except for most years during the 1950s, 1960s, and mid to late-1970s and also from 2003 to 2010, this San Francisco-based NFL team has been above average to superior competitively and often successful while playing clubs in both conferences of the league during regular seasons and any postseasons (Table A.6).

Since 1950, 49ers teams have been led by a number of superior and some inferior head coaches and their staffs. In number of wins, Coach George Seifert had 108 victories, Bill Walsh 102, and Steve Mariucci 60. For their leadership, Walsh was AP coach of the year in 1981 and also Jim Harbaugh in 2011. Alternatively, San Francisco head coaches with fewer than 10 wins each included Norman Strader, Monte Clark, Key Meyer, Pete McCulley, Fred O'Connor, Dennis Erickson, and Jim Tomsula.

To win games in seasons and postseasons, a few 49ers players established career, single season, and single game records for the franchise. Some career records and record holders, for example, were 35,124 yards and 244 touchdowns by quarterback Joe Montana, and 1,281 passes caught for 19,247 yards and 187 total touchdowns for 1,130 points by receiver Jerry Rice. During a single season, Frank Gore rushed for 1,695 yards in 2006; David Akers kicked 44 field goals and scored 166 points in 2011; and Aldon Smith had 19.5 sacks in 2012.

In a single game, Terrell Owens caught 20 passes; David Baker intercepted 4 passes; Ray Wersching and Jeff Wilkins each kicked 6 field goals; Fred Dean had 6 sacks; and players' Gore, Montana, and Rice each set records. Individually, these athletes had great performances for 49ers teams and contributed to their success while competing in the NFC and especially against such division rivals as the Cardinals, Seahawks, and Rams.

Several 49ers players won AP awards during their years with the club. The league's MVPs include quarterbacks John Brodie in 1970, Joe Montana in 1989 and 1990, and Steve Young in 1992 and 1994. They earned awards because of their high passer ratings and percentage of completions, and also by leading San Francisco to win games and perhaps titles and also championships.

Other San Francisco players receiving AP awards were offensive players of the year Jerry Rice (twice), Roger Craig, Joe Montana, and Steve Young; defensive player of the year Deion Sanders; defensive rookies of the year Bruce Taylor, Dana Stubblefield, and Patrick Willis; and comeback players of the year Bryant Young and Garrison Hearst. Besides Rice, Billy Wilson, and Hugh McElhenny became pro bowl MVPs. In addition to them, wide receiver Anquan Bolden was Walter Payton NFL Man of the Year in 2016.

Because of their outstanding careers in the sport, some 49ers are in the pro football Hall of Fame. Along with Coach Walsh and such players as Montana, Rice, Young, and McElhenny, two others honored, for example, were defensive tackle Leo Nomellini who played every 49ers game for fourteen consecutive regular seasons and named to an all-NFL team on both offense and defense, and fullback Joe Perry—who finished his career with 9,723 rushing yards on 1,929 carries with 71 touchdowns as a runner while adding 2,021 receiving yards on 260 catches and 12 touchdowns in 181 games. Also, Perry broke the NFL record for most career rushing yards.

Performance Highlights

Since 1988 San Francisco's most successful periods were 1970–1973, 1983–1990, 1992–1998, and 2011–2013. In large part, these playoffs and winning titles occurred because of quarterbacks John Brodie, Joe Montana, Steve Young, and Colin Kaepernick, rushers Ken Willard, Roger Craig, Ricky Watters, and Frank Gore, and receivers Gene Washington, Jerry Rice, and Michael

Crabtree. Alternatively, the team's worst back-to-back performances happened during 1950–1956, 1958–1969, 1973–1980, and 2003–2010. In retrospect, coaching problems and poor player performances contributed to the team's losses during these seasons.

At its home games in 68,500-seat Levi's Stadium, which opened in 2014, the club's attendances were above average for the league and greater than most teams in its conference. While the NFC's average was about 65,000, more than 70,000 spectators attended each 49ers game. Simply put, pro football is a popular sport in the San Francisco area especially when the 49ers win titles and compete in the playoffs.

Among thirty-one NFL venues, Levi's Stadium ranked third in a recent study. According to an article published about it in an edition of *Sporting News*, the author wrote:

> The NFL's newest facility took a big hit for its parking issues during its first year of operation [2014]. But this building in the heart of Silicon Valley represents the future in mobile technology where every fan in the seating bowl can order food and drink from their mobile device. The Pepsi and Bud Light themed areas in the upper deck of both end zones are good points to watch plays develop. The "Pepsi-space" has a 12-pack of seats designed like soda cans. Michael Mina's Bourbon Steak & Pub, the stadium's sports bar and restaurant, has been a big hit with well-heeled fans paying $500 a game for an all-inclusive tailgate feast. Tickets [are] not included.[7]

In the Entertainment Sports Programming Network's (ESPN) future power rankings, the network asked three experts to rate each NFL team for three seasons (2015–2017) on a scale of 0 to 100 percent in five categories including roster (excluding quarterback), quarterback, draft, front office, and coaching. In their analysis, the 49ers were twenty-second with a score of 66.3 after a disappointing 8–8 record in the 2014 season.

More specifically the team ranked twentieth in the front office (70.3), thirty-second in coaching (56.3), eighteenth in the nonquarterback roster (69.3), seventeenth at quarterback (64.3), and fourteenth in the draft (72). While several players retired, some coaches and a few front office personnel left the organization for various reasons in late 2014/early 2015. Other major concerns besides coaching are the development of quarterback Colin Kaepernick and how much the team's last three drafts will contribute in games.

Regarding the club's competitiveness, the 49ers hired Dr. Fergus Connolly to be director of elite performance. As a former consultant to teams in professional sports groups including the English Premier League and International Rugby, he helped coordinate performance protocols being utilized at the elite levels of sport. Furthermore, Connolly helped to train, develop, and manage the performance staffs of pro franchises and monitored, tested, and rehabilitated players and created supplementation and recovery nutrition programs for them.[8]

Seattle Seahawks

To comply with parts of its 1970 merger with the AFL, the NFL planned to expand from twenty-six teams in its 1975 season to twenty-eight in 1976. A few years earlier a group of Seattle business and community leaders formed Seattle Professional Football Inc. and announced its goal to acquire an NFL franchise for the city.[9]

During the summer of 1974, the league awarded a family ownership group, led by businessman Lloyd W. Nordstrom and such other investors as Herman Sarkowsky and David Skinner, an expansion franchise for $16 million. Then in December NFL Commissioner Pete Rozelle announced the official signing of the franchise agreement by Lloyd, who represented the Nordstrom family as majority partners for the consortium.

In March 1975, previous executive director of the NFL Management Council and a former University of Washington executive John Thompson was hired as the general manager of the new team. Three months later, Seattle Seahawks—a Seahawk being another name for a fish-eating Osprey bird of prey—was selected after a public naming-contest that included more than 20,000 entries and over 1,700 different names.

Historical Results

A member of the National Conference's Western Division in 1976, American Conference's Western Division from 1977 to 2001, and then the NFC's WD during the league's 2002–2015 seasons, the Seahawks played 628 total games and won approximately 50 percent of them. Among other teams in its conference as of their 2014 season, Seattle ranked twelfth in wins and seventh in winning percentage, and also ninth in division titles, tied for ninth with the Eagles each with three conference titles, tied for ninth with three other teams in number of NFL plus Super Bowl championships, and tenth in qualifying for the conference's playoffs (Table A.5).

Compared to just teams in the NFC's WD as of 2015, Seattle had fewer wins and a lower winning percentage than the 49ers but more total titles and also playoff appearances than both the Cardinals and Rams. Based on this data, the Seahawks have been competitive in their division but average to below average or mediocre while performing against others in their conference. In other words, the forty-year-old club has won only three conference titles and one Super Bowl in fifteen postseasons.

In contrast to the performances of thirty-one other NFL teams as of their 2015 season, the Seahawks ranked twenty-first in total wins, fourteenth in winning percentage, tied for fifteenth with the Raiders in division titles, tied for fourteenth with the Raiders and Eagles in conference titles, and also tied for fifteenth with several other teams in number of championships including Super Bowls, and fifteenth in qualifying for playoffs. These and other results prove that, except for most years during the mid to late-1970s to early 1980s and late 1980s to 1990s, and also 2000 to 2002, Seattle's NFL team has been average competitively while playing clubs as a group among all divisions of the league (Table A.6).

Since 1976 the Seahawks have been led by various superior and inferior head coaches during their regular seasons and in postseasons. In number of wins for the franchise, Mike Holmgren had 90 victories, Chuck Knox 83, and Pete Carroll 60. For their leadership of a Seattle team, Jack Patera was AP coach of the year in 1978 and Knox in 1984. Alternatively, coaches with the fewest wins included Mike McCormick, Jim Mora, Tom Flores, and Dennis Erickson. Through the NFL's 2015–2016 season, Coach Carroll was 55–33–0 with two Super Bowl appearances and one championship in four postseasons.

A few Seattle players established career, single season, and single game records for the franchise in various years. Career records, for example, include 9,420 rushing yards by Shaun Alexander; 29,434 yards passing by Matt Hasselbeck; 50 interceptions by Dave Brown; and 159 field goals and 810 points by Norm Johnson. During one season, Dave Krieg passed for 32 touchdowns in 1984; Bobby Engram caught 94 passes in 2007; Jon Ryan averaged 46.6 yards per punt in 2011; and Michael Sinclair had 16.5 sacks in 1998.

In a single game, three different Seattle quarterbacks passed for 5 touchdowns; Steve Largent caught 15 passes for 261 yards; Eugene Robinson and four other players each intercepted 3 passes; four players each had 5 field goals; and Shaun Alexander scored 5 touchdowns and 30 points. Between 1976 and 2014, these athletes had great years for Seahawks teams and helped them win games in regular seasons and perhaps in postseasons.

Besides awarding NFL coaches, each year the AP honors players for their performances at a position on the field. Seattle's Shaun Alexander, for example, became the league's MVP and offensive player of the year in 2005. As a running back, he led the NFL with 1,880 rushing yards and set a record with 28 touchdowns. After his team qualified as a wild card, it won games in the divisional playoff and NFC championship but lost to the Steelers in Super Bowl XL. Other AP award winners, besides Alexander, were offensive player of the year Kenny Easley in 1984 and Cortez Kennedy in 1992, and pro bowl MVP Warren Moon in 1998.

Eight players, who played one or more seasons for the Seahawks, are members of the pro football Hall of Fame. Of them, receivers Steve Largent and Walter Jones played most of their years with Seattle. During his 200-game career with the club from 1976 to 1989, Largent held six pass-receiving records including most receptions, consecutive games with a reception, yards on receptions, touchdowns on receptions, and seasons with at least 50 receptions and 1,000 yards. Offensive tackle Jones played in nine pro bowls, an all-pro six times, and on the all-decade team of the 2000s.

Performance Highlights

Since 1976 Seattle's most successful periods consecutively were 1983–1984, 1987–1988, 2003–2007, and 2012–2015. In large part, these playoffs and winning titles occurred because of such quarterbacks as Dave Krieg, Matt Hasselbeck, and Russell Wilson, rushers Curtis Warner, Shaun Alexander, and Marshawn Lynch, and receivers Steve Largent, Darrell Jackson, and Golden Tate. Alternatively, the team's worst back-to-back performances happened during 1976–1982, 1989–1998, 2000–2002, and 2008–2009. In retrospect, coaching problems and poor player performances contributed to these losing seasons of the Seahawks.

At its home games in 67,000-seat CenturyLink Field, which opened in 2002, the club's attendances have been above average among most teams in the conference. While the NFL's was between 60,000 and 65,000 each game, the Seahawks averaged from 65,000 to 70,000. Simply put, pro football is a popular sport in the Seattle area especially because the team appeared in nine playoffs since 2003 including three Super Bowls and winning one of them in 2013.[10]

Among thirty-one NFL venues, CenturyLink Field ranked fourth in a recent study. According to an article published about it in an edition of *Sporting News*, the author wrote:

> The stadium's roof canopy speaks more too European futbol than American football, but as a result, it's helped to produce one of the NFL's loudest venues. Plus, any building containing a suite for Jimi Hendrix, a Seattle native, and a German-themed beer hall, gets a big thumbs-up. In a region known for tasty microbrews, the Seattle Alehouse, situated one block south of the stadium and across the street from Safeco Field, stands out as the first location for Pyramid Brewery.[11]

In the Entertainment Sports Programming Network's (ESPN) future power rankings, the network asked three experts to rate each NFL team for three seasons (2015–2017) on a scale of 0 to 100 percent in five categories including roster (excluding quarterback), quarterback, draft, front office, and coaching. In their analysis, the Seahawks' score of 89.7 ranked second to the Green Bay Packers' 91.3.[12]

More specifically, Seattle's roster rated an 89.7, quarterback 87.3, draft 87.3, front office 92.3, and coaching 91.7. Because there is no young backup for Russell Wilson entering the last year of his rookie deal—he eventually signed a four-year, $87.6 million contract extension that included a $31 million signing bonus with $60 million guaranteed—the quarterback position was a weak spot in the rankings. Otherwise, the club was among the two best in four other categories.

While salary-cap space worried the experts, they were optimistic about the team calling their draft picks the backbone because of a 36–12–0 record in the past three regular seasons. The 2012 draft class comprised of quarterback Wilson, plus linebacker Bobby Wagner, offensive guard J. R. Sweezy, and linebacker Bruce Irvin, among others, has been an integral part of the Seahawks' consecutive Super Bowl appearances. With the addition of wide receiver Ricardo Lockett and defensive end Frank Clark in the 2015 draft, Seattle may have snagged two more eventual starters.

St. Louis Rams

After eight seasons and winning an NFL championship in Cleveland, the Rams moved to Los Angeles in 1946. While there, the club appeared in twenty-one playoffs and won several division titles but lost Super Bowl XIV to the Steelers in 1979. Due to financial problems and reorganizations, the franchise experienced several changes in owners that included Hollywood comedian, entertainer, and movie star Bob Hope.[13]

In 1980, the team moved its home games from Los Angeles Memorial Stadium to Anaheim Stadium. While playing in the National Conference's Western Division, the Rams finished third or fourth from 1990 to 1994 with a 19–45 record, and during these regular seasons, their attendance steadily declined from about 60,000 to 42,000 per game.

When Rams' owners Dominic and Georgia Frontierre negotiated with but failed to get permission from public officials to develop plots of land near Anaheim Stadium, they received approval from the league to move their team out of Southern California. Although Baltimore was originally a preferred site, the Frontierre's transferred the Rams to St. Louis, Missouri, in 1995 and agreed to share revenues from the sale of permanent seat licenses (PSLs) at the city's newly-constructed Trans World Dome with other NFL franchise owners.

Historical Results

A member of the NFC's Western Division from 1995 to 2001 and then the WD since 2002, the Rams played 336 games and won approximately 42 percent of them. Compared to other teams in the conference as of the league's 2015 season, St. Louis ranked sixteenth in number of wins and fourteenth in winning percentage, and also tied for fifteenth with three division titles and five playoffs each, tied for eleventh with two conference titles, and tied for ninth with the Saints, Buccaneers, and Seahawks in championships including a Super Bowl victory in 1999 (Table A.5).

Among only clubs in the conference's WD as of their 2015 season, the Rams had the fewest victories and second lowest winning percentage, and also more division and conference titles combined than the Cardinals, same number of championships as the Seahawks, and less playoffs than the 49ers and Seahawks. Based on these results, this twenty-one-year-old St. Louis–based franchise has been a low-performance team among those in its division and conference and thus not competitive during many NFL seasons since 1995 because of significant coaching and player problems, and other issues within the organization.

Compared to the performances of thirty-one other NFL teams as of the league's 2015–2016 season, the Rams ranked thirtieth in total wins, twenty-ninth in winning percentage, tied for twenty-sixth with the Cardinals and Titans in division titles, tied for seventeenth with the Panthers, Ravens, Bengals, and Colts each with two conference titles, tied for fifteenth with several other teams in winning championships, and tied for twenty-ninth with the Cardinals in qualifying for the playoffs. These and other results prove that, except from 1999 to 2001 and in 2003 and 2004, St. Louis's NFL team has been below average competitively while playing clubs in their division and conference and also others in the AFC (Table A.6).

To play games against rivals across the NFL during their 1995–2015 seasons, the Rams employed a few successful but mostly unsuccessful head coaches. In number of wins, Mike Martz had 56 victories and Dick Vermeil 25. In 1999, Vermail was AP coach of the year because his team won WD and NFC titles and then Super Bowl XXXIV at the Georgia Dome in Atlanta. Alternatively Jim Haslett, Joe Vitt, Steve Spagnuolo, Scott Linehan, and Rich Brooks each had more losses than wins while coaching in regular seasons.

Between 1994 and 2015, Rams players established career, single season, and single game records for the franchise. For example, career records include 10,135 rushing yards by Stephen Jackson; 46.6 yards per punt by Donnie Jones; 265 field goals and 1,223 points by Jeff Wilkins; 85 touchdowns by Marshall Faulk; and 81 sacks by Leonard Little.

During a single season, Kurt Warner passed for 41 touchdowns in 1999 and 2,105 yards in 2001; Isaac Bruce caught 119 passes for 1,781 yards in 1995; and Jones in 2008, Wilkins in 2003, and Faulk in 2000 each set punting, kicking, and scoring records respectively while Robert Quinn had 19 sacks in 2013. In a single game, Warner passed for 5 touchdowns; Keith Lyle intercepted 3 passes; Wilkins kicked 6 field goals; and Faulk scored 4 touchdowns and 24 points. Individually, these athletes had remarkable performances and in different ways became record holders who contributed to victories by Rams teams against opponents in the WD and other divisions of the NFC.

Each year the AP awards players for being outstanding while playing at their positions on the field. Quarterback Warner in 1999 and 2001, and running back Faulk in 2000, were each MVPs in the league. Warner became the second quarterback in history to pass for 40 touchdowns in a season, and in 2001, he set an NFL record with 4,830 passing yards, 36 touchdowns, a 68.7 completion percent, and a 101.4 passing rating. Faulk established an NFL record in 2000 by scoring 26 touchdowns and led the conference with 2,189 yards from scrimmage.

Other Rams winning AP awards as of 2015 were offensive player of the year Faulk during 1999–2001; offensive rookie of the year quarterback Sam Bradford in 2010 and running back Todd Gurley in 2016; and defensive rookie of the year Aaron Donald in 2014. Besides those honors, quarterback Marc Bulger was pro bowl MVP in 2004 and Warner the Super Bowl MVP in 1999.

Four Rams players, who spent one or more seasons in St. Louis, were inducted into the pro football Hall of Fame. Including guard Jackie Slater and running back Jerome Bettis each with the franchise for one year and Faulk for seven, the other member was cornerback/safety Aeneas Williams. Inducted in 2014, he played in 7 pro bowls, recorded 55 interceptions for 807 yards, scored 9 touchdowns, and was named to the NFL's all-decade team of the 2000s.

Performance Highlights

Since 1995, St. Louis's only successful periods consecutively were 1999–2001 and 2003–2004. In large part, these playoffs and winning titles occurred because of such quarterbacks as Warner and Bulger, rusher Falk, and also receivers Isaac Bruce and Torry Holt. Alternatively, the team's worst back-to-back performances happened during 1995–1998 and 2005–2015. In retrospect, coaching problems and unproductive player performances contributed to these losing seasons of the franchise.

At its home games in the 66,000-seat Edward Jones Dome, which opened in 1995, the club's attendances have been near the bottom among teams in the conference and league. While the NFL's was between 60,000 and 65,000 per game, the Rams averaged from 50,000 to 55,000 for several seasons. Simply put, pro football is not an extremely popular sport in the St. Louis area especially because the Rams appeared in only five playoffs since 1995 although winning a Super Bowl in 1999.[14]

Among thirty-one NFL venues, the Edward Jones Dome ranked twenty-seventh in a recent study. According to an article published about it in an edition of *Sporting News*, the author said:

> By now, everyone knows about the Rams' desire to get back to sunny Los Angeles after spending 20 years in St. Louis. The dome, part of a convention center complex, has served its purpose well during the past two decades and the team has creatively developed some novel clubs and premium seat additions. Whether the building ultimately loses its primary tenant remains to be seen. There are a few tailgating lots by the dome, as well as some nearby bars. A short cab ride away is Ballpark Village, a collection of bars and restaurants situated across the street from Busch Stadium that turn into football bars on game day.[15]

In ESPNs future power rankings, the network asked three experts to rate each NFL team for three seasons (2015–2017) on a scale of 0 to 100 percent in five categories including roster (excluding quarterback), quarterback, draft, front office, and coaching. In their analysis, the Rams ranked seventeenth with a score of 68.4. In descending order, the draft was 76.3, roster 74.7, coaching 73.3, front office 70, and quarterback 46.7.

For an overview, the Rams' front office placed thirteenth and coaching seventeenth because they made no significant changes in either area. Switching from Brian Schottenheimer to Frank Cignetti at offensive coordinator did not account for a full reassessment of the coaching situation. This team has many of the right players in their positions, but little enthusiasm and morale could simply reflect frustration with its lack of progress in the standings.

With a record of 7–8–1 to 7–9–0 and then 6–10–0 in three seasons under the current leadership, it is unclear whether a long-term quarterback actually exists on the roster. The club hopes that quarterback Nick Foles will be the solution and publicly expressed interest in re-signing him to a long-term contract before he played in a regular season game for them.[16]

FRANCHISE BUSINESS

Besides performing as teams in regular season and postseason games, NFL franchises are also commercial enterprises. To that end, their economic objective is to earn maximum revenue and obtain the greatest amount of profit on a fiscal basis from their operations. Although they share revenue with each other from such sources as national television contracts and other deals, it is important for them to efficiently allocate resources, determine and distribute payrolls, set nonpremium and premium ticket prices, and schedule investments in short- and long-term assets. To reveal and manage these activities, this section focuses on different parts of four NFC franchise's business and how these organizations rank and succeed or not succeed from a financial perspective.

Arizona Cardinals

A former Chicago sports figure and current member of the pro football Hall of Fame, Charles Bidwill purchased the NFL Cardinals in 1932 from businessman David Jones for $50,000 and owned the club until his death in 1947. His wife, Violet, then controlled the franchise for the next fifteen years followed jointly by sons Bill and Charles Bidwill Jr.[17]

Named a Cardinals vice president during his undergraduate days at Georgetown University, Bill Bidwill returned to Chicago from the Navy in 1956 to assist with family investments that included professional football. When the team moved to St. Louis in 1960, he returned to the organization full-time. Twelve years later, Bill bought his brother's share of the team for $6.5 million and became its only owner.

In 2007, Bill's son Michael took over day-to-day operations of the club. Before joining the Cardinals' front office in 1996, he was a prosecutor in the United States attorney's office in Phoenix, where he worked in the violent crimes unit. Unlike the league's three other third-generation owners, Michael has not been a member of the NFL's powerful finance, broadcasting, and management committees. Instead, he focused on his expertise including chairman of the stadium security and fan behavior committee and serving on the stadium committee.[18]

Team Financials

According to data and other financial information published in *Forbes* for sixteen franchises in the NFC as of their 2015–2016 season, the Cardinals ranked twelfth in market value at $1.54 billion, revenue at $308 million, and gate receipts at $55 million, and also tenth in operating income at $57 million, eighth in player expenses at $166 million, and seventh in its debt-to-value ratio at 10 percent. Among just WD teams in the conference, Arizona was third in market value, total revenue, and gate receipts, second in operating income and the debt ratio, and fourth in player expenses. Based on these results, this is an average to below-average franchise from a financial perspective within its division and conference (Table A.7).

Compared to thirty-one other NFL teams as of their 2015 season, the Cardinals were twentieth in market value and twenty-third in revenue, and also tied for twentieth with the Chiefs and Chargers in gate receipts, eighteenth in operating income, thirteenth in player expenses, and tied for eighteenth with the Titans in their debt-to-value percent. As such, this team has below-average amounts among the group of clubs in the league. Thus, the Cardinals are not a financially prominent NFL sports enterprise or significant business organization such as the Cowboys, Giants, and Redskins (Table A.8).

For several years a Chicago-based company named Team Marketing Report (TMR) has prepared and published a Fan Cost Index (FCI) for the home games of teams in professional sports leagues. To attend a game for a typical family with two kids, an FCI includes the costs of four average-priced tickets, two cheapest-priced draft beers, four each cheapest-priced soft drinks and hot dogs, parking for one car, and two each game programs and least-expensive, adult-size adjustable caps. Costs are determined by telephone calls with team representatives, venues, and concessionaires, and from asking questions during interviews.[19]

For the league's 2015 season, the Cardinals FCI was approximately $436 or twenty-first highest in the league with zero percent change from 2014. Listed from most to least in amount by item for one person, the team's non-premium tickets averaged about $82, a cap $20 and parking for one vehicle $14, beer more than $7, a soft drink and hot dog each about $4, and a program $3. For FCIs of other WD clubs in the NFC, the 49ers were first at $640, Seahawks seventeenth at $472, and Rams twenty-second at $431. Thus, the 49ers had the highest FCI in the league and Jaguars lowest at $347.

At $258 each, Arizona's premium tickets for seats at the University of Phoenix Stadium cost about 1 percent more than the league average. In short Phoenix is a mid-sized sports market where Cardinals teams, with only four playoff appearances since 1988, charge neither high nor too low prices for admission to their home games, in part, to maximize gate receipts and generate more revenue for the franchise.

Business Highlights

Using fifteen years of data on such things as NFL team performances, home-game ticket prices, and market populations and their median incomes, Emory University researchers created an equity index to determine which clubs had the most avid, engaged, passionate, and/or supportive fans before the NFL's 2015 season. Among the NFC's WD teams, the Cardinals ranked nineteenth and above the Rams at twenty-third and Seahawks at twenty-sixth but below the 49ers at tenth. According to this index, Arizona has more enthusiastic football fans than six NFC teams and seven in the AFC.[20]

In another Emory University index titled Social Media Equity, the Cardinals had the league's thirty-second or worst fan base in the league and inferior to the division's 49ers at sixth, Seahawks at twelfth, and Rams at twenty-eight. Although this index reflects whether teams over- or underperform with respect to their Twitter following, Arizona's fans are less involved or passionate about their hometown team on social media than those of thirty-one other NFL clubs. Interestingly, the Cowboys had the most dedicated and fervent fan base of teams in the NFC and Steelers of those in the AFC.

For other important business news about Arizona's NFL franchise, the website Complex Sports did a review of beer prices in the NFL's thirty-two markets and found patrons at Cardinals games are paying 60 cents per ounce for beer. Only Philadelphia at 71 cents per ounce and San Francisco at 63 cents were pricier. Since the NFL average for beer is 46 cents per ounce, a 20-ounce cup of it costs $9.20, but also about $12 for Cardinals fans. In another study involving beer the maker of breath analyzers, BACtrack, ranked NFL teams with the drunkest fans. Those of the Cardinals were fifth with an average blood alcohol content of 0.062 percent while the threshold for a DUI in Arizona is 0.08 percent.[21]

To highlight their performances, the Cardinals made history in July 2015 when they hired the first female in the sport, Jen Welter, to coach inside linebackers during training camp and the preseason. Even so, they were the best in football in 2014 until quarterback Carson Palmer tore his ACL in November in a win over the Rams and an 8–1–0 record. However, the team then went 3–4–0 and lost its opportunity for a wild card in the NFC to the Panthers. Although Palmer recovered, defensive coordinator Todd Bowles—considered among the best in the league—left to join the Jets in the AFC.

San Francisco 49ers

American heir and businesswoman Denise DeBartolo York and her husband John are owners and cochairpersons of the 49ers franchise. After graduating from Saint Mary's College of Indiana—the Holy Cross women's counterpart to adjacent Notre Dame—Denise joined the family business—named The DeBartolo Corporation— and became its executive vice president. Following her father Edward DeBartolo's death in 1994, she then was the company's co-chairwoman and sold all its malls.[22]

During the early 2000s, Denise and John gained control of the 49ers and other sports assets from her brother, Edward DeBartolo Jr. Since then they have transferred control of the team to their son, Jed York. A graduate of the University of Notre Dame with a bachelor of art in finance and history, he began his career as a financial analyst for Guggenheim Partners at their office in New York but resigned from the business a year later.

After leaving Guggenheim Partners, York's parents urged him to join the 49ers organization as the director of strategic planning, and later, they promoted him to vice president of strategic planning. In December 2008 Jed's father appointed him president of the club. When Jed became the operating head of the franchise, his parents provided economic resources but maintained their role of interacting with other owners and NFL executives. Nevertheless, in 2012, Jed was replaced by Gideon Yu but kept his title of chief executive officer.

Team Financials

According to data and other financial information published in *Forbes* for sixteen franchises in the NFC as of their 2015–2016 season, the 49ers ranked fourth in both market value at $2.7 billion and gate receipts at $77 million, tied for fourth with the Bears in player expenses at $168 million, and also third in total revenue at $427 million, operating income at $123 million, and their debt-to-value ratio of 21 percent. Among only WD clubs in the conference, San Francisco was the most valuable in the group with the highest revenue, gate receipts, and operating income, second in players expenses to the Seahawks, but also first in its debt-to-value ratio (Table A.7).

Compared to thirty-one other NFL franchises as of their 2015 season, the 49ers were fifth in market value, fourth both in total revenue and operating income, tied for fifth with the Jets in gate receipts, tied for eighth with the Bears in player expenses, and also fourth in its debt-to-value percent. Based on these results, this is a high-valued and financially lucrative and profitable franchise within its division and conference and also above average, including its debt ratio, among teams in both conferences (Table A.8).

As given before for the WD Cardinals in the NFL's 2015 season, the 49ers' FCI was $640 or highest in the league but 0.2 percent less than in 2014. Listed from most to least in amount by item for one person, the team's nonpremium tickets averaged $117, parking for one vehicle $40 and a cap $22, beer and a program each $10, and a soft drink and hot dog each $6. The

FCIs and rankings of other WD clubs in the NFC were respectively $472 and seventeenth for the Seahawks, $436 and twenty-first for the Cardinals, and $431 and twenty-second for the Rams.[23]

At $320 each, San Francisco's team had the league's seventh most expensive premium ticket price in 2015 and $65 or 26 percent higher than those of the typical team. Because of such things as the Bay Area's high cost of living, opening a new stadium, team's huge debt, popularity of pro football on the West Coast, and other factors, it costs a family of four to attend a game at Levi's Stadium more money than at any other venue in the NFL. If the team performs to fans' expectations in 2016 and thereafter, its prices will maximize gate receipts and earn an excess amount of operating income and revenue for the franchise.

Business Highlights

Using fifteen years of data on such things as NFL team performances, home-game ticket prices, and market populations and their median incomes, Emory University researchers created an equity index to determine which clubs had the most avid, engaged, passionate, and/or supportive fans before the NFL's 2015 season. Among the NFC's WD teams, the 49ers ranked tenth and ahead of the Cardinals at nineteenth, Rams at twenty-third, and Seahawks at twenty-sixth. According to this index, San Francisco has more enthusiastic football fans than the majority of franchises in both conferences but below the NFC's Cowboys, Giants, Bears, Packers, and Saints.

In another Emory University index titled Social Media Equity, the 49ers had the league's sixth best fan base in the league and superior to the division's Seahawks at twelfth, Rams at twenty-eighth, and Cardinals at thirty-second. Although this index reflects whether teams over- or underperform with respect to their Twitter following, San Francisco's football fans are committed and passionate about their hometown team on social media than those of twenty-six other NFL clubs. Interestingly, the Cowboys had the most dedicated and fervent fan base of teams in the NFC and Steelers in the AFC.

For other important business news about San Francisco's NFL franchise, an ABC affiliate in Northern California reported that fans are upset about Levi's Stadium. With licenses at $12,000 each and individual season tickets selling for about $2,000, that is a high price to pay to sit in the scorching sun for over three hours to watch a football game. Unlike Candlestick Park, which was located in a part of the city well known for its cold weather and gusty winds, Levi's is located in the heart of Silicon Valley—one of the hottest parts of the Bay Area. Unfortunately, the 49ers failed to take this into account when building the stadium.[24]

As a result, thousands of 49ers Season Builders Licenses have found their way on to the secondary market. Dealing with the public relations backlash after releasing a successful head coach, the current regime is not the most popular in Northern California. Couple that with the wide array of issues at Levi's Stadium including multiple problems with the turf, it is not going well for team officials.

To review this franchise's operations, the 49ers endured disappointing 2014 and 2015 seasons after three straight trips to the NFC title game. The club missed the playoffs and parted ways with Coach Jim Harbaugh after its 2014 season. Things were better for bean counters as the team opened their privately financed, \$1.2 billion, 68,500-seat stadium in Santa Clara. The team booked more than \$1 billion in ticket and sponsorship revenue ahead of the stadium's opening with much of the revenue earmarked to pay for the venue's construction costs. The team added 1,400 seats ahead of their 2015 season in part to fulfill requirements for hosting the Super Bowl. The new seating is part of \$17 million in stadium upgrades.

Seattle Seahawks

Although he liked team sports, Seattle billionaire Paul Allen had no burning passion for them or for any childhood dream to fulfill, or a midlife crisis to own a professional football franchise. Yet in a warehouse by the Ballard Bridge in June 1997, Allen delivered a sales pitch to the media and people in Washington State whereby he agreed to purchase the NFL Seahawks from disgruntled owner Ken Behring—who threatened to move the team to Southern California—but the deal depended on a make-or-break decision. That is, he would not buy the team unless the public voted in favor of a new stadium later in the month.

Within two weeks of the stadium vote, Allen's advisors pulled the trigger. A rumor circulated that he would still purchase the Seahawks from Behring even without a new stadium. As a result, Allen's campaign staff sent him to the warehouse with a film director and producer. In a thirty-second commercial ad, Allen agreed to save the Seahawks and do his part in building something for the future, personally and financially. In other words, the public should vote yes for a new stadium and exhibition center. After voters narrowly passed the measure, Allen committed \$130 million of his money for the two facilities. Then, he acquired the Seahawks franchise from Behring for \$288 million.

Team Financials

According to data and other financial information published in *Forbes* for sixteen franchises in the NFC as of their 2015 season, the Seahawks ranked eighth in both market value at \$1.81 billion and total revenue at \$334 million, and also they were tenth in gate receipts at $58 million, twelfth in operating income at $43 million, second in player expenses at $178 million, and tied for eleventh with the Packers in their debt-to-value ratio of 6 percent. Among only WD teams in the conference, Seattle had the second highest market value, total revenue and gate receipts, third most operating income and largest player expenses, but smallest percent of debt-to-value (Table A.7).

Compared to thirty-one other NFL teams as of their 2015–16 season, the Seahawks were sixteenth in market value, tied for thirteenth with the Steelers in total revenue, tied for sixteenth with the Colts in gate receipts, twenty-fifth in operating income, third in player expenses, and tied for twenty-fourth with the Packers and Browns in percent of their debt-to-value ratio. According to these rankings, Seattle is an average franchise from a financial perspective among clubs in its division and conference, and also with respect to those in the AFC (Table A.8).

As determined before for the WD Cardinals and 49ers in the league's 2015 season, the Seahawks FCI was approximately $472 or seventeenth highest in the league and 0.1 percent greater than in 2014. Listed from most to least in amount by item for one person, the team's nonpremium tickets averaged about $84, parking for a vehicle $50, a cap $18, one beer and a soft drink each $5, and a hot dog and program each $3. Among the NFC's other WD teams, their rankings and FCIs were respectively the 49ers first at $640, Cardinals twenty-first at $436, and Rams twenty-second at $431.[25]

At $202 each, Seattle's premium tickets for seats at Levi's Stadium were $53 or 26 percent lower than the league average and also less than those of the 49ers and Cardinals but more in price than tickets of the Rams. Thus, it costs a family of four to purchase nonpremium or premium tickets to attend a Seahawks home game only a few dollars below the amount paid to be at one of a typical team in the league. In retrospect, Seahawks fans received a discount in 2015 at CenturyLink Field when compared to NFL games at Levi's Stadium in San Francisco but not at University of Phoenix Stadium in Glendale or the Edward Jones Dome in St. Louis.

Business Highlights

Using fifteen years of data on such things as NFL team performances, home-game ticket prices, and market populations and their median incomes, Emory University researchers created an equity index to determine which clubs had the most avid, engaged, passionate, and/or supportive fans before the NFL's 2015 season. Among the NFC's WD teams, the Seahawks ranked twenty-sixth and below the 49ers at tenth, Cardinals at nineteenth, and Rams at twenty-third. According to this index, Seattle has fewer enthusiastic football fans than other franchises in the NFC but more than the AFC's Chiefs, Bills, Jaguars, Raiders, Browns, and Dolphins.

In another Emory University index titled Social Media Equity, the Seahawks had the league's twelfth best fan base in the league and superior to the WD's Rams at twenty-eighth and Cardinals at thirty-second but inferior to the 49ers at sixth. Although this index reflects whether teams over- or underperform with respect to their Twitter following, Seattle fans are more committed and passionate about their hometown team on social media than those of twenty other NFL clubs. Interestingly, the Cowboys had the most dedicated and fervent fan base of teams in the NFC and Steelers in the AFC.

For other important business news about Seattle's NFL franchise, tote bags are sold at CenturyLink Field. These one-of-a-kind products are the result of a partnership between the team and Alchemy Goods, a Seattle company which makes bags, wallets, belts, and the like out of everything from recycled bike tires to stadium banners, seatbelts, and more. Priced at $15 for a small lunch size bag and $22 for a grocery size, any proceeds from tote bag sales are transferred to the Washington State Coalition Against Domestic Violence.

Seahawks' owner Paul Allen cannot be accused of gouging his team's fans. With two consecutive trips to the Super Bowl, ticket demand for Seahawks home games was high before early 2015. With 105 consecutive sellouts at CenturyLink Field and a renewal rate of 99.6 percent in the league's 2013 and 2014 seasons, the club still managed to find a way to increase the availability of tickets.

Thanks to the redistribution of tickets that were previously sold to brokers, almost 20 percent of fans on the "Blue Pride" season-ticket waiting list were able to purchase season tickets prior to the 2015 season. In addition, about 4,000 single-game tickets were taken by the team from longtime ticket brokers in order to distribute them directly to fans. Of the 4,000 tickets recovered from brokers, 2,000 went to fans on the "Blue Pride" wait list. The team sold an additional 2,000 seats as single-game tickets using dynamic pricing during July 2015. The price for those tickets fluctuated based on market demand and eventually sold on Ticketmaster.com.[26]

For the first time ever, some other NFL teams have started using dynamic pricing, a system adopted by other professional sports league clubs in the past. Besides that change in policy by Seahawks officials, the newly added 1,000-seat Toyota Fan Deck also increased ticket availability for home games at CenturyLink Field.

St. Louis Rams

Stanley Kroenke, a sixty-three-year-old Missouri billionaire, became involved with bringing professional football back to St. Louis in 1993 when he failed to receive an expansion franchise. After the Rams moved from Los Angeles to St. Louis two years later, he joined the Rosenbloom family as a minority owner but increased his stake to 40 percent in 1997. In the summer of 2010, he bought the Rosenbloom's share of the team for $750 million.[27]

But first Kroenke had to deal with NFL rules against owning major league franchises in other pro football cities. Since he owned the NBA's Denver Nuggets and NHL's Colorado Avalanche, Kroenke agreed to turn over operational and financial control of those teams to his thirty-year-old son, Josh, by December 2014. He marked the occasion by making a rare appearance before the media.

For years, Kroenke has steadfastly maintained a low profile as owner of the Rams, earning the nickname "Silent Stanley." Besides the Rams, he also owns Major League Soccer's Colorado Rapids and the National Lacrosse League's Colorado Mammoth, and also invested enough of his money to become the largest shareholder in the English Premier League's Arsenal club.

Team Financials

According to data and other financial information published in *Forbes* for sixteen franchises in the NFC as of their 2015–2016 season, the Rams ranked fifteenth in both market value at $1.45 billion and total revenue at $290 million, sixteenth in gate receipts at $45 million, tied for fourteenth with the Vikings in operating income at $34 million, tied for sixth with the Eagles in player expenses at $167 million, and tied for eighth with the Eagles in their debt-to-value ratio of 8 percent. Among only WD clubs in the conference, St. Louis had the smallest amounts in the data except for its player expenses and the debt ratio percent (Table A.7).

Compared to thirty-one other teams in the league as of their 2015–2016 season, the Rams were tied for twenty-eighth with the Raiders in market value, and also they ranked thirtieth in total revenue, thirty-first in gate receipts, tied for twenty-ninth in operating income, tied for tenth in player expenses, and tied for sixteenth in the debt-to-value ratio. From a financial perspective, this is a struggling franchise and an inferior business enterprise. Certainly the team has economic, front office, and image problems, including its small market size, obsolete stadium, historical performances and unsuccessful coaching staffs, lack of enough support from civic organizations and local businesses, and leadership issues with respect to its owners and executives (Table A.8).

As explained for the WD Cardinals, 49ers, and Seahawks as of the NFL's 2015 season, the Rams FCI was approximately $431 or twenty-second highest in the league and 1 percent more than in 2014. Listed from most to least in amount by item for one person, the team's nonpremium tickets averaged about $73, a cap $28 and parking for one vehicle $20, beer $9, a program and soft drink each $5, and a hot dog between $4 and $5. Among other WD teams in the conference, they had rankings and FCIs respectively as follows: 49ers first at $640, Seahawks seventeenth at $472, and Cardinals twenty-first at $436.[28]

A premium ticket cost, on average, about $189 for a fan to attend a Rams home game in the Edward Jones Dome. This was $66 or 35 percent less than the league's average premium price. Since the club's FCI was $49 or 12 percent below the amount of a typical NFL team, a family of four could buy nonpremium or premium tickets and enjoy a pro football game in St. Louis cheaper than in the majority of stadiums within the league. These costs and prices, in turn, were set by the Rams organization to improve its home-game attendances and increase gate receipts and profit.

Business Highlights

Using fifteen years of data on such things as NFL team performances, home-game ticket prices, and market populations and their median incomes, Emory University researchers created an equity index to determine which clubs had the most avid, engaged, passionate, and/or supportive fans before the NFL's 2015 season. Among the NFC's WD teams, the Rams ranked twenty-third and below the 49ers at tenth and Cardinals at nineteenth but above the Seahawks at twenty-sixth. According to this index, St. Louis has fewer enthusiastic football fans than twenty-two franchises in the league but more than the NFC's Lions and Seahawks and also seven AFC teams.

In another Emory University index titled Social Media Equity, the Rams had the league's twenty-eighth best fan base in the league and superior to the WD's Cardinals at thirty-second but inferior to the 49ers at sixth and Seahawks at twelfth. Although this index reflects whether teams over- or underperform with respect to their Twitter following, St. Louis sports fans are more committed and passionate about their hometown team on social media than only four other NFL clubs. Interestingly, the Cowboys had the most dedicated and fervent fan base of teams in the NFC and Steelers in the AFC.

For other important business news about St. Louis's NFL franchise, chief executive officer and president of the Walt Disney Company Robert Iger has been appointed to oversee an effort to build an NFL complex in Carson, California. While he would serve as non-executive chairman of Carson Holdings only if NFL owners approve a stadium in Carson but reject Rams owner Kroenke's $1.86 billion stadium plan in Los Angeles suburb Inglewood, the announcement was meant to generate support for Iger's proposal. During early January 2016 the league's franchise owners approved the relocation of the Rams from St. Louis to play in a new privately funded stadium in Inglewood.[29]

For more information about the Rams' future, Kroenke wanted to leave St. Louis even though the city offered hundreds of millions of dollars in taxpayer money for a new stadium. Instead he preferred to build an open-air, $1.8-plus billion stadium with a canopy on a 238-acre complex formerly occupied by Hollywood Park racetrack and adjacent to The Forum in Los Angeles. The development may include a movie theater, performing arts center, housing, offices, and commercial businesses. Kroenke, who owns the land, had to compete against the San Diego Chargers and Oakland Raiders that requested to share a stadium in Carson.

During mid-December 2015, a committee of St. Louis aldermen approved a tentative financing plan for the construction of a new $1 billion stadium near the Gateway Arch along the Mississippi River. According to this proposal, the city will spend $150 million and Rams $250 million for the facility. In addition, the NFL will provide the team with a $200 million loan while seat licenses contribute approximately $160 million toward the cost. Through tax credits or bonds, the State of Missouri would fund the remaining amount.[30]

NOTES

1. Seasons, postseasons, and details about NFL organizations and their players and coaches since 1920 are in part contained in the *NFL Record & Fact Book 2014* (New York, NY: NFL, 2014) and "Teams," http://www.pro-football-reference.com, cited August 25, 2015.
2. For clubs in the WD and other divisions, online at "Teams," http://www.profootballhof.com, cited September 1, 2015.
3. "Rod Fort's Sports Business Data," http://www.sites.google.com, cited September 1, 2015.
4. The best source is "Ranking All 31 NFL Stadiums," http://www.sportingnews.com, cited August 31, 2015.
5. "2015 NFL Future Power Rankings," http://www.insider.espn.go.com, cited October 10, 2015, is the reading to review for this analysis.
6. See, for example, such sources as the "History of National Football League Franchises, 1920–Present," http://www.profootballhof.com, cited August 25, 2015, and "NFL Links," http://www.sportsecyclopdia.com, cited August 25, 2015.
7. Michael Potts, "Ranking All NFL Stadiums for 2015—From Worst to Best." http://www.whatculture.com, cited September 2, 2015.
8. David Fucillo, "49ers Name Dr. Fergus Connolly Director of Elite Performance," http://www.ninersnation.com, cited November 10, 2015.
9. Frank P. Jozsa, Jr., *National Football League Strategies: Business Expansions, Relocations, and Mergers* (New York: Springer, 2014), contains the history of NFL expansion teams.
10. For specific seasons of the league, there are "Rod Fort's Sports Business Data" and NFL attendances at http://www.espn.go.com.
11. "Ranking All 31 NFL Stadiums," http://www.sportingnews.com, cited August 31, 2015.
12. Besides "2015 NFL Future Power Rankings," see "Power Rankings: Rating the Likeability of Every NFL Franchise," http://www.foxsports.com, cited August 31, 2015.
13. For the founding and early history of the Rams and other NFL teams, see such websites as http://www.nfl.com and http://www.sportsencyclopedia.com.
14. See note 10 above for attendance of the team and others in the league.
15. Quote was from "Ranking All 31 NFL Stadiums," http://www.sportingnews.com, cited August 31, 2015.
16. Quarterback Nick Foles signed a two-year contract extension with the St. Louis Rams in August 2015. As expected, the deal pays him almost $14 million guaranteed. The exact amount

of guaranteed money is $13,792,000 and includes a $3 million signing bonus, a fully guaranteed base salary this season of $1,042,500, and a $2 million roster bonus to be paid on September 1.

There are also $4.5 million in not-likely-to-be-earned incentives available based on going to the pro bowl, playoff appearances, and wins. See Nick Wagoner, "Breaking Down Quarterback Nick Foles' Contract Extension," http://www.espn.go.com, cited December 13, 2015.

17. Several readings, including online sources, have information about the circumstances and reasons that encouraged current owners to purchase an NFL team.

18. Chris Smith, "Rising NFL Team Values Make Billion-Dollar Fortune for Arizona Cardinals' Bidwills," *Forbes* (September 28, 2015): 1.

19. Two sources are the "2015 NFL Fan Cost Index," http://www.teammarketing.com, cited November 20, 2015, and "2014 NFL Fan Cost Index," http://www.teammarketing.com, cited August 26, 2015.

20. See results of the fan equity and social media indexes in Manish Tripathi, "2015 NFL Fan Equity Rankings," https://scholarblogs.emory.edu, cited September 4, 2015, and Michael Lewis, "2015 NFL Social Media Equity Rankings," https://scholarblogs.emory.edu, cited September 4, 2015.

21. For this study see Patrick O'Grady, "Arizona Cardinal Hit High Point—With Beer Prices," http://www.bizjournals.com, cited November 9, 2015. Regarding the team's stadium financing, see Aaron Kuriloff, "Courts Sack Stadium Bond Buyers," *Wall Street Journal* (October 26, 2015): C1, C3.

22. "NFL Team Owners," http://www.biography.yourdictionary.com, cited December 24, 2015.

23. "2015 NFL Fan Cost Index" and Jon Greenberg, "2014 NFL Fan Cost Index," https: www.teammarketing.com, cited August 26, 2015.

24. Chris Nyugen, "Many Unhappy San Francisco 49ers Fans Selling Season Ticket Licenses," http://www.abc7news.com, cited November 11, 2015, and Ashlee Vance, "The San Francisco 49ers' New Stadium Is a Dud," *Business Week* (August 4, 2014): 1.

25. The same references for the FCIs, stadium rankings, and indexes of the Cardinals and 49ers were used as for the Seahawks and Rams. See notes above.

26. This business highlight is in John Boyle, "Seahawks Make More Tickets Available to Fans in 2015," http://www.seahawks.com, cited November 11, 2015.

27. Specific information about the business of the Rams, including its current owner, FCI, and equity and social media indexes, is in the sources cited in earlier notes for other WD teams.

28. From the "2014 NFL Fan Cost Index" to "2015 NFL Fan Cost Index" reflects the changes in average nonpremium and premium ticket prices and other expenses to attend games of NFL teams for a four-person family.

29. Darren Rovell, "Disney CEO Bob Iger Joins NFL Stadium Project in Carson, California," http://www.espn.go.com, cited November 12, 2015, and Eliot Brown, Jim Carlton, and Matthew Futterman, "Cities Rethink Sports-Team Deals," *Wall Street Journal* (January 14, 2016): B1, B2.

30. See "St. Louis a Step Closer to Stadium Financing Plan," *Charlotte Observer* (December 11, 2015): 5B; Ben Kesling, "St. Louis Officials Unveil Proposal for Stadium to Try to Keep Rams," *Wall Street Journal* (January 9, 2015): 1; "St. Louis Gives OK on $150 Million toward Stadium," *Charlotte Observer* (December 20, 2015): 11B.

Conclusion

The contents in chapters 1–4 and 5–8 of this book revealed how sixteen clubs, in the American Football Conference (AFC) and National Football Conference (NFC), respectively, each performed in seasons and postseasons of the National Football League (NFL). To measure and report their success from a financial perspective, these chapters also contained data and other information about them as franchises within their sports market.

To compare and analyze the performances of teams as a group within four divisions of the AFC and also NFC, Table 1.1 denotes some interesting results. First, AFC teams averaged fewer seasons and number of wins but a higher winning percentage than those in the NFC. Such AFC clubs, for example, as the Cleveland Browns, Houston Texans, and Tennessee Titans had each played less than twenty years in the league as of their 2015 season and averaged fewer than 110 wins in 261 games.

Second, seven AFC teams—led by the Denver Broncos and Miami Dolphins—each won more than 50 percent of their games, while the NFC's Tampa Bay Buccaneers and Arizona Cardinals, for example, lost about 60 percent of them. In other words, on average, NFC clubs combined played more seasons and won a larger number of games but proportionately had more losses than wins especially by those in the conference's South Division, which include the Atlanta Falcons, Carolina Panthers, New Orleans Saints, and Tampa Bay Buccaneers.

Third, NFC teams have won more total titles—division and conference—and also championships—NFL and Super Bowls—than those in the AFC. Such clubs as the Dallas Cowboys, New York Giants, Green Bay Packers, and San Francisco 49ers have been successful in postseasons while five teams in the AFC failed to win a conference title including, for example, the New York Jets, Jacksonville Jaguars, and Kansas City Chiefs. Despite its

Table 1.1: NFL Teams Historical Performance Records, Divisions by Conference

		Average			Total
American Football Conference	Seasons	Wins	Win%	Titles	Championships
East Division	46	365	.511	56	6
North Division	41	295	.461	46	8
South Division	21	166	.479	22	1
West Division	42	337	.507	52	5
National Football Conference					
East Division	77	563	.515	98	21
North Division	81	601	.520	91	26
South Division	40	267	.436	27	2
West Division	38	290	.467	46	7

Note: Abbreviations are National Football League (NFL) and Winning Percentage (Win%). Titles include total number of division and conference titles of teams in each division. Championships include NFL championships (1933–1965 seasons) and Super Bowls (1966–2015 seasons) for teams in each division. (Source: *NFL Record & Fact Book 2014* (New York: NFL, 2014) and statistics reported for teams at http://www.nfl.com.)

lower average winning percentage, the NFC has been the superior conference in the league's postseasons from a competitive viewpoint.

In contrast to the performances of sixteen clubs each in these conferences, Table 2.1 indicates that collectively NFC franchises had a higher average market value, earned more revenue, gate receipts, and operating income, and spent a greater amount for player expenses than their counterparts in the AFC. Furthermore, the conference's Dallas Cowboys, New York Giants, Washington Redskins, and San Francisco 49ers were leaders in financial data while in the AFC, such franchises as the Buffalo Bills, Cincinnati Bengals, Cleveland Browns, and Oakland Raiders each received relatively smaller inflows of cash from their operations.

As denoted in the table, the NFC's East Division franchises were the most valuable group with the largest average revenue, gate receipts, and operating income while those in the conference's West Division had the highest player expenses. Alternatively, the AFC's West Division was least lucrative of the eight groups except for their average market value and player expenses.

In fact, the conference's Buffalo Bills, Cincinnati Bengals, Cleveland Browns, Jacksonville Jaguars, Tennessee Titans, Kansas City Chiefs, Oakland Raiders, and San Diego Chargers each exist in small to mid-sized sports

Table 2.1 NFL Teams' Financial Data, Divisions by Conference

American Football Conference	Value	Revenue	Average Gate Receipts	OI	Player Expenses
East Division	2,262	373	70	99	157
North Division	1,693	322	57	50	169
South Division	1,836	334	57	80	149
West Division	1,611	310	55	54	160
National Football Conference					
East Division	3,012	457	85	146	162
North Division	1,857	319	57	54	160
South Division	1,563	315	58	56	162
West Division	1,875	339	58	64	169

Note: NFL is National Football League. Amounts are in millions of U.S. dollars. Value of a team is based on the current stadium deal (unless new stadium is pending) without deduction for debt (other than stadium debt). Revenue is net of stadium revenues used for debt payments. Gate Receipts include revenue from club seats. Operating Income (OI) is earnings before interest, taxes, depreciation, and amortization. Player Expenses include benefits and bonuses. (Source: Kurt Badenhausen, Michael K. Ozanian, and Christina Settimi, "NFL Team Values: The Business of Football," http://www.forbes.com, cited August 26, 2015.)

markets and struggle to generate enough money from home games at their stadiums and also from other sources such as advertising, radio, and television broadcasting, and the sale of clothing, merchandise, and memorabilia.

According to the data in table 2.1, the NFC was and continues to be the richest and most powerful and successful group of franchises as of 2015. Meanwhile the AFC's New England Patriots, New York Jets, and Houston Texans are also wealthy enterprises individually and ranked among the league's top ten based on their business operations. Lastly, if they construct and play in a new stadium locally and/or eventually relocate to the Los Angeles area—to join the NFC Rams—the AFC Raiders and Chargers will appreciate in value and significantly increase their revenue at home games.[1]

NOTE

1. An important business but controversial topic is the movement of an NFL team from its current site to another city in a small, mid-sized, or large sports market. To read about this issue, see such articles as James Nash, "L.A. Fans Pray for an NFL Team of Their Own," *Business Week* (June 1–7, 2015): 28; Kevin Clark, "NFL: The Race to Move to Los Angeles Is

On," *Wall Street Journal* (August 10, 2015): 1; Erica E. Phillips and Matthew Futterman, "St. Louis Rams Owner Plans Los Angeles Football Stadium," *Wall Street Journal* (January 5, 2015): 1; Daniel Kaplan, "L.A. May Pit Owners v. Owners," *SportsBusiness Journal* (August 17, 2015): 10; "St. Louis Gives OK on $150 Million toward Stadium," *Charlotte Observer* (December 20, 2015): 11B; "NFL Move Could Cause Divisional Move," *Wall Street Journal* (August 18, 2015): 1.

Appendix

Table A.1: Historical Performance Records, AFC Teams by Division

Teams	Seasons	Wins	Win%	Titles: Division	Titles: Conference	Championships: NFL	Championships: SB
East Division							
Buffalo Bills	46	328	.462	7	4	0	0
Miami Dolphins	46	414	.581	13	5	0	2
New England Patriots	46	399	.560	17	8	0	4
New York Jets	46	318	.446	2	0	0	0
North Division							
Baltimore Ravens	20	173	.540	4	2	0	2
Cincinnati Bengals	46	332	.466	9	2	0	0
Cleveland Browns	17	87	.321	0	0	0	0
Pittsburgh Steelers	83	590	.517	21	8	0	6
South Division							
Houston Texans	14	97	.433	3	0	0	0
Indianapolis Colts	32	271	.531	11	2	0	1
Jacksonville Jaguars	21	152	.452	2	0	0	0
Tennessee Titans	18	145	.503	3	1	0	0
West Division							
Denver Broncos	46	417	.585	15	8	0	3
Kansas City Chiefs	46	348	.488	6	0	0	0
Oakland Raiders	33	249	.486	9	3	0	2
San Diego Chargers	46	335	.471	10	1	0	0

Note: Teams are listed in alphabetical order by division as of their 2015 season. Abbreviations are the American Football Conference (AFC), National Football League (NFL), Super Bowl (SB), and winning percentage (Win%). Except for the Pittsburgh Steelers (1933–2014), the total period for other teams is from the league's 1970 to 2014 season. Seasons, Wins, Win%, Titles, and Championships exclude performances of any teams while playing in the All American Football Conference (1946–1949) and American Football League (1960–1969). The column NFL is number of championships before 1966. Performance data includes the Boston Patriots (1970) followed by the New England Patriots (1971–2014), Tennessee Titans (1998–2014) in Nashville, and Oakland Raiders (1970–1981 plus 1995–2014). It excludes the Baltimore Colts (1953–1983), Cleveland Browns' other franchises (1946–1995), Tennessee Oilers in Memphis (1997), Houston Oilers (1960–1996), and Los Angeles Raiders (1982–1994). (Source: "NFL Links," http://www.sportsecyclopdia.com cited August 25, 2015 and "Teams," http://www.pro-football-reference.com cited August 25, 2015.)

Table A.2: NFL All-Time Performance Rankings, AFC Teams by Division

				Titles		Championships	
Teams	Seasons	Wins	Win%	Division	Conference	NFL	SB
East Division							
Buffalo Bills	13th t	19th	22nd	19th	10th t	7th t	18th t
Miami Dolphins	13th t	12th	2nd	10th t	8th t	7th	9th t
New England Patriots	13th t	13th	4th	8th	3rd t	7th t	4th t
New York Jets	13th t	20th	24th	30th	28th t	7th t	18th t
North Division							
Baltimore Ravens	29th	26th	7th	25th	17th t	7th t	9th t
Cincinnati Bengals	13th t	16th	21st	15th t	17th t	7th t	18th t
Cleveland Browns	31st	32nd	32nd	32nd	28th t	7th t	18th t
Pittsburgh Steelers	4th t	4th	12th	4th	3rd t	7th t	1st
South Division							
Houston Texans	32nd	31st	27th	26th t	28th t	7th t	18th t
Indianapolis Colts	24th	22nd	10th	13th	17th t	7th t	12th t
Jacksonville Jaguars	26th t	28th	23rd	30th t	28th t	7th t	18th t
Tennessee Titans	30th	29th	13th	26th t	22nd t	7th t	18th t
West Division							
Denver Broncos	13th t	11th	1st	9th	3rd t	7th t	7th t
Kansas City Chiefs	13th t	14th	17th	20th t	28th t	7th t	18th t
Oakland Raiders	23rd	23rd	18th	15th t	14th t	7th t	9th t
San Diego Chargers	13th t	15th	20th	14th	22nd t	7th t	18th t

Note: NFL is National Football League. AFC is American Football Conference. The t is a tie in rank between one or more teams. (Source: "NFL Links," http://www.sportsecyclopdia.com, cited August 25, 2015 and "Teams," http://www.pro-football-reference.com, cited August 25, 2015.)

Table A.3: Financial Data, AFC Franchises by Division, 2015

Franchises	Value	Revenue	Gate Receipts	OI	Player Expenses
East Division					
Buffalo Bills	1,400	296	49	44	163
Miami Dolphins	1,850	322	57	41	169
New England Patriots	3,200	494	100	195	160
New York Jets	2,600	383	77	118	138
North Division					
Baltimore Ravens	1,930	345	68	59	184
Cincinnati Bengals	1,445	296	49	55	158
Cleveland Browns	1,500	313	50	34	167
Pittsburgh Steelers	1,900	334	61	54	170
South Division					
Houston Texans	2,500	383	65	114	151
Indianapolis Colts	1,875	321	58	90	141
Jacksonville Jaguars	1,480	315	54	67	140
Tennessee Titans	1,490	318	52	50	164
West Division					
Denver Broncos	1,940	346	70	65	170
Kansas City Chiefs	1,530	307	55	48	159
Oakland Raiders	1,450	285	40	39	158
San Diego Chargers	1,525	304	55	64	155

Note: NFL is the National Football League. AFC is the American Football Conference. Franchises are listed in alphabetical order, by division, as of the league's 2015 season. Amounts are in millions of dollars. Value of a team is based on the current stadium deal (unless new stadium is pending) without deduction for debt (other than stadium debt). Revenue is net of stadium revenues used for debt payments. Gate Receipts include revenue from club seats. Operating Income (OI) is earnings before interest, taxes, depreciation, and amortization. Player Expenses include benefits and bonuses. (Source: Kurt Badenhausen, Michael K. Ozanian, and Christina Settimi, "NFL Team Values: The Business of Football," http://www.forbes.com, cited August 26, 2015.)

Table A.4: NFL Financial Data Rankings, AFC Franchises by Division, 2015

Franchises	Value	Revenue	Gate Receipts	OI	Player Expenses
East Division					
Buffalo Bills	32nd	28th t	27th t	24th	16th t
Miami Dolphins	15th	16th t	18th t	26th	7th
New England Patriots	2nd	2nd	1st	2nd	19th
New York Jets	6th	6th t	5th t	5th	31st
North Division					
Baltimore Ravens	12th	12th	9th	17th	2nd
Cincinnati Bengals	30th	28th t	27th t	19th t	22nd t
Cleveland Browns	25th	21st t	26th	29th t	10th t
Pittsburgh Steelers	13th	13th t	15th	21st	4th t
South Division					
Houston Texans	7th	6th t	11th t	6th	27th
Indianapolis Colts	14th	18th	16th t	8th	29th
Jacksonville Jaguars	27th	20th	23rd	13th	30th
Tennessee Titans	26th	19th	24th t	22nd	15th
West Division					
Denver Broncos	11th	11th	7th	14th	4th t
Kansas City Chiefs	21st	24th	20th t	23rd	20th t
Oakland Raiders	28th t	31st	32nd	27th	22nd t
San Diego Chargers	22nd	25th	20th t	15th	26th

Note: NFL is National Football League. AFC is American Football Conference. OI is operating income. The t is a tie in rank between one or more franchises. (Source: Kurt Badenhausen, Michael K. Ozanian, and Christina Settimi, "NFL Team Values: The Business of Football," http://www.forbes.com, cited August 26, 2015.)

Table A.5: Historical Performance Records, NFC Teams by Division

				Titles		Championships	
Teams	Seasons	Wins	Win%	Division	Conference	NFL	SB
East Division							
Dallas Cowboys	56	480	.564	22	8	0	5
New York Giants	91	673	.528	24	11	4	4
Philadelphia Eagles	83	548	.474	13	3	3	0
Washington Redskins	79	554	.497	12	5	2	3
North Division							
Chicago Bears	95	731	.551	20	4	8	1
Detroit Lions	82	507	.441	8	4	4	0
Green Bay Packers	95	720	.552	23	9	9	4
Minnesota Vikings	55	449	.536	19	4	0	0
South Division							
Atlanta Falcons	50	330	.429	5	1	0	0
Carolina Panthers	21	166	.494	6	2	0	0
New Orleans Saints	49	331	.439	5	1	0	1
Tampa Bay Buccaneers	40	241	.383	6	1	0	1
West Division							
Arizona Cardinals	28	184	.411	3	1	0	0
San Francisco 49ers	66	520	.536	19	6	0	5
Seattle Seahawks	40	315	.502	9	3	0	1
St. Louis Rams	21	142	.422	3	2	0	1

Note: Teams are listed in alphabetical order by division as of their 2015 season. Abbreviations are the National Football Conference (NFC), National Football League (NFL), Super Bowl (SB), and winning percentage (Win%). The column NFL is number of championships before 1966. Performance data includes the Chicago Staleys (1921) and Green Bay Packers (1921) while in the American Professional Football Association (renamed National Football League in 1922), Dallas Cowboys in the Western Conference (1960), Phoenix Cardinals (1988–1993), St. Louis Rams (1995–2014), and the Seattle Seahawks while in the AFC (1976–2001) and NFC (2002–2014). It excludes the Boston Braves (1932), Boston Redskins (1933–1936), Chicago Cardinals (1921–1959) and St. Louis Cardinals (1960–1987), Cleveland Rams (1937–1945) and Los Angeles Rams (1946–1994), Decatur Staleys (1920), Portsmouth Spartans (1930–1933), and San Francisco 49ers (1946–1949) while in the All American Football Conference. (Source: "NFL Links," http://www.sportsecyclopdia.com, cited August 25, 2015 and "Teams," http://www.pro-football-reference.com, cited August 25, 2015.)

Table A.6: NFL All-Time Performance Rankings, NFC by Division

				Titles		Championships	
Teams	Seasons	Wins	Win%	Division	Conference	NFL	SB
East Division							
Dallas Cowboys	9th	9th	3rd	3rd	3rdt	7tht	2ndt
New York Giants	3rd	3rd	11th	1st	1st	3rdt	4tht
Philadelphia Eagles	4tht	6th	19th	10tht	14tht	5th	18tht
Washington Redskins	7th	5th	15th	12th	8tht	6th	7tht
North Division							
Chicago Bears	1stt	1st	6th	5th	10tht	2nd	12tht
Detroit Lions	6th	8th	25th	18th	10tht	3rdt	18tht
Green Bay Packers	1stt	2nd	5th	2nd	2nd	1st	4tht
Minnesota Vikings	10th	10th	8tht	6tht	10tht	7tht	18tht
South Division							
Atlanta Falcons	11th	18th	28th	23rdt	22ndt	7tht	18tht
Carolina Panthers	26tht	27th	16th	20tht	17th t	7tht	18tht
New Orleans Saints	12th	17th	26th	23rdt	22ndt	7tht	12tht
Tampa Bay Buccaneers	21stt	24th	30th	20tht	22ndt	7tht	12tht
West Division							
Arizona Cardinals	25th	25th	17th	26tht	22ndt	7tht	18tht
San Francisco 49ers	8th	7th	8th	6tht	7th	7tht	2ndt
Seattle Seahawks	21stt	21st	14th	15tht	14tht	7tht	12tht
St. Louis Rams	26tht	30th	29th	26tht	17tht	7tht	12tht

Note: NFL is National Football League. NFC is National Football Conference. The t is a tie in rank between one or more teams. (Source: "NFL Links," http://www.sportsecyclopdia.com, cited August 25, 2015 and "Teams," http://www.pro-football-reference.com, cited August 25, 2015.)

Table A.7: Financial Data, NFC Franchises by Division, 2015

Franchises	Value	Revenue	Gate Receipts	OI	Player Expenses
East Division					
Dallas Cowboys	4,000	620	94	270	148
New York Giants	2,800	400	92	105	165
Philadelphia Eagles	2,400	370	69	88	167
Washington Redskins	2,850	439	85	124	170
North Division					
Chicago Bears	2,450	352	67	85	168
Detroit Lions	1,440	298	52	36	156
Green Bay Packers	1,950	347	65	63	159
Minnesota Vikings	1,590	281	47	34	157
South Division					
Atlanta Falcons	1,670	303	57	25	187
Carolina Panthers	1,560	325	65	77	137
New Orleans Saints	1,515	322	63	70	162
Tampa Bay Buccaneers	1,510	313	48	55	163
West Division					
Arizona Cardinals	1,540	308	55	57	166
San Francisco 49ers	2,700	427	77	123	168
Seattle Seahawks	1,810	334	58	43	178
St. Louis Rams	1,450	290	45	34	167

Note: NFC is National Football Conference. NFL is National Football League Franchises are listed in alphabetical order by division as of their 2014 season. Amounts are in millions of dollars. Value of a team is based on the current stadium deal (unless new stadium is pending) without deduction for debt (other than stadium debt). Revenue is net of stadium revenues used for debt payments. Gate Receipts include revenue from club seats. Operating Income (OI) is earnings before interest, taxes, depreciation, and amortization. Player Expenses include benefits and bonuses. (Source: Kurt Badenhausen, Michael K. Ozanian, and Christina Settimi, "NFL Team Values: The Business of Football," http://www.forbes.com, cited August 26, 2015.)

Table A.8: NFL Financial Data Rankings, NFC Franchises by Division, 2015

Franchises	Value	Revenue	Gate Receipts	OI	Player Expenses
East Division					
Dallas Cowboys	1st	1st	2nd	1st	28th
New York Giants	4th	5th	3rd	7th	14th
Philadelphia Eagles	9th	8th	8th	9th	10th
Washington Redskins	3rd	3rd	4th	3rd	4th t
North Division					
Chicago Bears	8th	9th	10th	10th	8th t
Detroit Lions	31st	27th	24th t	28th	25th
Green Bay Packers	10th	10th	11th t	16th	20th t
Minnesota Vikings	18th	32nd	30th	29th t	24th
South Division					
Atlanta Falcons	17th	26th	18th t	32nd	1st
Carolina Panthers	19th	15th	11th t	11th	32nd
New Orleans Saints	23rd	16th t	14th	12th	18th
Tampa Bay Buccaneers	24th	21st t	29th	19th t	16th t
West Division					
Arizona Cardinals	20th	23rd	20th t	18th	13th
San Francisco 49ers	5th	4th	5th t	4th	8th t
Seattle Seahawks	16th	13th t	16th t	25th	3rd
St. Louis Rams	28th t	30th	31st	29th t	10th t

Note: NFL is National Football League. NFC is National Football Conference. OI is operating income. The t is a tie in rank between one or more franchises. (Source: Kurt Badenhausen, Michael K. Ozanian, and Christina Settimi, "NFL Team Values: The Business of Football," http://www.forbes.com, cited August 26, 2015.)

Bibliography

Abbot, Nicole. "Dynamic Profit-Maximization in the National Football League." Senior Thesis, Colorado College, 2002.

Alonzo, Austin. "Chiefs Kick Corporate Tailgating Up a Notch." http://www.bizjournals.com, cited December 1, 2015.

Bacon, John. "William Clay Ford: The Detroit Lions' Company Man." *Wall Street Journal* (March 12, 2014): 1.

Badenhausen, Kurt, Michael K. Ozanian, and Christina Settimi. "NFL Team Values: The Business of Football." http://www.forbes.com, cited August 26, 2015.

"Baltimore Ravens Go Solar with Constellation." http://www.baltimoreravens.com, cited September 23, 2015.

Battle, Tim. "ESPN's NFL Future Power Rankings Bode Poorly for Houston Texans." http://www.battleblog.com, cited September 24, 2015.

Beaton, Andrew. "The NFL's Least Optimistic Fans." *Wall Street Journal* (September 10, 2015): D6.

"Bengals, 49ers Stakes Change Hands." *SportsBusiness Journal* (December 19, 2011): 4.

Boyle, John. "Seahawks Make More Tickets Available to Fans in 2015." http://www.seahawks.com, cited November 11, 2015.

Broughton, David. "Saints Dominate Local Preseason Ratings." *SportsBusiness Journal* (July 28, 2014): 8.

Brown, Eliot, Jim Carlton, and Matthew Futterman. "Cities Rethink Sports-Team Deals." *Wall Street Journal* (January 14, 2016): B1, B2.

Brunkhorst, John Patrick. "Profit Maximization in the National Football League." Senior Thesis, Colorado College, 2007.

Brustein, Joshua. "Houston Running Back Arian Foster Is Going Public at the Perfect Time." *Business Week* (October 14–20, 2013): 1.

Burke, Monte. "Think the NFL Is in Decline Because of Head Trauma Issues? Think Again." *Forbes* (September 2, 2013): 1.

Byrne, Kerry. "A CHFF Epic: All-Time Franchise Rankings." http://www.coldhardfootballfacts.com, cited August 26, 2015.

"Carolina Panthers PSL." http://www.pslsource.com, cited November 5, 2015.

Chemi, Eric. "Why Arian Foster Has Zero Chance of Making $50 Million on the Field." *Business Week* (October 28–November 3, 2013): 1.

Clark, Kevin. "Management Secrets of the NFL: The League's Best Teams Share Front-Office Habits." *Wall Street Journal* (September 5, 2012): D7.

Clark, Kevin. "NFL: The Race to Move to Los Angeles Is On." *Wall Street Journal* (August 10, 2015): 1.

Ecker, Danny. "FanDuel among New Bears Corporate Partners." http://www.chicagobusiness.com, cited October 22, 2015.

Ecker, Danny. "Here's the Bears' 2015 Ad Campaign." http://www.chicagobusiness.com, cited December 8, 2015.

Ecker, Danny. "The Game Is Getting Harder for Chicago Ticket Brokers." http://www.chicagobusiness.com, cited October 22, 2015.

Fucillo, David. "49ers Name Dr. Fergus Connolly Director of Elite Performance." http://www.ninersnation.com, cited November 10, 2015.

Futterman, Matthew. "NFL's Money Machine Never Blinks." *Wall Street Journal* (September 10, 2015): B1, B2.

Gagnon, Brad. "The NFL All-Time Power Rankings of the Super Bowl Era." http://www.cbssports.com, cited August 26, 2015.

George, John. "Here's How You Can Take a Vacation with Some Eagles." http://www.bizjournals.com, cited October 20, 2015.

Gomes, Dean. "Power Rankings: Rating NFL Owners From 1–32." http://www.cover32.com, cited August 31, 2015.

Greenberg, Jon. "2014 NFL Fan Cost Index." https: www.teammarketing.com, cited August 26, 2015.

Gribble, Andrew. "Owner Jimmy Haslam Focused on Cleveland Browns' Ultimate Goal." http://www.clevelandbrowns.com, cited September 18, 2015.

Halter, Nick. "Vikings Redevelopment Plan Adds to Ongoing Eagan Retail Boom." http://www.bizjournals.com, cited October 21, 2015.

"History." http://www.nfl.com, cited August 25, 2015.

"History of National Football League Franchises, 1920–Present." http://www.profootballhof.com, cited August 25, 2015.

Hudson, Phil W. "Atlanta Falcons Ink Sponsorship Deal With Texas Vodka Distiller." http://www.bizjournals.com, cited November 5, 2015.

Joyner, K. C. "N.F.L. Sellouts Have Become Easier, But Not for Bills." http://www.nytimes.com, cited September 2, 2015.

Jozsa, Frank P., Jr. "An Economic Analysis of Franchise Relocation and League Expansion in Professional Team Sports, 1950–1975." Ph.D. diss., Georgia State University, 1977.

Jozsa, Frank P., Jr. *Football Fortunes: The Business, Organization and Strategy of the NFL* (Jefferson, NC: McFarland, 2010).

Jozsa, Frank P., Jr. *National Football League Strategies: Business Expansions, Relocations, and Mergers* (New York: Springer, 2014).

Kaplan, Daniel. "Among Wilson's Legacies: a Small-Market Team, A Prescient Vote." *SportsBusiness Journal* (March 31, 2014): 29.

Kaplan, Daniel. "Bengals, 49ers Stakes Change Hands." *SportsBusiness Journal* (December 19, 2011): 4.

Kaplan, Daniel. "Bucs Set Sail with Fresh Approach to Business." *SportsBusiness Journal* (September 2, 2013): 1.

Kaplan, Daniel. "Chargers, Raiders Retain Legends for L.A. Bid." *SportsBusiness Journal* (June 15, 2015): 7.

Kaplan, Daniel. "Dolphins See Potential for Tailgating Revenue." *SportsBusiness Journal* (August 17, 2015): 19.

Kaplan, Daniel. "Focus Group Helps Texans Program New Video Boards." *SportsBusiness Journal* (July 29, 2013): 6.

Kaplan, Daniel. "Future Bodes Well for Packers' Income." *SportsBusiness Journal* (July 14, 2014): 3.

Kaplan, Daniel. "Haslam, NFL Develop Plan B." *SportsBusiness Journal* (August 5, 2013): 4.

Kaplan, Daniel. "L.A. May Pit Owners v. Owners." *SportsBusiness Journal* (August 17, 2015): 10.

Kaplan, Daniel. "Lions' Variable Pricing Will Be the First for NFL." *SportsBusiness Journal* (January 27, 2014): 5.

Kaplan, Daniel. "NFL Projecting Revenue Increase of $1B over 2014." *SportsBusiness Journal* (March 9, 2015): 1.

Kaplan, Daniel. "NFL Votes to Allow Trust Ownership of Teams." *SportsBusiness Journal* (May 25, 2015): 3.

Kesling, Ben. "St. Louis Officials Unveil Proposal for Stadium to Try to Keep Rams." *Wall Street Journal* (January 9, 2015): 1.

King, Bill. "New Bills Owners' Passionate Vision of One Buffalo." *SportsBusiness Journal* (December 8, 2014): 1.

King, Bill. "Rooney Rule: Just Do the Right Thing." *SportsBusiness Journal* (May 19, 2014): 28.

King, Bill. "The Sit-Down: Art Rooney II, Pittsburgh Steelers." *SportsBusiness Journal* (August 4, 2014): 54.

Kuriloff, Aaron. "Courts Sack Stadium Bond Buyers." *Wall Street Journal* (October 26, 2015): C1, C3.

Lanks, Belinda. "Atlanta Falcons New Stadium Makes a Spectacle of Its Retractable Roof." *Business Week* (September 1, 2014): 1.

Lefton, Terry. "AT&T Naming Deal Years in the Making." *SportsBusiness Journal* (October 28, 2013): 28.

Lefton, Terry. "Eagles Making Sponsorship Connections." *SportsBusiness Journal* (September 7, 2015): 11.

Lefton, Terry. "In the Owner's Box, Listening, Learning." *SportsBusiness Journal* (April 22, 2013): 1.

Lefton, Terry. "Jets Stroll Down 'Silicon Valley' with an Eye on Engagement." *SportsBusiness Journal* (June 15, 2015): 13.

Lefton, Terry. "N.Y. Giants Make Rare Move, Extend Brand to Health Center." *SportsBusiness Journal* (April 1, 2013): 4.

Leuty, Ron. "Ousted Oakland Raiders Stadium Developer Kephart Gets the Last Word (Video)." http://www.bizjournals.com, cited October 11, 2015.

Lewis, Michael. "2015 NFL Social Media Equity Rankings." https://scholarblogs.emory.edu, cited September 4, 2015.

Madkour, Abraham. "Patriots Build on Stadium's Year-Round Appeal." *SportsBusiness Journal* (September 7, 2015): 1.

"Minnesota Vikings History Timeline." http://www.vikings.com, cited December 16, 2015.

Muret, Don. "Browns' New Fan Decks Raise Branding Profile for Sponsors." *SportsBusiness Journal* (August 18, 2014): 13.

Muret, Don. "Browns Sell Out Ticket Inventory for Event-Level Club." *SportsBusiness Journal* (August 3, 2015): 15.

Muret, Don. "Chiefs Busy Checking Mobile Concessions Tech at Arrowhead." *SportsBusiness Journal* (October 20, 2013): 16.

Muret, Don. "Cowboys Plug Feedback Tool Into App." *SportsBusiness Journal* (October 7, 2013): 10.

Muret, Don. "Dolphins Boxes to Offer Comforts of Home." *SportsBusiness Journal* (February 2, 2015): 3.

Muret, Don. "Finance Still Bullish on Naming Rights." *SportsBusiness Journal* (June 22, 2015): 3.

Muret, Don. "Jaguars Create New Category of Poolside Seating." *SportsBusiness Journal* (June 9, 2014): 17.

Muret, Don. "Post-Manning Colts Get Some Help Selling Season Tickets." *SportsBusiness Journal* (May 28, 2012): 14.

Muret, Don. "Titans Sign 10-Year Deal with ANC for Boards." *SportsBusiness Journal* (June 11, 2012): 8.

Nash, James. "L.A. Fans Pray for an NFL Team of Their Own." *Business Week* (June 1–7, 2015): 28.

"NFL Chronology." http://www.footballgeography.com, cited August 25, 2015.

"NFL Links." http://www.sportsecyclopdia.com, cited August 25, 2015.

"NFL Move Could Cause Divisional Move." *Wall Street Journal* (August 18, 2015): 1.

NFL Record & Fact Book 2014 (New York: NFL, 2014).

"NFL Team Owners." http://www.biography.yourdictionary.com, cited December 24, 2015.

Nguyen, Chris. "Many Unhappy San Francisco 49ers Fans Selling Season Ticket Licenses." http://www.abc7news.com, cited November 11, 2015.

O'Grady, Patrick. "Arizona Cardinals Hit High Point—With Beer Prices." http://www.bizjournals.com, cited November 9, 2015.

O'Keefe, Brian. "Reinventing Football." *Fortune* (November 18, 2013): 106.

O'Keefe, Kate. "Daily Fantasy Gears for Reality Check." *Wall Street Journal* (September 10, 2015): B1, B2.

Olson, Rochelle. "New Vikings Stadium Will Be Named for U.S. Bank." http://www.startribune.com, cited October 29, 2015.

Ourand, John. "Roll Out Small-Town Feel." *SportsBusiness Journal* (September 20, 2013): 39.

Ozanian, Mike. "Stephen Ross Wants F1 Because Fast Cars Will Make Dolphins Swim Faster." http://www.forbes.com, cited September 9, 2015.

"Packers Unveil 'Titletown' Development Plans for Area Near Lambeau Field." http://www.espn.go.com, cited October 22, 2015.

Palazzalo, Joe. "U.S. Justice Department Intervenes in Football Redskins' Trademark Case." *Wall Street Journal* (January 9, 2015): 1.

"Patriots: Suite New Digs." *SportsBusiness Journal* (September 7, 2015): 40.

Phillips, Erica E., and Matthew Futterman. "St. Louis Rams Owner Plans Los Angeles Football Stadium." *Wall Street Journal* (January 5, 2015): 1.

Potts, Michael. "Ranking All NFL Stadiums for 2015—From Worst to Best." http://www.whatculture.com, cited September 2, 2015.

"Power Rankings: Rating the Likeability of Every NFL Franchise." http://www.foxsports.com, cited August 31, 2015.

Quirk, James, and Rodney D. Fort. *Pay Dirt: The Business of Professional Team Sports* (Princeton, NJ: Princeton University Press, 1992).

Ramsey, Mike. "Nissan Buys 20-Year Naming Rights to NFL's Tennessee Titans' Stadium." *Wall Street Journal* (June 25, 2015): 1.

"Ranking All 31 NFL Stadiums." http://www.sportingnews.com, cited August 31, 2015.

"Ranking the Best and Worst NFL Stadiums." http://www.athlonsports.com, cited August 31, 2015.

Ringel, Benjamin. "A Quantitative Analysis of the Use and Efficiency of the Franchise Tag in the National Football League." B.S. Thesis, Pennsylvania State University, 2013.

Robinson, Joshua, and Matthew Futterman. "London Becomes NFL's New Frontier." *Wall Street Journal* (January 14, 2016): B1, B2.

"Rod Fort's Sports Business Data." http://www.sites.google.com, cited September 1, 2015.

Rovell, Darren. "Disney CEO Bob Iger Joins NFL Stadium Project in Carson, California." http://www.espn.go.com, cited November 12, 2015.

Salfino, Michael. "The Count: Luck Is on the Colts' Side." *Wall Street Journal* (September 15, 2014): B8.

Seiferheld, Steve. "Total Recall: Which On-Site Factors Make Fans Remember Brands?" *SportsBusiness Journal* (April 22, 2013): 15.

"Shadid Khan: The New Face of the NFL and the American Dream." *Forbes* (September 24, 2012): 1.

Shapira, Ian. "Federal Judge Orders Cancellation of Redskins' Trademark Registrations." http://www.washingtonpost.com, cited October 21, 2015.

Shea, Bill. "Detroit Bids to Host 2019 College Football Championship Game at Ford Field." http://www.crainsdetroit.com, cited October 21, 2015.

Smith, Chris. "Rising NFL Team Values Make Billion-Dollar Fortune for Arizona Cardinals' Bidwills." *Forbes* (September 28, 2015): 1.

Spanberg, Erik. "Panthers Double Up on New Private Clubs." *SportsBusiness Journal* (May 11, 2015): 8.

Sports Illustrated Almanac 2015 (New York: Sports Illustrated, 2014).

"St. Louis a Step Closer to Stadium Financing Plan." *Charlotte Observer* (December 11, 2015): 5B.

"St. Louis Gives OK on $150 Million toward Stadium." *Charlotte Observer* (December 20, 2015): 11B.

"Teams." http://www.profootballhof.com, cited September 1, 2015.

"Teams." http://www.pro-football-reference.com, cited August 25, 2015.

Terlep, Sharon. "A Mystery in the Lions' Den." *Wall Street Journal* (December 23, 2015): D6.

Terlep, Sharon. "Why Ticket Brokers Hate the Dolphins." *Wall Street Journal* (October 2, 2015): D8.

Tripathi, Manish. "2015 NFL Fan Equity Rankings." https://scholarblogs.emory.edu, cited September 4, 2015.

"2014 NFL Fan Cost Index." https://www.teammarketing.com, cited August 26, 2015.

"2015 NFL Fan Cost Index." http://www.teammarketing.com, cited November 20, 2015.

"2015 NFL Future Power Rankings." http://www.insider.espn.go.com, cited October 10, 2015.

Vance, Ashlee. "The San Francisco 49ers' New Stadium Is a Dud." *Business Week* (August 4, 2014): 1.

Veres, Joseph Andrew. "Touchdown! The Determinants of Team Success in the National Football League." Senior Thesis, Colorado College, 2007.

Vlassopoulos, Andreas. "Determinants of National Football League Franchise Revenue Generation." Senior Thesis, Colorado College, 2009.

Wagoner, Nick. "Breaking Down Quarterback Nick Foles' Contract Extension." http://www.espn.go.com, cited December 13, 2015.

Waller, Mark. "Business Insider Finds the New Orleans Saints Enjoy Highest Level of Devotion from Local Fans." http://www.nola.com, cited November 5, 2015.

Wilkerson, Chris. "Bucs Asking State to Chip In for Stadium Upgrades." http://www.bizjournals.com, cited November 5, 2015.

Woo, Stu. "New Jets Leaders Will Need a Patient Flight Plan." *Wall Street Journal* (December 31, 2014): 1.

Index

Adams, Bud, 55, 65, 76
Adams, Kenneth, 76–77
All American Football Conference (AAFC), 191
Allen, Paul, 206
American Professional Football Association (APFA), 113, 135
Arizona Cardinals: Team Performances, 187–190; Franchise Business, 201–203
Arrowhead Stadium, 87, 99, 100;
Associated Press (AP). *See* Team Performances
Atlanta Falcons: Team Performances, 161–165; Franchise Business, 175–178
AT&T Stadium, 112, 125

Baltimore Ravens: Team Performances, 29–33; Franchise Business, 42–45
Bank of America Stadium (BOA), 167, 180
Belichick, Bill, 11, 38
Benson, Tom, 180–181, 182
Bidwill, Bill, 188
Bisciotti, Stephen, 42–43
Blank, Arthur, 175–176
Bowlen, Pat, 95–96, 97, 98
Brady, Tom, 12, 13, 16
Brees, Drew, 94, 170, 171
Brown, Mike, 45–46
Brown, Paul, 35, 45
Buffalo Bills: Team Performances, 3–6; Franchise Business, 17–20

Carolina Panthers: Team Performances, 165–168; Franchise Business, 178–180
CenturyLink Field, 196–197, 208
Chicago Bears: Team Performances, 135–139; Franchise Business, 149–152
Cincinnati Bengals: Team Performances, 33–36; Franchise Business, 45–47
Cleveland Browns: Team Performances, 37–39; Franchise Business, 48–50

Dallas Cowboys: Team Performances, 109–113; Franchise Business, 123–126
Davis, Al, 88, 90, 101
Davis, Mark, 101
Dawg Pound, 38, 39
Denver Broncos: Team Performances, 81–85; Franchise Business, 95–98
Detroit Lions: Team Performances, 139–142; Franchise Business, 152–154

Edward Jones Dome, 200, 210
Elway, John, 83, 84
Entertainment Sports Programming Network (ESPN). *See* Team Performances
EverBank Field, 64

Fan Cost Index (FCI). *See* teams' Franchise Business
Favre, Brett, 144
FedEx Field, 122
FirstEnergy Stadium, 39, 49
Football Fortunes, 27n1–133n1, 185n1. *See also* Jozsa, Frank P. Jr.
Ford Field, 141
Fort, Rodney D., 27n1–133n1, 159n2, 185n1. *See also Pay Dirt*

Georgia Dome, 164
Gillette Stadium, 13, 24, 25
Glazer, Malcolm, 183
Green Bay Packers: Team Performances, 142–146; Franchise Business, 154–156

Halas, George, 136, 137, 178
Harbaugh, Jim, 138, 192, 206
Harbaugh, John, 31, 61
Haslam, Jimmy, 39, 48
Heinz Field, 42, 52
Houston Texans: Team Performances, 55–58; Franchise Business, 69–71
Howsam, Bob, 81
Huizenga, Wayne, 20
Hunt, Clark, 98

Indianapolis Colts: Team Performances, 59–61; Franchise Business, 71
Irsay, Robert, 30, 33, 71, 172

Jacksonville Jaguars: Team Performances, 62–65; Franchise Business, 74–76
Jones, Jerry, 123–124, 125
Jozsa, Frank P. Jr.: *See Football Fortunes National Football League Strategies*

Kansas City Chiefs: Team Performances, 85–88; Franchise Business, 98–100
Khan, Shadid, 74
Kraft, Robert, 13, 23
Kroenke, Stanley, 208–209, 210

Lambeau Field, 145, 156
Landry, Tom, 111, 124
Lerner, Al, 37, 48
Levi's Stadium, 193, 205, 207
Levy, Marv, 4, 87
Lincoln Financial Field, 118–119
Lucas Oil Stadium, 61
Luck, Andrew, 61, 73
Lurie, Jeffrey, 128–129

Madden, John, 89, 90
Major League Baseball (MLB), 34, 188
Major League Soccer (MLS), 98, 178
Manning, Peyton, 60, 83, 84, 85, 88, 97
Marshall, George Preston, 118, 119–120
McCaskey, Virginia Halas, 149, 152
McNair, Robert, 55–56, 69, 70
Mercedes-Benz Superdome, 171
MetLife Stadium, 16, 27, 115
Miami Dolphins: Team Performances, 7–10; Franchise Business, 20–22
Minnesota Vikings: Team Performances, 146–149; Franchise Business, 157–159
Modell, Art, 30, 37, 43
Most Valuable Player (MVP). *See* Team Performances
M&T Bank Stadium, 32, 44

Namath, Joe, 14, 15, 25
National Basketball Association (NBA), 25, 125, 182
National Football League Strategies, 185n13, 211n9. *See also* Jozsa, Frank P. Jr.
New England Patriots: Team Performances, 10–13; Franchise Business, 23–25
New Orleans Saints: Team Performances, 168–172; Franchise Business, 180–182
New York Giants: Team Performances, 113–116; Franchise Business, 126–128
New York Jets: Team Performances, 14–16; Franchise Business, 25–27
Newton, Cam, 166, 167, 168
Nissan Stadium, 67, 78
NRG Stadium, 58, 70

Oakland Raiders: Team Performances, 88–92; Franchise Business, 101–102
O.co Coliseum, 90–91

Parcells, Bill, 11, 12, 15, 114
Paul Brown Stadium, 36, 47

Pay Dirt, 27n1, 133n1, 159n2, 185n1. *See also* Quirk, James Fort Rodney D.
Payton, Walter, 137, 192
Pegula, Kim, 7, 17–18, 20
Pegula, Terry, 7, 17–18, 20
Philadelphia Eagles: Team Performances, 116–119; Franchise Business, 128–130
Pittsburgh Steelers: Team Performances, 40–42; Franchise Business, 50–36

Qualcomm Stadium, 94
Quirk, James: *See also Pay Dirt*

Ralph Wilson Stadium, 5–6
Raymond James Stadium, 174–175, 184
Rice, Jerry, 192, 193
Richardson, Jerry, 178
Rooney, Dan, 50–51, 172
Rozelle, Pete, 169, 172, 194

San Diego Chargers: Team Performances, 92–95; Franchise Business, 103
San Francisco 49ers: Team Performances, 191–194; Franchise Business, 203–206
Sanders, Barry, 140, 141
Seattle Seahawks: Team Performances, 194–197; Franchise Business, 206–208
Simpson, O.J., 4–5
Snyder, Daniel, 43, 122, 131, 133
Social Media Equity. *See* teams' Franchise Business
Soldier Field, 138, 151
Spanos, Dean, 103
Sports Authority Field at Mile High, 84, 97
St. Louis Rams: Team Performances, 197–201; Franchise Business, 208–211
Sun Life Stadium, 9, 21, 22

Tampa Bay Buccaneers: Team Performances, 172–175; Franchise Business, 183–185
TCF Bank Stadium, 148
Team Marketing Report (TMR). *See* teams' Franchise Business
Tennessee Titans: Team Performances, 65–68; Franchise Business, 76–78

University of Phoenix Stadium, 190

Warner, Kurt, 199
Washington Redskins: Team Performances, 119–123; Franchise Business, 131–133
Wilson, Ralph, 3, 6

York, Denise DeBartolo, 203–204

About the Author

A former college and semiprofessional athlete with an undergraduate degree in accounting and masters' degrees in business administration and economics, and also a doctorate in economics, Frank P. Jozsa Jr. is the author of several books on team sports in professional baseball, basketball, and football, and another on intercollegiate sports programs at American colleges and universities. His memoir, *A Hoosier's Journey: Athlete, Student, Teacher, and Author* were published by Dog Ear Publishing in 2011.

Besides books, Jozsa has written several articles published in journals, magazines, and newspapers. His dissertation, "An Economic Analysis of Franchise Relocation and League Expansion in Professional Team Sports, 1950–1975" was completed in 1977 at Georgia State University in Atlanta, Georgia. After teaching undergraduate and graduate courses in economics, finance, and statistics for three decades, Jozsa retired from Pfeiffer University in 2007.

www.ingramcontent.com/pod-product-compliance
Ingram Content Group UK Ltd.
Pitfield, Milton Keynes, MK11 3LW, UK
UKHW040909190926
475560UK00008B/52

9 781498 533942